MÔNICA FIÃES **BICALHO**

#HASHTAG ENGLISH 1
STARTER

LANGUAGE BOOSTER

Pearson

MISTO
Papel | Apoiando o manejo florestal responsável
FSC® C103535

Catalogue Publication Data

Hashtag English 1 Starter Language Booster
Authors: Mônica Fiães Bicalho
Pearson Educación de México, S.A. de C.V., 2023
ISBN: 978-607-32-5676-6
Area: Schools
Format: 20,5 × 24,7 cm Page count: 112

Product Vice President: Marianne Lewis ■ **ELT Director:** Marjorie Robles ■ **Product Managers:** Anita Heald, Priscila Marconi ■ **Product Developers:** Renata S. C. Victor, Carolina Andrade ■ **Editor:** Elaine Mendonça ■ **Art and Design Coordinator:** Anderson Ferreira ■ **Art and Design Editors:** Andréia A. Santa Rosa, Patricia Santos, Luiz Rubio ■ **Layout:** MRS Editorial ■ **Illustrators:** MRS Editorial ■ **Cover & Interior Design:** Apis Design ■ **Digital Development Supervisor:** Isabel Silva ■ **Digital Content and Development Editors:** Rafaela de Mendonça, Fernanda Patucci, Lara Tasso, Mirella Armentano ■ **Digital Content Authors:** 2014 Soluções Editoriais, Ohana Editorial, Bella Szyszkowska ■ **Audiovisual Coordinator:** Lucas Domingues ■ **Audiovisual Editor:** Lucas Motta ■ **Cover Photo:** Shutterstock ■ **R&P Coordinator:** Maiti Salla ■ **R&P team:** Maricy Queiroz, Cristiane Gameiro ■ **Content Support:** 2014 Soluções Editoriais (Editors: Carla Maurício Coelho da Silva Vianna, Fernanda Troeira Zuchini, Joyce Rocha Gomes, Marcos Carvalho Mendonça, Rebeca Pasqua de Andrade. Assistants: Cristine Zanela Monte, Elani Souza Gomes, Juliana Aga) ■ **Proofreading:** 2014 Soluções Editoriais, Silva Serviços de Educação ■ **Picture Credits:** Pearson Asset Library, Shutterstock, 123RF, Alamy Stock Photo

Contact: soporte@pearson.com

First published, 2023

ISBN PRINT BOOK: 978-607-32-5676-6

Printed in Brazil by Reproset RPSZ 221221

1 2 3 4 5 6 7 8 9 0 - 25 24 23 22

Avenida Antonio Dovalí Jaime #70
Torre B, Piso 6, Colonia Zedec Ed. Plaza Santa Fe
Delegación Álvaro Obregón, México, Ciudad de México, C. P. 01210

www.PearsonELT.com

Pearson

Pearson Hispanoamérica

Argentina ■ Belice ■ Bolivia ■ Chile ■ Colombia ■ Costa Rica ■ Cuba ■ República Dominicana ■ Ecuador ■ El Salvador ■ Guatemala ■ Honduras ■ México ■ Nicaragua ■ Panamá ■ Paraguay ■ Perú ■ Uruguay ■ Venezuela

LANGUAGE BOOSTER INDEX

The **LANGUAGE BOOSTER** is a separate book for you to review and practice the content of your Student's Book and engage in additional lessons in class and at home. The Language Booster is partially printed and partially worked on in the e-Language Booster, which consists of interactive consolidation activities. Each of the nine units in the print Language Booster follows the same structure as the Student's Book (Discover, Clarify, Understand, Develop, and Challenge). It also includes a page to reinforce the content covered in class (Assess). The additional pages at the end of the print Language Booster offer further practice. These are:

FOCUS ON CULTURE

This double-page section includes an authentic text, comprehension tasks, and a writing task.

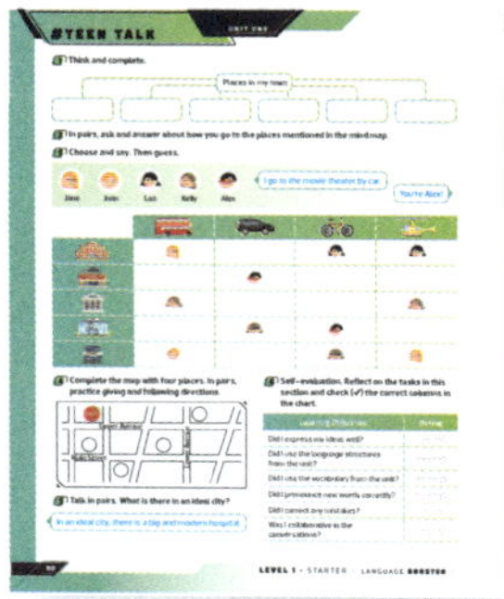

TEEN TALK

This single-page section contains communicative activities to practice the grammar and vocabulary of the unit. These activities include role-plays, information gap activities, interviews, and discussions.

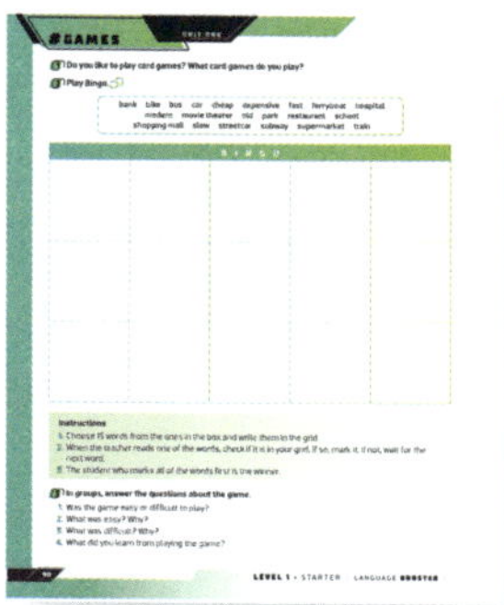

GAMES

The game pages contain nine games, one for each unit. These games review content in a fun way.

GRAMMAR GLOSSARY

The Grammar Glossary pages are designed for quick grammar reference and review.

The Language Booster also contains the audio tracks and the audio scripts from all the units.

Vocabulary

Greetings
Countries and Nationalities

1 **Read the conversation and check (✓) the correct option.**

Julia: Hi! My name is Julia. What's your name?
Ed: Hey! My name is Ed.
Julia: Nice to meet you, Ed.
Ed: It's nice to meet you, too, Julia. Are you from Canada?
Julia: No. I'm from France. Are you Canadian?
Ed: Interesting. My mother is French, too. And yes, I'm Canadian.
Julia: That's nice.

1. ☐ Julia is Canadian.
2. ☐ Ed's mother is from France. She is French.
3. ☐ Ed is Canadian.

2 **Answer the questions about the text.**

1. How does Julia ask Ed's name?

____

2. How does Ed ask what's Julia's nationality?

____

3 **Complete the chart writing the country or the nationality represented by each celebration.**

Celebration	Country	Nationality
 Tribal Dances during Carnival, Tapati Festival	Chile	1 ______
 New Year Festival	2 ______	Chinese
 Bastille Day	France	3 ______
 The Day of the Dead	4 ______	Mexican
 Boi Bumba	5 ______	6 ______

Reading

1 Listen to the conversation and check (✓) the country the boys are from. 02

1. ☐ Argentina 2. ☐ Vietnam

2 SCANNING. Read the text below and write the nationality of this festival.

____

This is a picture of the Children's Festival in Vietnam.

It is an annual event, and it's important for Vietnamese families.

Parents and children make their costumes and lanterns together.

The lanterns are colorful and in different shapes.

3 SKIMMING. Read the text again and mark the sentences T (True) or F (False).

1. ☐ This is a monthly event.
2. ☐ It is a special festival for families with children.
3. ☐ Vietnamese parents and children make their lanterns.
4. ☐ All their lanterns are in only one color and shape.

4 In groups of three, introduce a friend from Vietnam to another friend from school. Tell your school friend his / her age, nationality, and an interesting fact about Vietnam.

5 Complete with information about a friend.

His / Her name is ______________________.

He / She is ______________________ years old.

He / She is ______________________.

He / She is from ______________________

in ______________________.

Grammar

Verb *be*
Wh- questions
Possessive Adjectives

1 **Read the introductions below and circle the verb *be*.**

1. 

Hey, guys!
My name is Julia and I'm 18 years old.
I'm from Vitória, Espirito Santo. I'm a Brazilian student.
Nice to meet you all!

2. 

Hello, everyone.
My name is Haoyu. Nice to meet you!
I'm from Beijing, China. I'm a Chinese student living in Canada.
I'm 12 years old.

3. 

Hi!
My name is Adela. That is my sister Alea, and this is my grandmother Zaida.
I'm 10 years old, and Alea is 6 years old.
We're all from Damasco. We're Syrian.
Nice to meet you.

2 **Write the correct question(s).**

1. ______________________________
My name is Julia.
2. ______________________________
We're all from Damasco. We're Syrian.
3. ______________________________
I'm 11 years old.
4. ______________________________
I'm 10 years old, and Alea is 6 years old.

3 **Listen to the conversation between Alana and Marie. Then rewrite the sentences using possessive adjectives.** 03

1. Brutus is **Alana's** dog.
____
2. **Alana's** father gave the dog to her.
____
3. **All the dogs'** noses are cute.
____
4. Alana's mother is waiting at **Alana's and her mom's** house.
____

4 **Complete the chart with possessive adjectives.**

Subject	Possessive adjective
I	1 ______
You	2 ______
He	3 ______
She	4 ______
It	5 ______
You	6 ______
We	7 ______
They	8 ______

5 **Talk to your classmates and find out who has a pet. If you have a picture of your pet, you can show it. Use the possessive adjective to describe it.**

Use of English

1 Complete the dialogue with the words from the box.

Hello	I'm from	My	Nice to meet you	What's	years old

1.

[1] ________!

I'm Helena, and I'm 14 [2] ________. Are you new here?

[3] ________ your name? How old are you?

2.

Hi, Helena! [1] ____________!

[2] ____________ name is Chin-Sun, and I'm 13 years old.

[3] ____________ North Korea. Where are you from?

2 Complete the information below about a family member.

Name: ________________________________

Age: ________________________________

City / country: ________________________________

Nationality: ________________________________

3 Now introduce this family member to a friend.

Writing

1 **Read the text and check (✓) the correct option.**

CANCEL SEND

TO michelle9@hashtag.com

SUBJECT

Hi, Michelle.

How are you?

My name is Pedro. I'm Brazilian, and I'm now living in North Carolina, United States. Charlotte gave me your e-mail address. I think we are attending the same middle school. I'm 11 years old. How old are you? Where do you live? Near or far from school? Maybe we can go to a candy store after the first day of school.

See you.

Pedro

1. ☐ Michelle and Pedro go to the same middle school.
2. ☐ Michelle and Pedro are best friends.

Prepare to Write

2 **You are moving to another city, and you are going to write an e-mail to a friend of a friend who lives there. Write down the information needed.**

- Greeting

___

- Say your name and age

___

- Ask your new friend's age

___

- Say where you are from

___

- Give a piece of personal information

___

- Ask for personal information

___

- Say goodbye

___

Write

3 **Write your e-mail. Use the information in Activity 2 and the text in Activity 1 as a model.**

CANCEL SEND

TO

SUBJECT

Check and Change

4 **Read your e-mail and check that the information appears in the same order as in Activity 2. Are all the elements in your text? Check vocabulary and grammar. Use the information in this unit.**

Publish

5 **Write a clean copy of your e-mail.**

#ASSESS

Vocabulary

1 **Complete the conversation with the words from the box.**

Hi	I'm from	My name is	Nice to meet you	Peruvian

Teacher: Hello, everybody. Welcome to our first English class. [1] ________________ Danielle, I'm 45 years old, and [2] ________________ Poland. Please introduce yourselves.

Student 1: [3] ________________, Danielle. [4] ________________. I'm Beatrice, and I'm 13 years old. I'm from Cusco, Peru. I'm [5] ________________, and I live with my parents in Poland.

Grammar

2 **Complete the sentences with the missing word.**

1. __________ you 18 years old?
2. I have a friend. __________ name is Paula.
3. Jake is in the library with __________ brother.
4. __________ your mother's name?
5. __________ is he from?

Reading

3 **Read about two different greeting gestures in two different countries. Then complete the sentences.**

Hi, everyone.
My name is Sai. I'm 11 years old. I'm from Mumbai, India. I'm an Indian student living in New Delhi. When we greet each other around here it's common to use the Namaste gesture in formal situations. I place both hands in a prayer position like this. Namaste.

Hello, guys!
This is my little brother Aakar. I'm 13 years old, and my name is Aaron. Aakar is four years old. We are from Nepal.
Sticking out the tongue is a Nepali gesture to greet someone. Aakar is greeting you and saying *nice to meet you all.*

1. Text 1 is about the ________________.
2. Sai is an ________________ student.
3. It's common to use the Namaste gesture in ________________ situations.
4. Sticking out the ________________ is a greeting gesture in Nepal.
5. Aaron is Aaakar's ________________. They are Nepali.

Listening

4 **Listen and circle the correct information.** 04

1. Diogo is from **Guatemala / Costa Rica**.
2. Miguel is **ten / twelve** years old.
3. Maya is from **Hawaii / Argentina**.
4. Maya says her father is **Brazilian / Canadian**.
5. Miguel **is / isn't** a little nervous.
6. The OK gesture means everything **is / isn't** fine.
7. The OK gesture **is / isn't** a greeting gesture.

Writing

5 **Now you have the chance to write a note introducing yourself and describing the greeting gesture you use with your friends when you meet.**

Speaking

6 **Tell a classmate about the note you wrote in Activity 5. Are your greeting gestures different?**

Vocabulary

Places in Town
Means of Transportation

1 **Read the text and check (✓) the correct statements about it.**

Hi, I'm Andrea. I'm 13, and I'm from Trenton, New Jersey, in the United States. Trenton is a small and old town. My whole family lives here. There's a very good hospital, and there are two big supermarkets on Green Street, but there aren't any big shopping malls. There isn't a park in my neighborhood, but there are two sports centers. The public transportation system isn't very good, but there are bike lanes in my neighborhood, and I go to school by bike. My town is great! What about you? Where are you from? Tell me about your town.

1. ☐ Trenton is a big city in the state of New Jersey, in the United States.
2. ☐ There is a hospital in Andrea's neighborhood.
3. ☐ There are bike lanes in Andrea's neighborhood.

2 **Read the text again and complete the sentences.**

1. There are two ______________ in Andrea's neighborhood.
2. Trenton is a small and old ______________.
3. The public ______________ system isn't good in Trenton.
4. Andrea ______________ her town.

3 **Use the words from the box to complete the chart. Then add other words under the correct category.**

bank   ferryboat   movie theater   shopping mall   streetcar   subway

Places in town	Means of transportation
1 ______________	4 ______________
2 ______________	5 ______________
3 ______________	6 ______________
______________	______________
______________	______________
______________	______________

Reading

1 **Listen to the dialogue and write the New Wonders of the World mentioned and the countries where they are found.** 05

___

2 **Match each Wonder to its corresponding picture.**

1. Christ the Redeemer
   Rio de Janeiro, Brazil
2. Taj Mahal
   Agra, India
3. Great Wall of China
   Huairou, China
4. Colosseum
   Rome, Italy
5. Petra
   Ma'an, Jordan
6. Machu Picchu
   Cuzco, Peru

a. 
___

b. 
___

c. 
___

d. 
___

e. 
___

f. 
___

3 **SKIMMING. Read the text quickly. What are the New Wonders of the World mentioned?**

___

The New Seven Wonders of the World are all over the world. There is, for example, Petra, in Jordan. There is also the Colosseum, in Italy, and there is the Great Wall of China. In South America, there are two of the New Seven Wonders: a Peruvian one and a Brazilian one. Do you know any of them? People like to visit these places, and they are very famous.

4 **SCANNING. Read the text again and mark the sentences T (True) or F (False).**

1. ☐ The New Seven Wonders of the World are in Europe.
2. ☐ The Colosseum is Chinese.
3. ☐ There are two New Wonders of the World in South America.
4. ☐ There is a New Wonder of the World in Argentina.

5 **Which is your favorite Wonder among the New Seven Wonders of the World?**

My favorite Wonder is Christ the Redeemer, in Brazil.

6 **Record your answer to Activity 5 on an audio recording device.**

Grammar

There + Verb *be*

1 Which places are there in the neighborhood where you live? Check (✓) them.

1. ☐ banks
2. ☐ restaurants
3. ☐ schools
4. ☐ hospitals
5. ☐ shopping malls
6. ☐ supermarkets

2 What places are there in your school neighborhood? List them.

____

____

____

____

3 Complete the sentences with the correct form of *there* + verb *be*.

1. ______________ a great public park in New York city.
2. In my neighborhood, ______________ a lot of supermarkets. I love all of them!
3. ______________ any banks on this street.
4. ______________ good schools near here?
5. ______________ a shopping mall on Third Street?

4 Unscramble the words to form questions.

1. a / around / shopping mall / there / Is / here / ?

____

2. any / school yard / Are / children / there / in / the / ?

____

3. bank / a / this / on / avenue / there / Is / ?

____

4. Buenos Aires / there / Are / any / in / monuments / ?

____

5. city / in / there / Is / public / hospital / a / your / ?

____

5 Julian is going to visit Thomas, but he can't remember his address. Listen to the audio message he sent Thomas and complete it. 06

Hi, Thomas. I think I'm at the [1] ______________ station in your [2] ______________. I can't remember your address... Please, help me! [3] ______________ a park near your street? [4] ______________ a lot of small markets on the main avenue? That's what I see from here... Please send me your location. Bye!

6 Write questions to ask a classmate. Use *there is* and *there are* to ask if any of these places exist near his / her house.

a hospital	a subway station
bike lanes	movie theaters

____

____

____

____

7 Answer the questions you wrote in Activity 6.

____

____

____

____

____

____

Use of English

1 **Charlie is 13 years old. He lives in a small town in Texas. How do you think he goes to school? Check (✓) the options. Add another alternative.**

1. ☐ By bus
2. ☐ By ferryboat
3. ☐ By car
4. ☐ On foot
5. ☐ ____________________.

2 **Read the text and check your predictions in Activity 1. Then complete it with the words from the box.**

a big park	cheap	neighborhood
supermarkets	there aren't	there isn't

Hello, everyone! I'm Charlie, and I live in Jefferson, Texas. It's a small old town, but I love it! In my [1] ____________, there aren't any shopping malls or [2] ____________, but there is [3] ____________, and there are two sports centers. [4] ____________ a school near my house, but there are bike lanes, so I go to school by bike. The public transportation system isn't good, and [5] ____________ different options of means of transportation for everyone. My favorite thing about my town is the restaurants; they are [6] ____________! What about your town? What's it like?

3 **Circle the correct form of *there* + verb *be* to complete the sentences.**

1. **Is there** / **Are there** any banks on Silver Avenue?
2. **There isn't** / **There aren't** a good subway system in my city.
3. **There is** / **There are** 13 students in my classroom.
4. **Is there** / **Are there** a cheap restaurant here?
5. **There is** / **There are** a sports center on Third Street.
6. **There isn't** / **There aren't** any streetcars in my city.

4 **Complete the sentences about you.**

1. In my neighborhood, there aren't any ____________________, but there are ____________________.
2. There is a / an ____________________ on my street.
3. There isn't a / an ____________________ near my house.
4. The public means of transportation in my city are ____________________.

Writing

1 Read Kaya's profile. What is it about?

____

	Kaya
Full name	Kaya Okoro Masondo
Nickname	Kaka
Nationality	South African
Age	15
My City East London, South Africa	port city
	simple and welcoming
	good train network

Prepare to Write

2 Eduardo is planning to write a profile about him and his town. Write his ideas from the box in the correct sections.

> 13 years old   Colombian
> Dudu   Eduardo García
> good public transportation system   green areas
> Salamina (Colombia)   small and old

Me	My town
1 ____________	5 ____________
2 ____________	6 ____________
3 ____________	7 ____________
4 ____________	8 ____________

Write

3 Write Eduardo's profile. Use the information in Activity 2 and Activity 1 as a model.

	Eduardo
Full name	1 ____________
Nickname	2 ____________
Nationality	3 ____________
Age	4 ____________
My City Salamina, Colombia	5 ____________
	6 ____________
	7 ____________

Check and Change

4 Read the profile and make sure you included all the pieces of information in Activity 2.

Publish

5 Write a clean copy of the profile.

#CHALLENGE

UNIT ONE

#ASSESS

Vocabulary

1 Based on the vocabulary studied in this unit, write:

1. Three places in town ______________________________.
2. Three means of transportation ______________________________.

Grammar

2 Complete the questions and answer them. Write short answers.

1. **A:** ______________ any cheap supermarkets in your town or city?
   B: ______________________________
2. **A:** ______________ an Italian restaurant in your school neighborhood?
   B: ______________________________
3. **A:** ______________ a modern shopping mall in your town or city?
   B: ______________________________
4. **A:** ______________ any bike lanes in your town or city?
   B: ______________________________

Reading

3 Read the text and complete the sentences.

Hey! I'm Harry. I'm 18 years old, and I'm a student here in London, but I'm from Cali, Colombia. London is a big city and I like it, but it's very expensive! In London, there are great museums and there are good schools, too. In my neighborhood, there isn't a restaurant, but there are small cafés. We call the subway *the underground* here in London. The London underground rail network, the Tube, is modern and fast.

1. Harry isn't English, he is ______________.
2. London is an ______________ city.
3. There are great museums in ______________.
4. *The underground* is another name for ______________ in London.
5. The Tube is modern and ______________.

Listening

4 Listen to the dialogue and circle the correct words / phrases to complete it. 07

Tour Guide: Hello, everyone! I'm Noah. I'm [1] **twenty / thirty** years old. I'm [2] **Bolivian / Mexican**, but I live in the United States. I really like to travel, so it's great to have you here. Today we will visit the amazing Chichén Itzá, a Mayan city on the Yucatán Peninsula in Mexico. There are a lot of [3] **monuments / parks** and temples there. I hope you guys enjoy the tour.

Student 1: Are there any [4] **restaurants / malls** there?

Tour Guide: Sure. [5] **There are three / There is one** on our way to the temple.

Writing

5 Now you are the tour guide. You are going to write a text introducing yourself and describing one of the Seven Wonders of the World you read about on page 12. Use the dialogue in Activity 4 as a model.

Speaking

6 Record yourself reading the text you wrote in Activity 5.

Vocabulary

Numbers and Classroom Objects
Alphabet

1 Write the numbers.

1. 37 ____________
2. 81 ____________
3. 59 ____________
4. 17 ____________
5. 23 ____________
6. 100 ____________

2 Read the text and check (✓) the correct option.

Mike: Hi, Anne. What is this?
Anne: Hey, Mike. This is a marker.
Mike: Oh, and how do you spell it?
Anne: M-A-R-K-E-R.
Mike: OK, thanks!
Anne: You're welcome.

1. ☐ Anne is asking questions.
2. ☐ Mike spells the word.
3. ☐ Anne spells the word to Mike.

3 Label the classroom objects with the words from the box.

backpack
bulletin board
desk
eraser
laptop
marker
pen
whiteboard

1.  ____________
2.  ____________
3.  ____________
4.  ____________
5.  ____________
6.  ____________
7.  ____________
8.  ____________

4 List six school supplies you have that are different from your classmates.

1. ____________
2. ____________
3. ____________
4. ____________
5. ____________
6. ____________

Reading

1 SKIMMING. Read about different types of classrooms. Then match each picture to the corresponding text.

1 In the U.K., some children don't have a classroom. Their classroom is in the forest, and there are no desks! This is Forest School.

2 Some children in India use the train platform as their classroom. This classroom is for children with not much money. There are no whiteboards, desks, or chairs.

3 In Denmark, there is a school called the Orestad Gymnasium School. There are no classrooms. The students work in big, round, open rooms. There are lots of cushions.

a.  ☐

b.  ☐

c.  ☐

2 SCANNING. Read the texts again and mark the sentences T (True) or F (False).

1. ☐ There are lots of cushions in the Orestad Gymnasium School.
2. ☐ All children in India use the train platform as a classroom.
3. ☐ The classroom in Forest School is full of technology.
4. ☐ At Forest School, students go outside every day.
5. ☐ Platform school is expensive.

3 Look at the pictures in Activity 2 and write in the clouds the objects you see.

Singular

Plural

4 Listen to a Forest School teacher reading the class contract he has with his students. Use the words from the box to complete the sentences. 08

best	English	everyone	help	laugh	students	teacher

1. Speak only in ______________.
2. Always listen to other ______________ and to the ______________.
3. ______________ each other.
4. Try your ______________.
5. Don't ______________ at other students.
6. Respect ______________.

Grammar

Articles
Plural Nouns
Demonstrative Pronouns

1 **Read parts of an interview and circle the correct word. Then listen to identify who gave that information.** 03

1. "I have **a** / **an** small, red desk, pens and pencils, and books." ____________
2. "My highlighters and my backpack. I love my new backpack. **It's** / **They're** big and black." ____________
3. "I have **an** / **a** new desk. It's very big and pretty. I have **a** / **an** computer, but I like notebooks, too." ____________

2 **Listen to the interview again and check (✓) the true sentences.** 10

1. ☐ Mark has lots of highlighters.
2. ☐ Mark has a big desk.
3. ☐ Gaby is not new to this school.
4. ☐ Gaby's two favorite objects are her highlighters and her pencil case.
5. ☐ Farid is in Egypt.
6. ☐ Farid has a desk, pens, pencils, and no books.

3 **Unscramble the words and form sentences.**

1. class / students / many / in / are / the / How / there / ?

   ____
2. desk / are / backpacks / the / on / there / ten / .

   ____
3. books / teacher's / aren't / on / desk / there / five / the / .

   ____

4 **Complete the sentences with *this*, *these*, *that*, and *those*.**

1. 

   ____________ are my school pencils.
2. 

   ____________ is Anna's new backpack. It's blue.
3. 

   ____________ are Jessica's notebooks.
4. 

   ____________ is a bulletin board.

5 **Write four sentences similar to the ones in Activity 4. Use *this*, *these*, *that*, and *those*.**

____

____

____

____

Use of English

1 Complete these texts with the words from the boxes.

backpack	big	desk	notebooks

1. This is my study place. There is a [1] ____________ desk and a new chair. Both the desk and chair are blue. On my [2] ____________, there is a white laptop and two [3] ____________. The notebooks are black. Oh, and there is a backpack here, too. There are pencils, markers, and books in my [4] ____________.

laptop	markers	new	online

2. This is my study place. All my classes are [1] ____________. This is my [2] ____________. It is a good laptop, but it's old. There are many books in my bedroom. They are [3] ____________. These are my pencils, pens, and [4] ____________. I use them a lot when I study.

Writing

1 **Read the online comment below.**

< **allboutme23** ⋮

Hello, everyone! How are you today? This is my study space at home. Is it similar or different to your space? Comment below, please.

♥ 5 comments

Begoña33 Hi! I love your space! The colors are pretty, and I like your board 😃. My desk is small, and my chair is old. There are many things on my desk: a pencil case with pens, pencils, an eraser, and markers, one red and one green. I have three big notebooks. My friend Santi has a small tablet. I have a computer but no tablet. I have two plants, one big and one small. They are very pretty and green. I have headphones for my online classes and my cell phone.

Prepare to Write

2 **Think about your ideal study space. Complete the mind map below.**

My study space

Objects	Technology	Other
		plants pictures

3 **Now it's your turn to write a comment. Check (✓) the elements you want to include in your comment.**

1. ☐ greetings
2. ☐ personal introduction
3. ☐ introduction of the space
4. ☐ objects
5. ☐ technology
6. ☐ other decorative objects
7. ☐ a friend or classmate's things
8. ☐ opinion

Write

4 **Write the first draft of your online comment.**

< ____________ ⋮

____

____

____

____

____

____

____

____

____

____

Check and Change

5 **Read your online comment and check that you have included the elements checked in Activity 3. Check vocabulary and grammar. Use the information in this unit.**

Publish

6 **Write a clean copy of your comment.**

Vocabulary

1 Write what there is and what there isn't in your study space. Use colors to describe the objects.

1. There is / are ______________________.
2. There isn't / aren't ______________________.

Grammar

2 Circle the correct answer.

1. **These / This** sticky notes are green.
2. **A:** What's this on your desk?
   B: Oh, it's my new **chair / tablet**.
3. You have **a / an** old cell phone.
4. Those **markers / marker** are really good.
5. What are **those / that** at the back?

Reading

3 Read the social media post. What is it about?

Coolglasses

Hi! I'm Alana. Look at my new study space. I think it's very nice and clean. I had my dad's help; he's a decorator. It's the perfect space for an influencer. It's all white (I love it!) with yellow and black. There are plants, too. I have a new desktop computer, not a laptop. It's very big. My new chair is small. On my desk, there is a notebook. It's black and pretty. There are old pens and pencils on my desk, too, but no markers. These are interesting books, and these are my new headphones. Do you like my study space? Leave your comments below.

5 comments

1. ☐ New things in Alana's space.
2. ☐ Alana's new study space.
3. ☐ The things on Alana's desk.

Listening

4 Listen and mark T (True) or F (False). 11

1. ☐ They are in class.
2. ☐ There are three students in class.
3. ☐ The Post-its are green, pink, and yellow.
4. ☐ Lucas spells the word correctly.
5. ☐ Carmen spells a word.

Writing

5 Write about two different study places at school.

1. Study place: ______________________

2. Study place: ______________________

Speaking

6 Tell a classmate about one of the study places in Activity 5.

Vocabulary

Family Members
Jobs

1 **Read Gina's e-mail and answer the questions.**

CANCEL SEND

TO

SUBJECT G Angela is 80!

Hi,
In July, G Angela is 80! 😃
I have an idea for a gift – a book with family pictures! Please, send me your favorite pictures.
Lots of love,
Gina

1. How old is her grandma now? ______________________

2. Do you like Gina's gift idea? ______________________

2 **Match the pictures to the e-mails.**

a.

b.

c.

CANCEL SEND

Hey Gina,
Here is my favorite picture of me and my daughter Liza. I'm a lawyer now, and I can work from home. I think Liza's 6 months old in this picture!
Love,
Uncle Zak [ ]

CANCEL SEND

Dear Gina,
Here is a picture of your grandma, uncle Mike, cousins Lyla and Jacob, aunt Zoe, and Grandpa! Grandma and Grandpa are volunteer chefs at a community center now. Great idea, isn't it?
Lots of love,
Dad [ ]

CANCEL SEND

Hey sister,
How are you? Here is my favorite picture. Great-grandma Birdy in her lovely sweater. Can you believe she's 80 years old and still working? She's an English teacher at a school near her house.
Love youuuuuuu
Jade xxxx [ ]

3 **Underline the jobs in the e-mails.**

Reading

1 Listen to Gina. Does she have a big family or a small family? 12

____

2 USING PRIOR KNOWLEDGE. What are single-parent families and nuclear families?

____

3 Read the text and match the themes to the correct paragraphs.

Single-parent...

Single-parent Families vs. Nuclear Families

There are many single-parent families in the world. 23% of families in the United States are single-parent families. In Mexico, only 7% of families are single-parent families, and 10% in Brazil.

Sometimes single-parent families have less money. Nuclear families have two parents, so two parents can work and get more money than single-parent families.

Single-parent families have more support from extended families: grandparents, uncles, aunts, and cousins. Single-parent families are not better or worse than nuclear families. Both types of family are special.

☐ Extended families
☐ Money
☐ Data

4 MONITORING COMPREHENSION. Read the text again and mark the sentences T (True) or F (False).

1. ☐ 10% of families in the United States are single-parent families.
2. ☐ Parents in nuclear families are old.
3. ☐ Extended families are parents, brothers, and sisters.

5 Is your family a single-parent family or a nuclear family? Write about it.

____
____
____
____
____
____
____

Grammar

Possessive 's and Possessive Adjectives

Whose

1 Listen and check (✓) Gina's favorite thing. 13

1.  [ ]

2.  [ ]

2 Now listen again and complete the text. 14

This is [1] ________ favorite thing. I wear it every day. It's small and silver. There is a blue stone in it. My best friend Sarah [2] ________ favorite thing is also a ring, but [3] ________ ring has a pink stone. It's a sign of [4] ________ friendship. What's [5] ________ favorite thing?

3 Look at the pictures and complete the dialogues with the words from the box.

's	their	whose

1. 

A: ________ diary is this?

B: It's Luana ________.

2. 

A: Whose video game is this?

B: It's ________ video game.

4 Think about some things you and your family have. Write sentences using 's.

This is my sister's favorite book.

____

____

#UNDERSTAND

UNIT THREE

Use of English

1 **Read the messages and circle the possessive adjectives.**

Chat

Today

Mari

Hey! Whose are these? They are at my house!

Sofi
They're Raul's earphones. @Raul, those are your earphones, right?

Raul
No, my earphones are white and purple. 😟

Mari
Oh, maybe they're Pablo's earphones.

Raul
Yes! I think so.

Mari

What about this jacket?

Sofi
It's not my jacket.

Mari
OK, don't worry. I think it's Dani's jacket. I can talk to him!

2 **Read the text in Activity 1 again and find other examples of possessions that are not indicated by possessive adjectives.**

____

3 **Read the text again and mark the sentences T (True) or F (False).**

1. ☐ Raul's earphones are pink and white.
2. ☐ Raul's earphones are at Mari's house.
3. ☐ That is Sofi's jacket.
4. ☐ Mari thinks that is Dani's jacket.

4 **Correct the false statements in Activity 3.**

____

____

Writing

1 **Read about Maddie and her family.**

Maddie (Madison) Ziegler is an American young dancer, actress, author, and model. She's 19. Her middle name is Nicole. She is often on TV, in movies, music videos, or dance shows. Maddie's younger sister, Mackenzie, is 17 and is also a dancer.

Their parents are divorced. Their mother remarried, and her sisters live with their mom and stepfather. They have two older half-brothers from their father's previous marriage and two older step siblings from their stepfather's previous marriage.

Maddie's confident and strong. She has long, blond hair and a beautiful smile.

Prepare to Write

2 **Think about your family. Organize the information you want to mention about each member. Make notes.**

☐ name ☐ age ☐ job ☐ family relations

Write

3 **Write a short text describing your family. Use your notes from Activity 2 and the text in Activity 1 for help.**

____

____

____

____

____

Check and Change

4 **Read your text and make sure you included the information from your notes in Activity 2.**

5 **Edit your text. Make any necessary adjustments.**

Publish

6 **Write a clean version of your text.**

Vocabulary

1 Read the text and circle all the family members.

My name's Jackson. My family is not very big. I have two siblings, Jack and Piper. My parents are divorced. My father remarried. My father has one sister, Annette and my mother has one sister too, Layne. I have no cousins on my father's side, but I have three cousins on my mother's side, Ashley, Dean, and Edward. My father's parents are Eloise and Miles. My mother's parents are Tucker and Juliet.

Grammar

2 Ask and answer questions about possessions. Follow the model.

a.

Angelica

b.
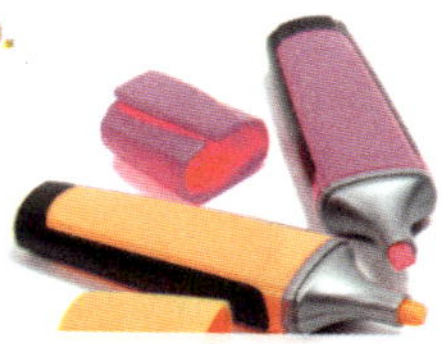
Manuel

c.

Meghan

d.

Rajesh

1. Whose backpack is this?
It's Angelica's backpack.

2. ______________________________
____

3. ______________________________
____

4. ______________________________
____

Reading

3 Read the text and mark the sentences T (True) or F (False).

Hi, my name's Oliver and this is my uncle George. He's my mother's brother. Her other brothers' names are Joe and John. Uncle George is really cool. He's a guitarist in a rock band. The band's name is *Yeah, right!* The other members' names are Carla, Jackie, Mike, and Steve. Carla is my aunt. She's Uncle George's wife, and she's great, too. Aunt Carla's favorite group is Nirvana. Their children's names are Cory and Tommy. They have their grandfather's names. Cory's just six months old, and Tommy's almost two.

1. ☐ Oliver's uncles are John, Joe, and George.
2. ☐ John is a guitarist in a rock band.
3. ☐ Joe is Oliver's uncle.
4. ☐ Cory and Tommy are Carla and George's sons.

Listening

4 Listen and check (✓) the correct picture. 15

1.

☐

2.

☐

Writing

5 How are the family relations in your favorite TV show? Write about them in your notebook. Use the possessive 's and possessive adjectives.

Speaking

6 How is your family similar to or different from the families in the pictures in Activity 4? Audio record your answer.

Vocabulary

Routines

1 **Read the text and mark the sentences T (True) or F (False).**

My Perfect Day

Hello! My name is Nia. My perfect day is Sunday. On Sundays, I wake up late, at 9 or 10 a.m., but I don't get up immediately. I read a book in bed, a novel, or a comic for 20 or 30 minutes. I have a quick breakfast in the kitchen, take a shower, and get dressed in sports clothes. I play volleyball with my friends for an hour. That's my weekend exercise. I go home and have lunch with my parents and siblings at 2 or 2:30 p.m. Sometimes my grandparents come, too. In the afternoon, I watch a show or a movie. I go to bed at 10 p.m. But before that, I read or listen to music. I really like Sundays.

1. ☐ On Sundays, Nia wakes up late and gets up immediately.
2. ☐ Nia likes to read in bed on Sunday mornings.
3. ☐ Nia has breakfast in bed.
4. ☐ On Sundays, Nia's grandparents sometimes have lunch with Nia's family.
5. ☐ Nia chats with her friends online, and then she goes to bed.

2 **Now Nia is writing about her routine on weekdays. Use the verbs from the box to complete the sentences.**

do	don't have	finish	get up
go	play	take a shower	walk

1. I ________________ early.
2. I ________________ in the morning.
3. I ________________ to school.
4. I ________________ lunch at school.
5. My classes ________________ at 1 p.m.
6. I ________________ homework in the afternoon.
7. I ________________ video games online in the evening.
8. I ________________ to bed early.

3 **Write five sentences about your routine on Sundays. Use the text in Activity 1 as a model.**

1. ____
____
2. ____
____
3. ____
____
4. ____
____
____
5. ____
____
____

Reading

1 **Listen to the interview and underline the correct sentences about Samia.** 16

1. Samia goes to school only in the morning.
2. After school, Samia stays in school to do ballet.
3. Samia has tennis classes on Saturdays.
4. On Saturdays, Samia goes to the market with her dad.
5. On weekends, she plays video games and chess.
6. On Sundays, she goes to bed at 10 p.m.

2 **USING PRIOR KNOWLEDGE. You are going to read about Joe Novogratz, from Colorado. What is his nationality?**

____

3 **MONITORING COMPREHENSION USING DETAILS. Read the text and complete the sentences about it.**

Joe Novogratz
posted 3 hours ago

Hello! I live in Colorado, in the United States. We have a lot of snow during the winter. So on the weekends my family and I usually go skiing. But during the week, my routine is different. I start school at 8 a.m. and finish at 2:15 p.m. My sister and I go to the same school. We take the bus in the morning, but my father picks us up in the afternoon. We go home, and we do our homework.

After school, I sometimes play hockey. I take drum classes, too. I love playing the drums!

On weekdays, I go to bed at 10:00 or 10:15 p.m., but on weekends, I go to bed at 11 p.m. or 12 a.m.

Is your routine like my routine? Tell me about it.

5 comments

1. There is a lot of snow during the winter in ______________.
2. Joe has different ______________ on the weekends and weekdays.
3. Joe and his ______________ go to school by bus.
4. He ______________ plays hockey.
5. Joe goes to ______________ late on weekends.

4 **Write a short paragraph to answer Joe's question at the end of the text in Activity 2.**

____
____
____
____
____
____
____
____
____
____
____
____
____
____
____
____
____
____

Grammar

Simple Present — Affirmative and Negative

1 Check (✓) the correct alternative(s) to complete the sentence about yourself.

My routine is

1. ☐ good. I'm happy with my daily habits.
2. ☐ good, but I want to change it.
3. ☐ terrible. I have a lot of unhealthy habits.
4. ☐ not good on weekdays, but I love my weekends!
5. ☐ great. I can say I have a healthy routine, and I like it.

2 Read the social media post below and complete the sentences with the verbs in parentheses.

Lisa C
posted 3 hours ago

Hello, lovelies! How are you today? I like my daily routine, but I [1] ____________ (want) to make some changes to it. So I [2] ____________ (have) a few questions for you. Here they are:

1. I [3] ____________ (not study) in the morning; my classes [4] ____________ (start) at 1:00 p.m.

Do you go to school in the morning or in the afternoon?

2. After school I [5] ____________ (do) my homework and [6] ____________ (watch) TV.

What do you do after school? What about on weekends?

3. I [7] ____________ (not go) to bed late. And you?

Do you go to bed early or late?

5 comments

3 Read Davi's comment to Lisa's post and complete it with the verbs from the box.

come	do
not finish	not go
not wear	study

5 comments

Davi Hello, LisaC! I'm from Rio de Janeiro, Brazil. I'm 13. I start school at 7 a.m. and I [1] ____________ until 12 p.m. At my school, we [2] ____________ a uniform. After school, I go home and [3] ____________ my homework. Sometimes my friend Janet [4] ____________ to my house, and we [5] ____________ together. On weekends I go to the beach and rest. I [6] ____________ to bed early.

4 Now here is Mila's comment to Lisa's post. Complete it with adverbs of frequency. The initial letters are there to help you.

5 comments

Mila Hey, Lisa! I'm from the Philippines. I'm 12. I go to school in the afternoon, so I don't [1] u____________ get up early. But my sister goes to school in the morning, so she [2] a____________ gets up very early. My mother [3] s____________ works from home. But my father [4] n____________ works from home; he works at an office downtown.

#UNDERSTAND

UNIT FOUR

Use of English

1 **Check (✓) the healthy habits.**

1. ☐ sleep well
2. ☐ exercise
3. ☐ eat fast food
4. ☐ go to bed late
5. ☐ skip breakfast
6. ☐ have a balanced diet
7. ☐ drink water

2 **Which habits from Activity 1 do you follow? Which ones don't you follow? Write sentences in the Simple Present, in the affirmative and negative forms.**

1. ______________________________
2. ______________________________
3. ______________________________
4. ______________________________
5. ______________________________
6. ______________________________
7. ______________________________

3 **Now complete the sentences below. Use *always*, *usually*, *sometimes*, or *never*.**

1. I ______________ get up late on weekends.
2. My first class at school ______________ starts at 9 p.m.
3. I ______________ brush my teeth after lunch.
4. My classmates and I ______________ exercise at the gym after school.
5. My family ______________ have pizza on weekends.

4 **Read and circle the correct alternatives to complete the text.**

Sportspeople and Their Routine

Sportspeople train very hard. They often [1] **practices / practice** in the morning and in the afternoon, for about 8 hours a day. They train on weekdays and on weekends. Sometimes they [2] **plays / play** their sport. They [3] **always / never** eat a lot of nutrient-dense foods. They [4] **don't skip / doesn't skip** a training session and always follow their coach's instructions. Their routine sometimes [5] **include / includes** superstitions. Some athletes never wear a certain color, and others have a lucky charm.

Writing

1 Read Karla's profile on a roommate website.

Name	Karla Martinez
City	Mexico City
Why I am a good roommate	I'm friendly, and I always cook delicious food.
Routine	I get up at 7:00 a.m. I am a morning person! I leave the house at 7:30 a.m, and I come home at 3:30 p.m. I always chat with my friends online in the evening — I have a lot of friends! I go to bed early.

Prepare to Write

2 You are going to write your profile for a roommate website. Organize the information you want to share. Make notes.

Name	
City	
Why I am a good roommate	
Routine	

Write

3 Write a profile describing yourself for a roommate website. Use your notes from Activity 2 and the texts on the previous pages as models.

____

____

____

____

____

____

____

____

____

____

____

____

____

____

____

____

Check and Change

4 Read your text and make sure you included:

- [ ] your personal information.
- [ ] information about why you are a good roommate.
- [ ] your routine.
- [ ] adverbs of frequency.

5 Edit your text. Make sure all the items in Activity 4 are included.

Publish

6 Write a clean version of your text.

Vocabulary

1 Match the columns.

1. go	☐ up
2. get	☐ to bed
3. take	☐ homework
4. chat	☐ a shower
5. play	☐ video games
6. have	☐ with friends
7. watch	☐ series
8. do	☐ breakfast

Grammar

2 Rewrite the sentences making them true for you. Use one of the frequency adverbs studied in this unit.

1. I have breakfast in bed.
2. I go to bed late on weekdays.
3. I walk to school.
4. I take a shower after I get up.
5. I go on social media in the morning.
6. I chat with my friends online.

Reading

3 Read the paragraph about Luan and mark the sentences T (True) or F (False).

Luan is from Boston, Massachusetts, in the United States. He is 14 years old. He goes to school in the morning, and he prefers to sleep early. He gets up at 7:00 a.m., takes a shower, and gets dressed. Then he has breakfast with his family and walks to school. His classes don't finish before 3:30 p.m., so he usually gets back home around 4:00 p.m. every day. He plays baseball for the school team. On weekends, he likes to exercise, and he always meets his friends to watch movies or play video games.

1. ☐ Luan doesn't have time to meet his friends on weekends.
2. ☐ He has classes in the morning and in the afternoon.
3. ☐ He doesn't like to exercise.
4. ☐ He takes the bus to school.
5. ☐ He has breakfast, and then he takes a shower to go to school.

Listening

4 Listen and complete the sentence about Ayari's routine on weekdays. 17

She [1] ____________ late from school because she has [2] ____________, and she [3] ____________ at the school club after that.

Writing

5 Read the text in Activity 3 again. Does Luan have a healthy routine? Why?

____
____
____
____
____

Speaking

6 Record a voice message with your answer to Activity 5.

Vocabulary

Rooms in a House
Furniture

1 **Read Christopher's e-mail to Cameron. How does he feel about his new apartment?**

____

CANCEL SEND

TO Cameron

SUBJECT new apartment

Hey, Cam!
How are you?
The new apartment is so cool!
My brother and I have a really big bedroom.
My mom has a big bedroom with a bathroom.
My brother and I share the other bathroom.
There is a living room and a room where we have dinner. There is a balcony with an amazing view of the city. The kitchen is small, but it's not a problem.
The neighborhood is nice and quiet.
Come visit me soon! 😃
Chris

2 **Read the e-mail again and mark the sentences T (True) or F (False). Then correct the false sentences to make them true.**

1. ☐ There is a laundry room in Christopher's new apartment.
____
2. ☐ Christopher shares a bedroom with his brother.
____
3. ☐ Christopher and his brother share a bathroom with his mom.
____
4. ☐ The apartment has a living room and a dining room.
____
5. ☐ The apartment doesn't have a balcony.
____
6. ☐ The kitchen isn't small.
____

3 **List the rooms of the house mentioned in the e-mail in Activity 1.**

____
____
____
____
____
____

4 **Solve the puzzle below and find out what the hidden word is. Use the letters twice, if necessary.**

1. TCHENKI
2. TECOSL
3. OCCUH
4. RRAERTREIGOF
5. EOSWRH
6. VETOS

5 **What pieces of furniture do you find the most important in a home? Write a sentence in your notebook.**

UNIT FIVE #DISCOVER

Reading

1 Listen to Lizzie's description of her new home. Where does she live now? 18

____

2 Read Lizzie's diary about her first day in her new home. Put the paragraphs 1–4 in the correct order.

____

1. April 18

Hey,

Here I am in our new home. It's very small!! Dad has a bedroom at the front. My bedroom is at the back. I have space for a bed... and nothing else!

2.

Anyway, I want to stay positive for dad. Let's see what happens tomorrow.

Lizzie xxx

3.

I think about our old house because it's so big and comfortable. My old bedroom is really big, and there's a balcony. And our beautiful garden... we don't have a garden now.

4.

There's a kitchen and a living room on the boat. We have a wood fire, so it's cozy, I guess. But the bathroom is SO small!!! Our old house has two bathrooms!

3 Read Lizzie's diary again. How are her old and new homes different? Complete the table below.

Lizzie's old home	Lizzie's new home
• 1 ______	• 1 small bathroom
• big bedroom with a balcony	• 3 ______
• 2 ______	• cozy
• beautiful garden	• 4 ______

4 GENERATING QUESTIONS. Read the text in Activity 2 again. Why is Lizzie hesitant about her new home?

____

____

5 RESEARCH. What different homes from around the world do you know? Which ones do you want to know more about? Which ones do you prefer?

1. Homes I know #about: _______________
2. Homes I want to know about: _______________
3. Homes I prefer: _______________

Grammar

Simple Present – Questions and Short Answers
Prepositions of Place

1 **Look at Gloria's bedroom. Does your bedroom look like this one?**

____

2 **Write six sentences about Gloria's bedroom. Use *there is / there are* and prepositions of place (*in, on, next to, under, behind, between*).**

1. ______________________
2. ______________________
3. ______________________
4. ______________________
5. ______________________
6. ______________________

3 **Use the verbs from the box to ask questions in the Simple Present.**

clean	do	eat	have	keep	open	watch

1. Where __________ your parents usually __________ TV?
2. __________ your grandma __________ big trees in her yard?
3. __________ you __________ the bathtub?
4. __________ your family __________ in the dining room?
5. How __________ the chef __________ the cans?
6. What __________ you __________ in the balcony?
7. __________ you __________ your dresses in the closet?

4 **Answer the questions in Activity 3. Use a dictionary, if necessary.**

1. ______________________
2. ______________________
3. ______________________
4. ______________________
5. ______________________
6. ______________________
7. ______________________

#UNDERSTAND

UNIT FIVE

#DEVELOP

UNIT FIVE

Use of English

1 **What places are there in your neighborhood? Write four sentences. Use *there is / isn't* and *there are / aren't*.**

In my neighborhood, there is a movie theater.
In my neighborhood, there aren't any parks.

____

____

____

____

2 **Read the text about Slab City and complete the table.**

Welcome to Slab City

Slab City is a *free-city* in California, in the United States. There aren't any police officers or laws. There isn't any electricity. It's a place to escape from modern life.

There are stores and people buy food and supplies there. But there aren't any offices, and there isn't a post office. It's a surprise that there's a very nice library and a concert venue.

The community has many art installations. There isn't an art gallery, but they put their art outside in the street. Life in Slab City is very simple and creative.

There is...	There isn't...

There are...	There aren't...

3 **Write three sentences comparing your city to Slab City. Use a dictionary, if necessary.**

In my city, there are lots of police officers.

____

____

____

4 **Label the pictures with the prepositions from the box.**

behind | between | in | next to | on | under

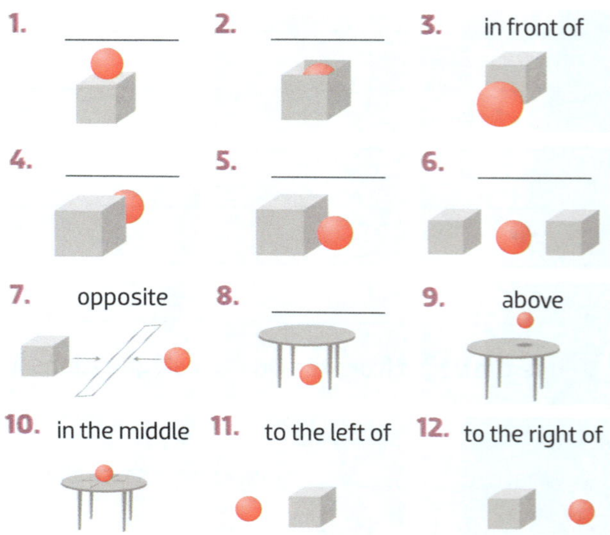

5 **Complete the questions using the verbs in parentheses in the Simple Present. Then write short answers.**

1. **A:** ________ you ________ (live) in an apartment?
   B: Yes, I ________.
2. **A:** ________ your teacher ________ (have) a vegetable garden?
   B: No, she ________.
3. **A:** ________ your friends ________ (know) what sustainable houses are?
   B: Yes, they ________.

Writing

1 **Read about New Zealand. Check (✓) the best title for the blog post.**

1. ☐ New Zealand and Its Special Caves
2. ☐ New Zealand and Its Diverse Landscapes
3. ☐ New Zealand is Different!

Welcome to...

New Zealand is a long and narrow island country in the Pacific Ocean. The landscape of New Zealand is diverse. There are beaches, mountains, and an active volcano. At the top of the volcano, there is a lake. Very impressive, right? The islands have beautiful and quiet rural areas and several big cities. The weather is different depending on the area of the island: it goes from extremely wet to semi-arid.

New Zealand has a natural attraction, the amazing Waitomo Glowworm Caves. They are magical. You take a little boat and sail through the caves. The views are awesome!

Prepare to Write

2 **You are going to write a post about a travel destination. Think about what you would like to include in your text and make notes. Here are some suggestions.**

activities to do · cities and towns · countryside · family-friendly places · geography · landscapes · location · pet-friendly places · summer / winter tourism · weather · weird / unusual place

______

______

______

______

Write

3 **Choose a travel destination and write your post. Use your notes in Activity 2 and the text in Activity 1 for help. Remember to use *there is / there are* and prepositions of place.**

Check and Change

4 **Read your post and make sure you included:**

- ☐ a destination.
- ☐ *there is / there are.*
- ☐ prepositions of place.
- ☐ reasons for visiting the destination.

5 **Edit your post. Make sure all the elements in Activity 4 are included.**

Publish

6 **Write a clean version of your post.**

#CHALLENGE

UNIT FIVE

Vocabulary

1 **Where can you find the pieces of furniture below? Write the rooms of the house.**

1. 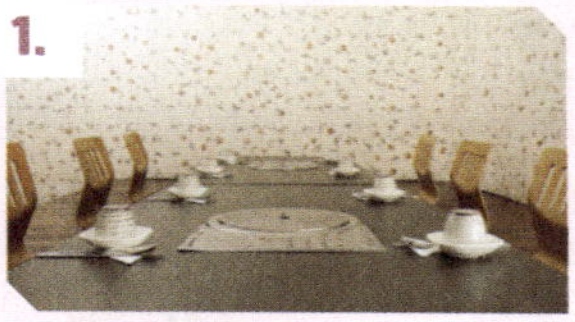

a big table: ____________

2. 

a sink: ____________

3. 

a couch: ____________

4. 

a big bed: ____________

Grammar

2 **Underline the correct options to complete the phone conversation. Then listen and check.** 19

H: Hotel Receptionist **G: Guest**

H: Good morning! Paradise Hotel. How can I help you?

G: Good morning. I have a reservation for next week, and I have some questions. [1] **Does** / **Do** the bedrooms have a TV? We watch our favorite show every day after dinner.

H: Yes, they [2] **does** / **do**. [3] **There is** / **There are** a remote control for the TV, too.

G: Perfect. And are there any bus stops [4] **on** / **next to** the hotel?

H: No, [5] **there aren't** / **there isn't**.

G: I see. Last question. Is there somewhere I can connect my laptop?

H: Yes, there is one power outlet [6] **in** / **behind** the bedroom and two in the living room. And there is also Wi-Fi.

G: Great! Thank you very much for the information. See you next week!

Reading

3 **Read the text and answer the questions.**

Cave Homes

In Matmata, Tunisia, some people live in underground caves. These homes are hundreds of years old. They aren't modern, but they're very comfortable. The houses have a circular courtyard, and the rooms are around the courtyard. They have a door and small windows. The town receives many tourists, and the houses are open for them only to visit. Some caves are hotels these days.

1. How old are the cave homes?

____

2. Are cave homes comfortable?

____

3. Can tourists visit the cave homes?

____

Listening

4 **Listen to a hotel radio advertisement and complete the sentences.** 20

1. There is a restaurant ____________ the reception desk.
2. The ____________ are big and comfortable.
3. There is a big balcony in the ____________.

Writing

5 **Write three sentences to describe the bedroom in the picture.**

Speaking

6 **Read your sentences in Activity 5 and record yourself. Share your recording with a classmate, if possible.**

Vocabulary

General Abilities

1 Use can and the information from the box to write captions for the pictures.

dance	play chess	play the piano
solve math problems	swim	walk fast

1.

He ______________________.

2.

She ______________________.

3.

She ______________________.

4.

He ______________________.

5.

He ______________________.

6.

He ______________________.

2 Read and mark the sentences T (True) or F (False).

1. ☐ I can play volleyball, but I can't play basketball.
2. ☐ Piano is my favorite instrument. I can play it very well.
3. ☐ My best friend can dance, but I can't.
4. ☐ I am not very good at math. I can't solve all math problems.

3 Order the words to make questions.

1. glasses / Can / read / you / without / ?
____
2. cook / pasta / you / Can / ?
____
3. study / Can / and / listen to / simultaneously / you / music / ?
____
4. Can / foreign / you / languages / four / speak / ?
____

4 Answer the questions in Activity 3 with your own information. Use short answers.

1. ______________________
2. ______________________
3. ______________________
4. ______________________

5 Rewrite the sentences from Activity 1 so they are true for you.

1. ______________________
2. ______________________
3. ______________________
4. ______________________
5. ______________________
6. ______________________

Reading

1 **ACTIVATING PRIOR KNOWLEDGE. Who was Stephen Hawking?**

____

2 **Listen and read. What else do you know about Stephen Hawking?** 21

This is Stephen Hawking, a famous British scientist, professor, and author. His books help people understand science.

At age 21, he is diagnosed with a degenerative disease and he dies in 2018, at 76.

He is one of the most famous scientists of the century.

3 **Read the text in Activity 2 again and complete the fact file below.**

1. Name:
2. Birth:
3. Death:
4. Nationality:
5. Occupations:

4 **ACTIVATING PRIOR KNOWLEDGE. Check (✓) the item that refers to visualization techniques.**

1. ☐ dancing
2. ☐ writing your goals
3. ☐ storytelling

5 **Read the text and mark the sentences T (True) or F (False).**

Athletes and Visualization

How can visualization help athletes? Athletes create mental pictures of the objectives they want to reach and that increases their confidence and well-being, which helps them perform better.

Visualization is often part of athletes' training and competition routines. Effective visualization techniques involve visualizing success, using mental repetition to improve a skill, using the senses (with pictures, for example), etc.

1. ☐ The visualization technique is not part of the training of athletes at the moment.
2. ☐ Visualization means creating a mental picture of what you want to happen.
3. ☐ In visualization, a person must see, hear, or feel what he / she wants to happen.
4. ☐ Visualization does not improve athletes' performances.

6 **Research into visualization and athletes from your country. Which athletes practice this technique before competitions? Make notes.**

____
____
____
____

Grammar

Can / Can't for Abilities
Imperatives

1 Look at the pictures below and write what people can do. Use the clues in parentheses.

1. 

(read) __________
____

2. 

(play musical instruments)
____

3. 

(sing) __________
____

4. 

(ride a bike) __________
____

5. 

(dance) __________
____

6. 

(drive) __________
____

7. 

(write poems) __________
____

8. 

(jump rope) __________
____

2 Change the sentences in Activity 1 into the negative form.

1. __________
2. __________
3. __________
4. __________
5. __________
6. __________
7. __________
8. __________

3 Complete the rules for the school swimming pool with the verbs from the box in the imperative form. Then listen and check. 22

listen   play   respect   run   shout

1. __________ to the swimming instructors.
2. __________ around the pool.
3. __________ with electronics near the pool.
4. __________ at other people.
5. __________ everybody and have fun!

4 Talk to your family. Write a list of rules for your home. Use the imperative form.

1. Wash your dishes after meals.
2. __________
3. __________
4. __________
5. __________

#DEVELOP

UNIT SIX

Use of English

1 **Write three questions asking for permission in your school.**

Can I go to the toilet?

____

2 **Read and complete the dialogues below.**

1. **A:** Do you like to dance?

   B: Yes, I love it. And you? [1] __________ you dance?

   A: Yes, I can. [2] __________ I turn on the music for us to dance?

   B: [3] __________, you can. Go ahead!

2. **A:** It's really hot today. [4] __________ I open the window?

   B: Of course, you can. I'm studying for my English class. [5] __________ you speak [6] __________?

   A: [7] __________, I can.

   B: Oh, please, help me.

   A: Sure. I'll just open the window first.

3. **A:** [8] __________ I use your phone for a moment? I need to call my mom about our chess class.

   B: Sure, you can. [9] __________ play chess?

   A: No, I [10] __________, not yet. But I'm learning. And you?

   B: I [11] __________ play chess, but I will learn someday.

3 **Now read the dialogues again and complete the table.**

Asking for permission	Asking about an ability

4 **Read the extracts from the dialogues in Activity 2. Underline the ones in the imperative form.**

1. I need to call my mom about our chess class together.
2. Go ahead!
3. Oh, please, help me.
4. I'm studying for my English class.

5 **Rewrite the sentences in the negative imperative form.**

1. Go away after the end of the class.

   ____

2. Bring your laptop to school.

   ____

3. Consult your book to do the activity.

   ____

4. Read this text before the exam.

   ____

Writing

1 **Read about a Brazilian web influencer and check (✓) the ability mentioned in the text.**

Lorrane Silva, also known as *Pequena Lo*, is a Brazilian psychologist who is famous on the Internet because she can make funny videos and tell jokes. She is 24 years old and uses crutches and a scooter to move. She says she can use the humor around her condition to her advantage.

1. ☐ Pequena Lo can make jokes.
2. ☐ Pequena Lo can play chess.
3. ☐ Pequena Lo can speak Mandarin.

Prepare to Write

2 **Read the abilities below and underline the ones your family or people who live with you have.**

code   cook very well   dance tango   play a musical instrument   play basketball   play soccer
play the piano   run a marathon   speak a foreign language   swim   use sign language

Write

3 **Choose a person who lives with you and has a special ability. Write about this person and his / her ability / abilities.**

____

____

____

____

____

____

____

____

____

____

____

____

____

____

Check and Change

4 **Edit your text. Make sure you included *can* or *can't* for abilities.**

Publish

5 **Write a clean version of your text.**

#CHALLENGE

UNIT SIX

Vocabulary

1 Match the columns and write sentences about yourself with can / can't.

1. Play ☐ zumba
2. Dance ☐ soccer
3. Practice ☐ Japanese
4. Speak ☐ mindfulness
5. Use ☐ sign language

1. ______________________
2. ______________________
3. ______________________
4. ______________________
5. ______________________

Grammar

2 Complete the conversation with can / can't.

A: Adam D: Danielle

A: Hi, Danielle. How are you today? Feeling better?

D: Hello, Adam. I'm totally fine and relaxed today.

A: Really? That's great.

D: Yes. I [1] __________ meditate every day now and I can run, too.

A: That's amazing. I [2] __________ meditate, but I can run. [3] __________ you teach me?

D: Yes, I [4] __________. Maybe tomorrow we [5] __________ run together and talk more about meditation.

A: Sorry. I [6] __________ run tomorrow. I have a swimming class. How about Wednesday?

D: Sure. See you on Wednesday morning.

3 Read the text and check (✓) the best title for it.

Do you know why successful people are always learning? Because they see life as a lifelong learning journey. Here is a list of five skills you can learn to help you achieve success in your life. And keep on learning!

1. Speak a new language
2. Play a musical instrument
3. Write academic texts
4. Meditate
5. Draw or take pictures

1. ☐ Visualization in Sports
2. ☐ Skills to Success
3. ☐ How to Be Famous

Listening

4 Listen to three people talk about their abilities. Order the pictures in the correct sequence. 23

Writing

5 Write about three things you can't do, but you would like to. Use your notebook.

I can't cook, but I would like to.

Speaking

6 Choose two members of your family. Record an audio about their abilities.

My mom's name is Jane. She can dance very well.

Vocabulary

Days and Months
Ordinal Numbers

1 **Read the text and check (✓) the pictures that relate to the benefits mentioned.**

Many cities around the world celebrate World Car Free Day every year on September 22. Drivers don't use their cars for a day. The event highlights the benefits of a car-free day, such as reduced air pollution and the promotion of walking and biking in a safer environment.

1. 

2. 

3. 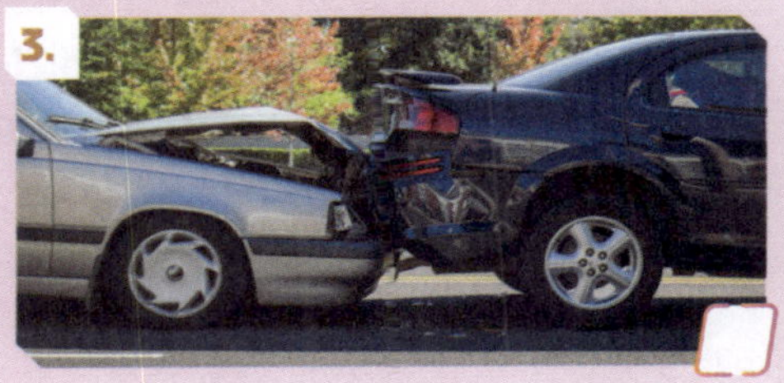

4. 

2 **Read the text again and complete the sentences.**

1. World Car Free Day is celebrated on ____________.
2. On World Car Free ____________, drivers don't use their cars.
3. The ____________ benefit of a day without a car mentioned in the text is reduced air pollution.
4. Many cities around the world ____________ World Car Free Day.

3 **Do you think World Car Free Day and Earth Day are similar? Why?**

Yes, in my opinion they are similar because they are environmental events.

____

____

____

____

4 **Look at the tickets and mark the sentences T (True) or F (False).**

1. ☐ The bus leaves in the morning.
2. ☐ The passenger has to go to the fourth gate.
3. ☐ The trip is on December 06.

4. ☐ The concert is in the evening.
5. ☐ The seats are in the first row.
6. ☐ The concert is on the weekend.

Reading

1 **Listen and answer. What will they celebrate at school?** 24

____

2 **Listen again and complete the sentences below.** 25

1. This year, school members of the __________ will celebrate a whole __________________ of __________________. It's on April ________.
2. This year we will celebrate __________________ Environmental __________________.
3. Each one will be responsible to choose a ________ in our calendar.
4. I love __________________. I hope there is a day for them in the __________________.

4 **EVALUATING DETAILS. Read the calendar again and answer the questions below.**

1. Is there a day to celebrate turtles? When is it?

____

2. Is there a day to celebrate vegetarianism? When is it?

____

3. According to this calendar, when do we celebrate World Water Day?

____

4. What do all these dates have in common?

____

5 **Choose a date you like from the calendar and explain why you think it is important.**

I think International Youth Day is important because young people are the future of the planet.

____

____

3 **Read the Annual Conservation and Environmental Days Calendar below.**

Annual Conservation and Environmental Days

JANUARY
1st New Year's Day– Resolve to go GREEN!

FEBRUARY
2nd World Wetlands Day
11th International Day of Women & Girls in Science

MARCH
3rd World Wildlife Day
2nd Friday Solar Appreciation Day
20th/21st Spring (Vernal) Equinox
21st International Day of Forests
22nd World Water Day
23rd World Meteorological Day
Last Saturday Earth Hour

APRIL
3rd World Aquatic Animal Day
Week before Earth Day National Environmental Education Week
22nd Earth Day
26th National Healthy Schools Day
Last Friday Arbor Day

MAY
First full week International Compost Awareness Week
2nd Saturday International Migratory Bird Day
16th Endangered Species Day
3rd Friday Bike-to-work Day
22nd International Day for Biological Diversity
23rd World Turtle Day

JUNE
1st Saturday National Trails Day
5th World Environment Day
8th World Ocean Day
15th Global Wind Day
21st/22nd Summer Solstice

JULY
11th World Population Day
26th International Day for the Conservation of the Mangrove Ecosystem

AUGUST
12th International Youth Day

SEPTEMBER
4th National Wildlife Day
21st International Day of Peace
21st Zero Emissions Day
22nd World Car Free Day
22nd/23rd Fall (Autumnal) Day

OCTOBER
1st Week Junk Mail Awareness Week
1st World Vegetarian Day
4th World Animal Day
8th Hydrogen Fuel Cell Day
17th International Day for the Eradication of Poverty

NOVEMBER
1st World Vegan Day
5th World Tsunami Awareness Day
15th America Recycles Day

DECEMBER
21st/22nd Winter Solstice

Source: https://projectgreenschools.org/annual-conservation-and-environmental-days-to-celebrate/. Accessed on January 31, 2022.

Grammar

Wh- question Words
Wh- questions and Prepositions of Time

1 Look at the pictures below and complete the dialogues. If necessary, refer to the table on page 48.

1.

A: [1] ______________ Car Free Day?

B: It is on [2] ______________.

A: [3] ______________ does it celebrate?

B: It celebrates the benefits of a day without [4] __________.

2.

A: [5] ______________ World Oceans Day?

B: It is on [6] ______________.

A: [7] __________ does it celebrate?

B: It celebrates the role of [8] ______________ in the world.

3.

A: [9] ______________ is International Day of Peace?

B: It is on [10] ______________.

A: [11] ______________ does it celebrate?

B: It celebrates the ideals of [12] ______________.

2 **Unscramble the words to make questions. Then answer the questions with true information about yourself.**

1. Is / when / birthday / your / ?

____

____

2. singer / your / who / favorite / is / ?

____

____

3. best friend / Where / live / your / does / ?

____

____

4. go / time / usually / What / to sleep / do / you / ?

____

____

3 **Complete the sentences with *in*, *on*, or *at*.**

1. My birthday is ______ July 21st.
2. The appointment is ______ Thursday ______ 7:30 a.m.
3. Our Halloween party is ______ October.
4. The grocery store closes ______ 6:00 p.m.

4 **Ask a family member about a date he / she thinks is important to celebrate. Then record what he / she said.**

What date do you think is important to celebrate? **Why**? **When** do you celebrate it?

My aunt thinks it's important to celebrate Arbor Day because trees give us clean air. We celebrate Arbor Day on **the last Friday of April**.

Use of English

1 **Write five special dates celebrated in your country and when you celebrate them.**

In Brazil, Carnival is a very special date. It's in February or March.

____

____

____

____

2 **Complete the sentences using the phrases from the box.**

dance and play	go to a party or ask for candies
special or new clothes	stay with family or friends

1. In some countries, it's a tradition to wear ______________ on New Year's Eve.
2. In Brazil, children ______________ on Halloween.
3. Carnival is a huge party in South America, people go to the streets to ______________.
4. On Christmas, it is common for people to ______________ and eat delicious food.

3 **Label the pictures with the special dates from Activity 2.**

4 **Match the *Wh–* questions to their corresponding answers.**

1. **When** is Halloween?
2. **What** do you do on New Year's Eve?
3. **Where** does your family celebrate Christmas?
4. **Who** do you spend Carnival with?

- ( ) With friends.
- ( ) It's on October 31st.
- ( ) At home.
- ( ) I party with my family and friends.

Writing

1 Read and check (✓) the American special date the text is about.

1. ☐ Independence Day
2. ☐ Easter
3. ☐ Thanksgiving

Also called Fourth of July, or July 4th, it is the nation's annual celebration of nationhood in the United States. The special date commemorates the passage of the Declaration of Independence by the Continental Congress on July 4, 1776.

It is a national holiday with parades, concerts of patriotic music, and fireworks. It is also a symbol of national power and American qualities — even the freedom to stay home and barbecue.

Prepare to Write

2 Think about Independence Day in your country and answer the following questions.

1. Is it a special date for the people in your country? Why?
____
____
2. When is it celebrated?
____
3. What do you do on this special day?
____
____
4. Who do you celebrate the date with?
____
____
5. Where do you celebrate it?
____

Write

3 Write a blog post about Independence Day in your country. Use your answers from Activity 2.

____
____
____
____

Check and Change

4 Read your blog post and make sure you included:

☐ the name of the special date.
☐ what is celebrated.
☐ how you celebrate the date.
☐ a picture to make your post more appealing.

5 Edit your text. Make sure all the elements in Activity 4 are included.

Publish

6 Write a clean version of your text.

your_post

____
____
____
____
____
____
____

#CHALLENGE

UNIT SEVEN

Vocabulary

1 **Complete Anna's schedule with ordinal numbers and days of the week. Then answer the questions.**

June

1st	**SUNDAY**	
	Stay home to watch a movie and relax	
2nd	**MONDAY**	
	7:00 a.m. – 11:30 a.m.	School
	2:10 p.m. – 3:00 p.m.	English Class
	4:00 p.m. – 5:00 p.m.	Homework
1 ______	2 ______	
	7:00 a.m. – 11:30 a.m.	School
	3:15 p.m. – 4:45 p.m.	Dance class
	4:00 p.m. – 5:00 p.m.	Homework
3 ______	4 ______	
	7:00 a.m. – 11:30 a.m.	School
	2:10 p.m. – 3:00 p.m.	English Class
	4:00 p.m. – 5:00 p.m.	Homework
5th	5 ______	
	7:00 a.m. – 11:30 a.m.	School
	3:15 p.m. – 4:45 p.m.	Dance class
	4:00 p.m. – 5:00 p.m.	Homework
6 ______	7 ______	
	7:00 a.m. – 11:30 a.m.	School
7th	**SATURDAY**	
	Play with friends all day	

1. What time does school finish?
______
2. What time is Anna's English class?
______
3. What time does Anna have dance class?
______
4. What time does Anna's dance class finish?
______
5. What time does Anna finish her homework?
______

Grammar

2 **Complete with *Wh-* questions and *in*, *on*, or *at*. About Anna's schedule**

1. **A:** ______ is Anna ______ Tuesday ______ 10:00?
B: She is at school.
2. **A:** ______ does she go to her English class?
B: ______ Tuesdays and Thursdays ____ 2:10 p.m.
3. **A:** ______ does she do ______ Saturdays?
B: She plays with friends all day.

Reading

3 **Read about a special day in the United States. Then check next year's calendar to answer the question.**

Martin Luther King Jr. Day, in the United States, is a holiday celebrated on the third Monday in January. The holiday honors the achievements of Martin Luther King Jr., a Baptist preacher who advocated the use of nonviolent means to end racial segregation.

When is this holiday celebrated next year?

______

Listening

4 **Listen and order the green events.** 26

- [ ] World Ocean Day
- [ ] World Aquatic Animal Day
- [ ] World Vegan Day

Writing

5 **Create a special date and write a short text about it in your notebook. Choose a date and the activities to celebrate this day.**

Speaking

6 **Talk about the special day you created in Activity 5 and audio record yourself.**

Vocabulary

Hobbies and Free-time Activities

1 **Read the text below and write the hobbies mentioned under the correct pictures.**

Positive hobbies contribute to the development of moral, social, academic, and creative skills, especially in children. If a child has positive hobbies, they will possibly have a better future, both professionally and personally. They have more creative energy and more confidence to make their own decisions. In addition, hobbies can be excellent for creating new things, learning, and having fun. Playing musical instruments, singing, gardening, taking pictures, reading, etc. are some hobbies a child can have.

1.

2.

5.

3.

4.

2 **Read the text in Activity 1 again and mark the sentences T (True) or F (False). Correct the false ones.**

1. ☐ Having a hobby is not important for the development of a child.

____

2. ☐ Hobbies help develop a lot of skills in kids.

____

3. ☐ Hobbies give children confidence to make decisions.

____

4. ☐ Reading and gardening are not examples of positive hobbies.

____

3 **Write about an eco-friendly hobby you have or would like to have.**

____

____

Reading

1 Listen and answer. What hobbies or free-time activities are they talking about? 27

1. ______________. 2. ______________.

2 Listen again and complete the sentences below. 28

1. This year I'm ______________ my ______________ at an ______________.
2. I ______________ so happy and grateful for that.
3. My mom ______________ in an office at the ______________.
4. I'm ______________ for buying some things for my ______________.
5. One of my hobbies is ______________.

3 Read the text below about shopping. Does the text encourage people to have this hobby?

____

It's nice to have a hobby like this, but it can become a problem in our lives and on our planet.

Money: Frequently purchasing things that are not necessary is bad for saving money or using it for a better future.

Close relationships: Parents may think that it is not good to buy too many things, which can cause disagreements in the family.

Time: Money is not the only limited and valuable commodity we waste when we buy too much. We also waste time.

Resources: Every time we buy things that are not necessary, we contribute to pollution and help industries destroy the environment.

4 SCANNING. Read the text again and answer the questions below.

1. According to the text, is shopping a positive and responsible hobby?

____

2. Shopping as a hobby can bring a lot of problems in four main areas. Which ones?

____

3. Why can shopping as a hobby be harmful to the environment?

____

4. Do you agree with the ideas in the text? Why? Why not?

____

5 Do you like shopping? Why? Why not? Audio record your answer and send it to a classmate.

Grammar

Present Continuous – Affirmative, Negative, and Questions
Object Pronouns

1 **Look at the pictures and answer the questions.**

1. 
What are they doing?
____
____

2. 
What is he doing?
____
____

3. 
Is she listening to music? What is she doing?
____
____

4. 
Is he driving a car? What is he doing?
____
____

5. 
What are they doing?
____
____

2 **Unscramble the words below to make questions. Answer them using affirmative and negative short answers.**

1. watching / Clara / Is / now / a movie / ?
____
____

2. a musical / Are / instrument / playing / they / ?
____
____

3. Are / studying / for / the final exam / you / on Tuesday / ?
____
____

4. the park / Is / she / running / in / ?
____
____

3 **Complete the sentences with the correct object pronouns.**

1. I'm going to school with (they) ______________.
2. I'm so tired. Maybe they can drive (we) ______________ there.
3. I love (he) ______________ so much!
4. My mother is buying a laptop for (you) ______________.
5. Look at (I) ______________ when I'm speaking, please.
6. Would you like to check (the bag) ______________ before we go?

4 **Correct the sentences. Rewrite them with the object pronouns.**

1. I want <u>she</u> to help me.
____
2. They would like <u>we</u> to go on the trip, too.
____
3. She paints <u>they</u> for Carnival.
____
4. We help <u>he</u> with his homework.
____

#DEVELOP

UNIT EIGHT

Use of English

1 **Use the verbs below to write true sentences about you and hobbies / free-time activities.**

Love: I love reading non-fiction books.

1. Like: ______________________________
2. Don't mind: ______________________________
3. Don't like: ______________________________
4. Can't stand: ______________________________

2 **Complete the dialogues below.**

1. **A:** ______________________________

   B: I love that. I go to the movies every week.

2. **A:** What do you think of red sneakers?

   B: ______________________________. They are casual.

3. **A:** What do you think about shopping as a hobby?

   B: ______________________________. I prefer outdoor activities and positive hobbies.

   A: ______________________________

   B: Oh, I love hiking. It's my favorite hobby.

3 **Answer the questions.**

1. What do you think about social media?

   ____

2. What do you think of web influencers?

   ____

3. What do you think of volunteering as a hobby?

   ____

4. What do you think about your mom?

   ____

4 **Rewrite the questions in Activity 3 using object pronouns.**

1. What do you think about ______________?
2. What do you think of ______________?
3. What do you think of ______________ as a hobby?
4. What do you think about ______________?

Writing

1 **Read and check (✓) the hobby the text is about.**

With their big heads and eyes, the vinyl figures are inspired by pop culture elements, characters from TV shows and movies, singers, etc. There are over 8,000 different figures in the market. They are a worldwide trend, and many people show pictures of their collections on the Internet. But why should you have a collection? People simply become fans of characters on TV. So imagine having your idols as little plastic dolls that you can display at home.

1. ☐ Collecting funko pops.
2. ☐ Collecting stamps.
3. ☐ Collecting Barbie dolls.

Prepare to Write

2 **Think about an interesting type of hobby and make notes.**

Write

3 **Write a paragraph about the hobby you chose in Activity 2 for a personal profile on a friendship app.**

Check and Change

4 **Read your text and make sure you included:**

☐ a description of the hobby.

☐ why you chose to write about this hobby.

5 **Edit your text. Make sure the elements in Activity 4 are included.**

Publish

6 **In your notebook, write a clean version of your text.**

Vocabulary

1 List the clothing items and accessories in the picture.

____

____

____

____

Grammar

2 Complete the dialogue using the verbs in parentheses in the Present Continuous.

Tim: What [1] ________ you [2] ________ (watch), Anna?

Anna: It's a documentary about a park in Canada.

Tim: [3] ________ you [4] ________ (enjoy) it?

Anna: Yes, I am, but it is a little long. I [5] ________ (not / pay) attention anymore... LOL

Reading

3 Read the personal profile and answer the questions.

Hello, I'm fourteen years old and my name is Tom. My parents, two brothers, and I live in Los Angeles. My brothers and I go to California Middle School. It's a big school, but everyone is nice. It's awesome! Art and theater are two of my favorite subjects. I'm a very inventive person!

I go swimming and play tennis and volleyball on the weekends. I also take piano lessons, but I'm not very good at playing musical instruments!

My dream is to pursue a career as an actor. I hope that one day I'll be able to appear on TV and in movies.

1. How old is Tom?

____

2. What are his hobbies?

____

____

3. How many brothers does he have?

____

4. What is his dream?

____

Listening

4 Listen and number the hobbies in the order they are mentioned. 29

- [ ] Learning to code
- [ ] Collecting coins
- [ ] Taking care of dogs

Writing

5 Imagine you started a new hobby that you love. Write a message telling a friend about it and invite him / her to join you.

____

____

____

Speaking

6 You are going to do your favorite free-time activity and a friend is going with you. But he / she doesn't know what to wear. Describe your clothes to him / her. Audio record yourself.

FOCUS ON CULTURE

1 Would you like to move to another country? Why? Discuss in pairs.

2 **MAKING PREDICTIONS.** What do you think a naturalization ceremony is? Think, and then read the text to check your predictions.

Naturalization...

A naturalization ceremony is an official event in the United States when immigrants become American citizens. Here are some people's stories:

I am from Pakistan, but my family and I are in the United States because there are more opportunities. The education system here is good for my children. I am American now.
Walia, 53

I am Russian, and I am the only immigrant in my company, but today there is a party in my office because it is my naturalization ceremony day. There are cakes, American flags, and balloons from my coworkers. It is a beautiful gesture.
Anna, 53

I am from the United Kingdom, but my wife is American. I say that I am here in the United States because of love! There are 13,000 other people here today. It is very exciting!
Simon, 54

Source: <https://www.theguardian.com/us-news/2017/feb/06/the-day-i-became-a-us-citizen-proud-grateful-and-hopeful>. Accessed on Feb. 15, 2022.

3 **CHECKING PREDICTIONS.** Read the text again and answer the questions.

1. Where is Walia from?

____

2. Where is Anna from?

____

3. Where is Simon from?

____

4 Write Walia, Anna, or Simon.

1. ________________ is at a party.
2. ________________ is married to an American.
3. ________________ is in the United States with her children.
4. ________________ is happy with her coworkers.
5. ________________ is one of many people at the ceremony.

5 Read the profiles. In pairs, take turns asking and answering the questions.

what / name   how / old   where / from   why / in the United States

Where are you from?

I'm from Brazil.

Juan

Basic Info
Age: 14
Nationality: Honduran
In the United States because:
his mom is married to an American

Meera

Basic Info
Age: 13
Nationality: Indian
In the United States because:
her parents are university professors here

6 Choose one of the profiles and write a short text about that person, including the reason why he / she is in the United States.

1 **PREDICTING. Read the title of the text. What cities in the world do you think are walkable?**

____

Walkable Cities

Walkable Cities

The best cities in the world to walk around are London, Paris, Bogota, and Hong Kong, according to a report. In these cities, citizens are close to car-free spaces, schools, and medical clinics so they don't need to travel by car.

In Bogota, Colombia, the city blocks are small. Most people are less than 100m away from parks, streets for pedestrians, and squares.

Alexandra Gomes, from the London School of Economics, says that walking is essential to life in a city. In the United States, there are lots of sidewalks. However, everything is far apart so in many states and cities it is impossible to go to a grocery store or to school on foot. In Indianapolis, only 4 % of people live close to education and medical clinics.

There are plans to change this is the future. Many cities around the world have plans to make their cities more pedestrian friendly.

Source: <https://www.theguardian.com/cities/2020/oct/15/study-reveals-worlds-most-walkable-cities>. Accessed on Feb. 15, 2022.

2 **SCANNING. Read the article. Check (✓) the countries with walkable cities, cross (✕) the ones without walkable cities, and draw (–) in the countries that aren't mentioned.**

1. ☐ Australia
2. ☐ Colombia
3. ☐ China
4. ☐ France
5. ☐ Spain
6. ☐ The United Kingdom
7. ☐ The United States

3 **Read the text again and mark the sentences T (True) or F (False). Then correct the false sentences.**

1. ☐ A walkable city means that residents are close to education and medical clinics.
2. ☐ Bogota is walkable because people are more than 100m away from parks.
3. ☐ Walking is an important part of life in a city.
4. ☐ There aren't many sidewalks in the United States.
5. ☐ You need a car in the state of Indianapolis.

____

____

____

____

____

____

4 **Is the city you live in walkable? Discuss in pairs.**

In my town / city, it is easy to go to... on foot.

In my town / city, it is difficult to go to... on foot.

5 **Think about your city and complete the sentence.**

I think my city is ____________ because there are / aren't ____________.

6 **In groups, list ideas to improve urban mobility in your city.**

____

____

____

____

____

____

7 **In groups, present the ideas discussed in Activity 6 to the class. Vote for the best ones.**

#FOCUS ON CULTURE

1 Look around your school. Is it big or small? How many students are there? Discuss in groups.

2 What is unusual about City Montessori school in Lucknow? Read the text and check your predictions.

City Montessori

City Montessori school in Lucknow, India, is a big school. There are 52,000 students at the school. In each of the 1,050 classrooms, there are approximately 45 students aged from five to 17 years old. Because the school is very large, there are 20 campuses across the city. There is even a department specifically for writing congratulation letters!

The school is popular because it gets good results. 40 % of students' grades on the HSC exams are over 90 %, so students can get into good universities in India and abroad. The teachers' salaries are good because of the large class size. There are also *notebook checkers* who are teachers' assistants that help during class time. Every month the teacher visits the homes of five students. They make simple observations, for example they suggest that the television is not in the student's study space.

Source: <https://www.theguardian.com/teacher-network/2015/dec/16/52000-students-and-1050-classrooms-inside-the-worlds-largest-school>. Accessed on Feb. 15, 2022.

3 **SKIMMING. Read the text again and answer. Why is City Montessori school in Lucknow popular?**

____

4 **MONITORING COMPREHENSION USING DETAILS. Circle the correct alternatives to complete the sentences about the text.**

1. There are **forty-five** / **fifty-five** students per classroom.
2. **Fourteen** / **Forty** percent of students get good grades on the HSC exams.
3. A good grade is **ninety** / **seventy** percent.
4. There **are** / **aren't** students who are eighteen years old.
5. There are **twelve** / **twenty** campuses around the city.

5 **Compare your school to City Montessori school in Lucknow. Answer the questions.**

1. How many students are there in your school? ______________________
2. How many classrooms are there? ______________________
3. How old are the students in your school? ______________________
4. What is the passing grade in your school? ______________________
5. Are there teachers' assistants helping in class? ______________________

6 **Write a short paragraph about your school.**

7 **Read your paragraph from Activity 6 to the class. Compare your text to your classmates'.**

1 What jobs can teenagers do?

____

2 MAKING AND CHECKING PREDICTIONS. What are some summer jobs for teenagers in the U.K.? Read the article and check your predictions.

____

____

A Job for the Summer +

www.workingteens.com

A Job for the Summer

In the United Kingdom, it is very popular for teenagers to get a job for the summer vacation. Sometimes it is difficult because you need experience. But a good academic and school record and good references are useful. Volunteer work is also helpful.

Most jobs for teenagers are in shopping malls and supermarkets. The salary for a store assistant in a regular store is around $6 (14–16 years old) or $9 (18–20 years old) per hour. In a supermarket, workers earn $12 per hour, but in some supermarkets the minimum age is 18. If you are 18 or over, there are a lot of jobs in food delivery services. Some, like Just Eat, offer a fully insured e-bike or moped and pay up to $14 per hour. You can work from the age of 13, but there aren't many jobs for teenagers this age. There is modeling or acting, but there is a lot of competition! An easy option for 13-year-olds is a paper round – delivering newspapers every morning at 6 a.m. Is that a job for you?

Source: <https://www.telegraph.co.uk/family/parenting/teenagers-summer-jobs-everything-need-know-helping-teen-find/>. Accessed on Feb. 15, 2022.

3 READING FOR DETAILS. Read the text again and complete the sentences.

1. Teenagers' salaries in the U.K. are by ______________ .
2. The salary for a 15-year-old store assistant is $ ______________ .
3. The salary for an 18-year-old supermarket assistant is $ ______________ .
4. A seventeen-year-old ______________ work as a food delivery driver.
5. There aren't many jobs available for teenagers aged ______________ .

4 Look at the profiles. In pairs, talk about possible summer jobs for each person.

Rita can be a store assistant. She can earn six dollars an hour. She can't be a supermarket assistant or a food delivery driver.

Rita, 14

Zara, 19

Patrick, 13

Alex, 17

5 Look online for some jobs for teenagers in your country and create the ads.

1 **ACTIVATING PRIOR KNOWLEDGE. What do you think is important for a teenager's health and well-being? Think and check (✓).**

1. ☐ a stable daily routine
2. ☐ a lot of time on social media
3. ☐ being with family
4. ☐ exercising
5. ☐ money to go shopping
6. ☐ eating fruit and vegetables

2 **Read the text. Which options from Activity 1 are mentioned?**

____

____

____

Teenagers Like...

www.simpleteenlife.com

Teenagers Like the Simple Things in Life

Close friends, playing sports, and a stable home life are more important to teenagers' happiness than their parents' salaries, according to a study by the Institute for Social and Economic Research at the University of Essex. The study involves children and teenagers aged 10 to 15.

They need to have access to the Internet, but if they use it for more than one hour a day, they don't do other social activities.

Teenagers who invite their friends for dinner once a fortnight and who go swimming once a month are also happier.

Diet is a factor in happiness, too. Teenagers who eat less than five portions of fruit and vegetables a day or who eat fast foods most days are less happy.

The study concludes that children need to have lots of opportunities for social contact. Money is important to teenagers, but only because it provides ways to enjoy leisure time with family and friends.

Source: <https://www.theguardian.com/society/2012/oct/06/teenagers-value-the-simple-things>. Accessed on Feb. 15, 2022.

3 **MONITORING COMPREHENSION USING DETAILS. Read the text again and mark the sentences T (True) or F (False).**

1. ☐ Teenagers want their parents to be rich.
2. ☐ Happy teenagers sometimes go swimming.
3. ☐ Teenagers need offline social contact
4. ☐ Eating fast food doesn't affect happiness.
5. ☐ Teenagers want money for experiences, not things.

4 **Talk in pairs. Read the sentences in Activity 3 again. Do you agree or disagree with them?**

I agree that teenagers want their parents to be rich.

5 **The text in Activity 2 is from 2012. Do you think teenagers' lives are different now? Write a paragraph about what makes teenagers happy nowadays.**

6 **Read your paragraph from Activity 5 to the class. Compare your ideas to your classmates'.**

1 **What makes a city unsustainable? Discuss in pairs.**

2 **MAKING PREDICTIONS. What is *quirky*? Read the text and check (✓) its correct definition.**

1. ▢ innovative and imaginative
2. ▢ unusual in an interesting way
3. ▢ strange and scary

Quirky Ideas...

Quirky Ideas to Make Cities Sustainable

City life has many benefits, but a sustainable lifestyle is not one of them. Pollution, traffic, and loss of green spaces are just some of the daily difficulties for city residents. Here are two interesting solutions to make cities sustainable.

____

Not everyone in cities loves cars. Bikes are popular, too. But where can we keep your bike safe? In Tokyo, there is an eco-cycle underground bicycle park. It is seven meters wide and there is space for 204 bikes. You touch a button and the park delivers your bike to you automatically in 13 seconds.

____

Today's cities sometimes look like they're built more for cars than people. The pop-up park is a simple idea. Take an empty parking lot, money, and a pot of plant or two, and make your own private park.

Source: <https://www.theguardian.com/sustainable-business/2015/apr/16/ten-quirky-ideas-for-making-our-cities-more-sustainable>. Accessed on Feb. 15, 2022.

3 **Read the text again and write the subheadings in the correct places.**

Pop-up park	Underground storage

4 **Answer the questions about the text in Activity 2.**

1. Where is the eco-cycle underground bicycle park?

____

2. How many bikes can go into it?

____

3. Why is the pop-up park a good idea?

____

4. What do you need for a pop-up park?

____

5 **In pairs, plan a pop-up park event for your town / city. Think about the questions below.**

Where is it?	**Is it free?**
Who is it for?	**What is there?**

____

____

____

____

6 **Write an e-mail to the mayor of your town/city presenting your idea for a pop-up park.**

CANCEL SEND

TO

SUBJECT

1 **Do you know anyone with disabilities? How are you related?**

2 **SKIMMING. What is a *bugbear*? Read the text and find out. Then (✓) its correct definition.**

1. ☐ Something that makes you feel annoyed.
2. ☐ A small animal that is a mixture of insect and mammal.
3. ☐ A person with a lot of annoying characteristics.

Four Things...

Four Things You Should Stop Saying and Doing to People with Disabilities

Four people with disabilities reveal their everyday bugbears.

1. I don't like it when people say I am *brave* or *inspiring* just because I am at the mall on my own. I find this phrase very patronizing. Don't say this to me unless I fly to the moon or fight a tiger!
2. It's irritating when people talk to me like I am a child. People think they need to speak in a loud, slow voice. I have a hearing aid. I can ask you to speak loud if I need you to!
3. You don't ask non-disabled people about their medical history, so why would you do this to me? It's an unnecessary and rude question.
4. People try to help me lock up my bike in the street. In restaurants they cut up my food before they serve me. It's frustrating and sometimes embarrassing.

Source: <https://www.theguardian.com/inequality/2017/nov/15/seven-things-you-should-stop-saying-doing-to-disabled-people>. Accessed on Feb. 15, 2022.

3 **Read the text again and write the number of the paragraph next to its corresponding command.**

☐ Don't use baby-talk.
☐ Don't help me without asking.
☐ Don't ask what my disabilities are.
☐ Don't call me brave.

4 SUMMARIZING. Check (✓) the correct sentence about the text.

1. ☐ The text is about things many people do that disabled people don't like.
2. ☐ Some people think that people who can't hear also can't understand well.
3. ☐ It is normal to ask everyone about their medical problems.
4. ☐ It is offensive to think that disabled people can't do things.

5 Work in pairs. What other bugbears do you think you could add to the article? Make notes.

6 Choose one of your ideas from Activity 5 and write a paragraph about it.

7 In pairs, present your ideas from Activity 5 to your classmates. Consider the ideas presented by the other pairs and vote for the best ones.

1 ACTIVATING PRIOR KNOWLEDGE. Look at the picture. What do you know about the festival of Diwali?

2 READING FOR DETAILS. Read the text and answer the questions.

Diwali

Diwali is an important religious festival in Hinduism and Sikhism. It lasts five days. The date is decided by the Hindu calendar, but in the Gregorian calendar it is usually in October or November. The name *Diwali* comes from the Sanskrit *dipavali*, which means *rows of lights*. The Diwali festival symbolizes the victory of light over darkness.

However, a few days after this year's festival, residents of many big Indian cities are in semi-darkness. Why? Because of smog from firecrackers. In the Diwali celebrations, people give candy and light traditional lamps, but they light millions of firecrackers. These firecrackers cause toxic fumes. Atul Chauhan is a professional athlete in the capital city of Delhi. He says that he needs to train for a competition, but he can't. "I get tired within 20 minutes. It's like something inside your eyes, you can't see properly." The government wants to introduce more green "crackers". These aren't noisy and emit less pollution.

Source: <https://www.theguardian.com/world/2018/nov/08/firecrackers-from-diwali-celebrations-shroud-delhi-in-toxic-smog>. Accessed on Feb. 15, 2022.

1. What religions celebrate Diwali?

____

2. How long does the festival last?

____

3. When is the festival?

____

4. What does the festival celebrate?

____

3 **Read the text again, look at the pictures, and check (✓) the elements of the festival that have positive consequences and cross (✕) the ones that have negative consequences.**

1. 

2. 

3. 

4 **In pairs, talk about the similarities and differences between Diwali and your country's carnival celebrations.**

5 **Write a short text about your country's carnival celebrations.**

1 **Match the pictures to the hobbies.**

1. beekeeping
2. model building
3. gardening
4. rock and fossil collecting
5. birdwatching
6. falconry

a.

b.

c.

d.

e.

f.

2 **SKIMMING. Read the text. What areas can the hobbies in Activity 1 contribute to?**

____

Hobbies such as...

Hobbies such as Beekeeping or Model Building Are the Key to a Technical Career

Children and teenagers who have certain hobbies are more likely to work with math, science, and engineering when they are adults, according to a study. These are key areas in the industry of the future.

Government ministers want schools to create opportunities for students to participate in these activities, such as gardening, rock and fossil collecting, and birdwatching. Teachers are connecting with hobbyists to provide inclusive opportunities for their students.

Some schools are already working with beekeepers and falconry. Julia Pigott, a beekeeper, works with two school projects in Cumbria. She says, "It is like all practical things where you have a practical element... You really get the children's interest".

Source: <https://www.theguardian.com/lifeandstyle/2017/oct/21/hobbies-key-to-childrens-interest-in-maths-science-engineering. Accessed on Feb. 15, 2022.

3 **Read the text again and mark the sentences T (True) or F (False).**

1. [ ] Jobs in science are important for the future.
2. [ ] Government ministers are talking to hobbyists about opportunities.
3. [ ] Some schools have projects in beekeeping and birdwatching.
4. [ ] Children like practical activities.

4 **READING FOR DETAILS. Work in pairs. Which of the hobbies in Activity 1 would you like to take up? Why? Make notes.**

____

____

____

____

5 **Research where you can do each of the hobbies in Activity 1. Write a short text with information about the hobbies and the places where you can do them.**

6 **Read your text from Activity 5 to your classmates. Vote for the best texts.**

TEEN TALK

1 Share personal information in pairs.

2 Look and role play.

Where are you from?

I'm from France. I'm French.

Student A

Student B

3 Complete Profile A with information about a new student. Then ask and answer questions to complete Profile B.

Profile A

Name: ______________________

Age: ______________________

Nationality: ______________________

Profile B

Name: ______________________

Age: ______________________

Nationality: ______________________

4 Work with a different classmate. Take turns telling your classmate about the profiles in Activity 3.

Her name's Joana. She's 14. She's from the U.K.

5 Ask and answer questions about the participants of the International Teen Summit.

6 Self-evaluation. Reflect on the tasks in this section and check (✓) the correct columns in the chart.

Learning Objectives	Rating
Did I express my ideas well?	☆☆☆
Did I use the language structures from the unit?	☆☆☆
Did I use the vocabulary from the unit?	☆☆☆
Did I pronounce new words correctly?	☆☆☆
Did I correct any mistakes?	☆☆☆
Was I collaborative in the conversations?	☆☆☆

1 Think and complete.

Places in my town

2 In pairs, ask and answer about how you go to the places mentioned in the mind map.

3 Choose and say. Then guess.

I go to the movie theater by car.

You're Alex!

4 Complete the map with four places. In pairs, practice giving and following directions.

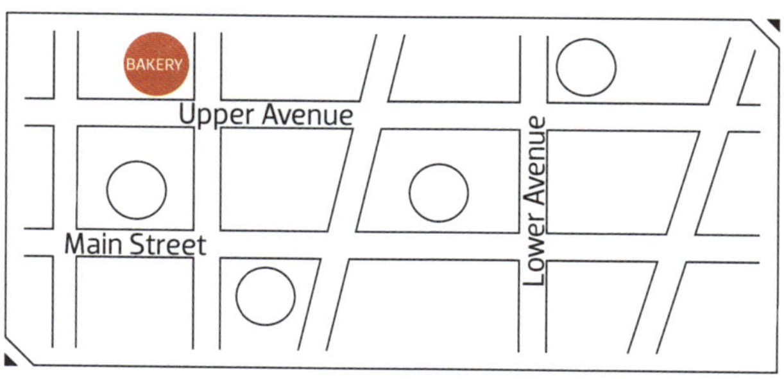

5 Talk in pairs. What is there in an ideal city?

In an ideal city, there is a big and modern hospital.

6 Self-evaluation. Reflect on the tasks in this section and check (✓) the correct columns in the chart.

Learning Objectives	Rating
Did I express my ideas well?	☆☆☆
Did I use the language structures from the unit?	☆☆☆
Did I use the vocabulary from the unit?	☆☆☆
Did I pronounce new words correctly?	☆☆☆
Did I correct any mistakes?	☆☆☆
Was I collaborative in the conversations?	☆☆☆

1 Look around your classroom and count. How many are there?

desks	whiteboards	books	chairs

2 Look at the picture below. Talk to a classmate about each item.

How many pens are there?

There is one pen.

3 Role play the situations in pairs.

Student A

1. You are the teacher. Respond to Student B.
2. You are the student. Ask how to spell *notebook*.
3. You are the teacher. Ask students to turn on their cameras.

Student B

1. You are the student. Ask the teacher to repeat.
2. You are the teacher. Respond to Student A.
3. You are the student. Respond to Student A.

4 Look at the picture. Ask and answer questions about it.

What are those?

They are books.

5 Compare schools in your country to boat schools.

On a boat school, the classroom is small.

6 Self-evaluation. Reflect on the tasks in this section and check (✓) the correct columns in the chart.

Learning Objectives	Rating
Did I express my ideas well?	☆☆☆
Did I use the language structures from the unit?	☆☆☆
Did I use the vocabulary from the unit?	☆☆☆
Did I pronounce new words correctly?	☆☆☆
Did I correct any mistakes?	☆☆☆
Was I collaborative in the conversations?	☆☆☆

1 Work in pairs. Tell your classmate about three family members.

2 Choose a person. Answer your classmate's questions so he / she can guess who you are.

> Are you a man or a woman?
> Are you a pilot?

1.

Samia

2.

Renan

3.

Andre

4.

Andy

5.

Sophie

3 Match the hats to the people in Activity 2.

> Whose hat is this?

> It's Andre's hat. It's his hat.

1. 
2. 
3. 
4. 
5. 

4 Work in pairs. Ask and answer questions to complete the family tree.

Student A

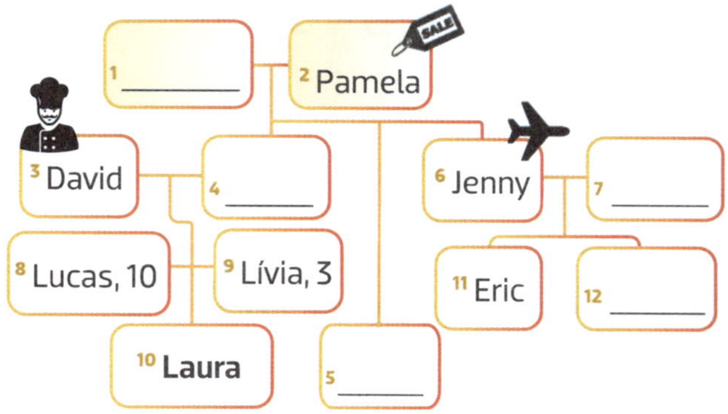

Student B

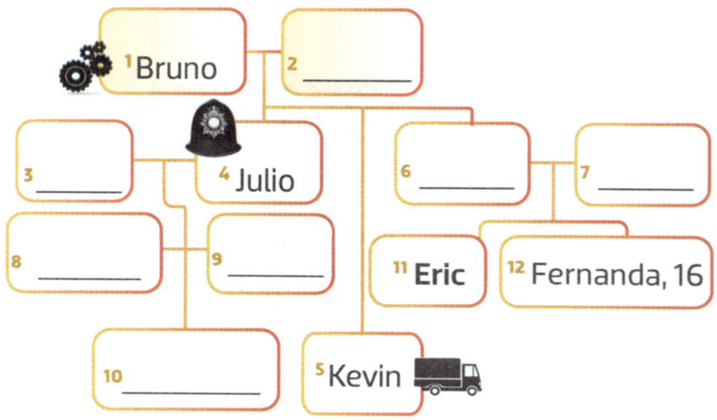

5 Discuss in pairs. What workers does a community need?

6 Self-evaluation. Reflect on the tasks in this section and check (✓) the correct columns in the chart.

Learning Objectives	Rating
Did I express my ideas well?	☆☆☆
Did I use the language structures from the unit?	☆☆☆
Did I use the vocabulary from the unit?	☆☆☆
Did I pronounce new words correctly?	☆☆☆
Did I correct any mistakes?	☆☆☆
Was I collaborative in the conversations?	☆☆☆

1 Talk in pairs. What do you do every day?

2 Number the pictures in the order you do the activities related to them. Then talk to a classmate. Change roles.

3 Tell another classmate about your daily routine.

4 Work with another classmate. Complete the chart with your assumptions about his / her daily routine. Then talk to your classmate and check your answers.

I think you never exercise.

	always	usually	sometimes	never
exercise	☐	☐	☐	☐
go on social media before school	☐	☐	☐	☐
watch a movie in the evening	☐	☐	☐	☐
have dinner with your parents	☐	☐	☐	☐
sleep for more than six hours	☐	☐	☐	☐

5 Read Vanessa's answers to a questionnaire. Then write complete sentences. Do you think she has healthy habits?

1. ☒ I sleep for 7 to 9 hours a night.
2. ☑ I chat with my family. *sometimes*
3. ☑ I watch a movie before bed. *always (series)*
4. ☒ I exercise for 30 minutes. *never haha!*
5. ☑ I have breakfast, lunch, and dinner. *usually*
6. ☑ I brush my teeth in the morning and the evening. *and after meals!*

____

____

____

____

____

____

____

____

____

____

6 Self-evaluation. Reflect on the tasks in this section and check (✓) the correct columns in the chart.

Learning Objectives	Rating
Did I express my ideas well?	☆☆☆
Did I use the language structures from the unit?	☆☆☆
Did I use the vocabulary from the unit?	☆☆☆
Did I pronounce new words correctly?	☆☆☆
Did I correct any mistakes?	☆☆☆
Was I collaborative in the conversations?	☆☆☆

1 Discuss the questions in pairs.

- Do you live in a house or an apartment?
- How many bedrooms are there in your home?
- What other rooms are there in your home?

2 Work in pairs. Role play.

1. Student A

Ask about:
- number of bedrooms
- number of bathrooms
- big yard
- balcony

Student B

Small apartment
2 bedrooms, 1 bathroom
✓ kitchen and living room (combined)
✓ balcony
✓ laundry room

2. Student B

Ask about:
- number of bedrooms
- big kitchen
- laundry room
- yard

Student A

House in the country
6 bedrooms, 4 bathrooms
✓ very large yard
✓ 2 porches
✓ 2 living rooms

3 Choose a room and ask your classmate about it.

bathroom bedroom kitchen living room

What is there in your kitchen?

4 Draw the items below in the picture. Then describe your picture to your classmate. Are your pictures similar?

book cat poster table

5 What is important to have in a home? Discuss in pairs.

6 Self-evaluation. Reflect on the tasks in this section and check (✓) the correct columns in the chart.

Learning Objective	Rating
Did I express my ideas well?	☆☆☆
Did I use the language structures from the unit?	☆☆☆
Did I use the vocabulary from the unit?	☆☆☆
Did I pronounce new words correctly?	☆☆☆
Did I correct any mistakes?	☆☆☆
Was I collaborative in the conversations?	☆☆☆

1 Choose a family member and tell your classmate which of the activities below he / she can and can't do.

code dance play chess run fast
sing speak another language swim

My brother can code, but he can't speak another language.

2 Take the challenge with a classmate. Check (✓) or cross (✗) in the chart.

Can you... ?

	Me	My classmate
say the alphabet backward		
count up to 30 in 20 seconds		
draw a dog		
sing a hit song in English		

3 Based on the chart in Activity 2, tell another classmate about what you and your classmate can and can't do.

I can't say the alphabet backward, but Ramon can.

4 Answer the questions in pairs.

1. Paulo is in a wheelchair. What can he do? What can't he do?

____

____

2. Fernanda is blind. What can she do? What can't she do?

____

____

5 Work in pairs. Read and decide who says each sentence.

1. ______________________________

Don't move!

2. ______________________________

Be quiet, please.

3. ______________________________

Don't eat that. It's hot!

4. ______________________________

Be careful here.

5. ______________________________

Brush your teeth!

6. ______________________________

Run fast!

6 Self-evaluation. Reflect on the tasks in this section and check (✓) the correct columns in the chart.

Learning Objectives	Rating
Did I express my ideas well?	☆☆☆
Did I use the language structures from the unit?	☆☆☆
Did I use the vocabulary from the unit?	☆☆☆
Did I pronounce new words correctly?	☆☆☆
Did I correct any mistakes?	☆☆☆
Was I collaborative in the conversations?	☆☆☆

1 Work in small groups. Talk about your birthdays.

My birthday is on November 24th.

2 Look and answer. What time is it?

1. 

____

2. 

____

3. 

____

4. 

____

5. 

____

6. 

____

3 Complete the chart with five daily routine activities you do. Then talk to two classmates and make notes about them.

Me	Time	My classmate

4 Choose a special date. Ask your classmate questions using the words from the box.

What When Where Who

Where do you celebrate New Year's Eve?
What do you do?

5 Ask questions to complete the fact sheet.

Student A

____

____________ **Day**

When: October 23

Where: ____________

Join in! ____________
Draw pictures about climate change in chalk on the sidewalk.

Student B

Youth Climate Action Day

When: ____________

Where: All around the world.

Join in!
Ride colorful bikes in the city center.

6 Self-evaluation. Reflect on the tasks in this section and check (✓) the correct columns in the chart.

Learning Objectives	Rating
Did I express my ideas well?	☆☆☆
Did I use the language structures from the unit?	☆☆☆
Did I use the vocabulary from the unit?	☆☆☆
Did I pronounce new words correctly?	☆☆☆
Did I correct any mistakes?	☆☆☆
Was I collaborative in the conversations?	☆☆☆

1 Tell your classmate about three hobbies you have.

2 Choose a profile. Make sentences about this person's hobbies. Have your classmate guess who the person is.

This person doesn't like shopping.

Olivia
go shopping
make videos
go to the beach

Pablo
hang out with friends
go to the beach
go shopping

Samuel
read comic books
go shopping
make videos

3 Work in pairs. Ask and answer questions to complete William's schedule.

It's Monday morning. What is William doing?

He's studying at school.

Student A

	Mon	Tues	Weds	Thurs	Fri
Morning	study at school	______	study at school	study at school	study at school
Afternoon	play soccer	×	visit Grandma and Grandpa	×	______
Evening	______	watch TV	______	do homework at Becca's house	______

Student B

	Mon	Tues	Weds	Thurs	Fri
Morning	______	study at school	study at school	______	study at school
Afternoon	play soccer	×	______	×	help at Mom's store
Evening	do homework	______	help Dad to make dinner	______	play at the arcade with Dan

4 Carol is shopping. What is she doing to be a responsible consumer?

1. ☐ buying bottles of water
2. ☐ drinking from a reusable water bottle
3. ☐ geting plastic bags in stores
4. ☐ using a reusable bag
5. ☐ shopping for new products
6. ☐ looking in thrift stores

5 Self-evaluation. Reflect on the tasks in this section and check (✓) the correct columns in the chart.

Learning Objectives	Rating
Did I express my ideas well?	☆☆☆
Did I use the language structures from the unit?	☆☆☆
Did I use the vocabulary from the unit?	☆☆☆
Did I pronounce new words correctly?	☆☆☆
Did I correct any mistakes?	☆☆☆
Was I collaborative in the conversations?	☆☆☆

GAMES

1 Do you like board games? What board games do you play?

2 Play the *Greetings Game* in groups.

Instructions

1. Take turns to flip a coin to move along the path (heads = 1 step; tails = 2 steps).
2. Follow the instructions in each square you step on or over (incorrect or incomplete sentences mean the student has to miss a turn).
   - **Words:** Introduce yourself using the word presented.
   - **Words with questions marks (?):** Choose a player and ask him / her a question using the word presented.
   - The chosen player answers the question (incorrect or incomplete sentences mean the student has to miss a turn).
3. The first player to get to the end is the winner.

3 In groups, answer the questions about the game.

1. Was the game easy or difficult to play?
2. What was easy? Why?
3. What was difficult? Why?
4. What did you learn from playing the game?

1 Do you like to play card games? What card games do you play?

2 Play Bingo.

bank bike bus car cheap expensive fast ferryboat hospital
modern movie theater old park restaurant school
shopping mall slow streetcar subway supermarket train

B I N G O				

Instructions

1. Choose 15 words from the ones in the box and write them in the grid.
2. When the teacher reads one of the words, check if it is in your grid. If so, mark it. If not, wait for the next word.
3. The student who marks all of the words first is the winner.

3 In groups, answer the questions about the game.

1. Was the game easy or difficult to play?
2. What was easy? Why?
3. What was difficult? Why?
4. What did you learn from playing the game?

1 What kinds of games do you usually play with your friends?

2 Play the *Snakes and Ladders Game* in groups.

Instructions

1. All players start on number 1.
2. Roll the die to move along the board.
3. Use the key. If you are correct, you stay there. If not, go back to START.
4. The first player to reach number 30 is the winner!

Key

Picture = spell the word
Color = say the color
? = say a question you ask in the classroom
Snake's head = go down
Ladder = go up

3 In groups, answer the questions about the game.

1. Was the game easy or difficult to play?
2. What was easy? Why?
3. What was difficult? Why?
4. What did you learn from playing the game?

1 What is your dream job? Discuss in pairs.

2 Play the game in pairs.

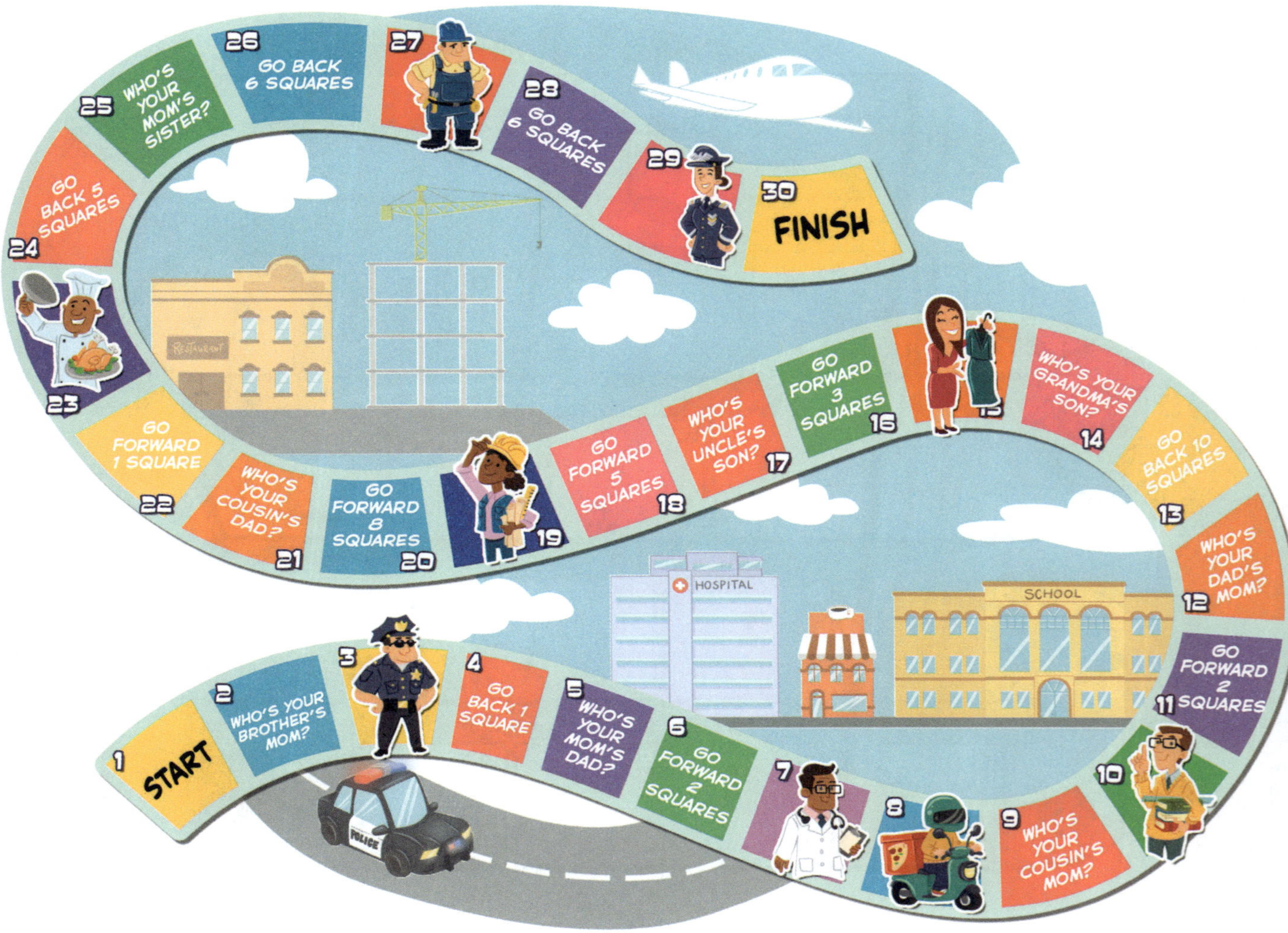

Instructions

1. Flip a coin. If it is heads, move one space. If it is tails, stay where you are.
2. If you land on a picture, make a sentence about the job, e.g. *He's a teacher*.
3. If you land on a question, ask the question to your classmate.
4. The winner is the player who gets to FINISH first!

3 In groups, answer the questions about the game.

1. Was the game easy or difficult to play?
2. What was easy? Why?
3. What was difficult? Why?
4. What did you learn from playing the game?

1 What is your routine like? Make notes in your notebook and share them with your classmates.

2 Play the *Routines Tiddlywinks Game* in pairs.

Instructions

1. Flip your counter and try to land on a colored circle.

2. Use the key.

Key

Yellow = Try again. 0 points.

Green = Identify a routine activity and use it in an affirmative sentence about you. 2 points.

Blue = Identify a routine activity and use it in a negative sentence about you. 5 points.

Red = Identify a routine activity and use it in an affirmative or negative sentence about someone else. 10 points.

3 In groups, answer the questions about the game.

1. Was the game easy or difficult to play?

2. What was easy? Why?

3. What was difficult? Why?

4. What did you learn from playing the game?

1 **How many rooms are there in your house? Talk in pairs.**

2 **Play Battleships.**

	A	B	C	D	E
10					
20					
30					
40					
50					

My points: ______

Instructions

1. Write ten words from this unit in any of the squares on the board.
2. Take turns trying to find your classmate's words.
3. If you *hit* a square with a word in it, your classmate says the word. You make a sentence with the word and score one point if the sentence is correct.
4. For every correct sentence, you score a point and your classmate draws a cross through the word in his / her board.

Is there a word in E40?

Yes, there is. The word is *kitchen*.

There is a kitchen in my house.

3 **In groups, answer the questions about the game.**

1. Was the game easy or difficult to play?
2. What was easy? Why?
3. What was difficult? Why?
4. What did you learn from playing the game?

1 What is your best ability? Talk in pairs and compare your talents.

2 Play the *Abilities Game* in pairs.

Instructions

1. Individually, check (✓) or cross (✕) the pictures.
2. Take turns asking and answering questions about the characters in the picture.

Can Luisa dance samba?

No, she can't!

Oh, no. She *can* dance ballet.

3 In groups, answer the questions about the game.

1. Was the game easy or difficult to play?
2. What was easy? Why?
3. What was difficult? Why?
4. What did you learn from playing the game?

1 In pairs, name as many special dates as you can in 60 seconds. How many did you manage to name?

2 Play the game in small groups.

Instructions

1. Get a die and counters for each student.
2. Roll the die and follow the instructions in the spot it lands.
3. Instructions for each spot:
   - **Challenge:** The following opponent has to challenge the one who is playing by writing a date, a time, or drawing a picture of a special date.
   - **Calendar:** The player has to roll the die and write the numbers it shows until it turns into a date and say it.
   - **Clock:** The player has to roll the dice and write the numbers it shows until it turns into a time and say it.
   - **Special Date Pictures:** The player has to name the special date.
4. The player who reaches *You Win* first has to be challenged one more time! If he / she gets it right, he / she wins the game!

3 In groups, answer the questions about the game.

1. Was the game easy or difficult to play?
2. What was easy? Why?
3. What was difficult? Why?
4. What did you learn from playing the game?

1 Talk in pairs. What are your hobbies?

2 Play *The Stars Game* in groups.

Instructions

1. Have all players put their counters in the center of the board (START).
2. Decide on a player to start the game.
3. The first player rolls the die and chooses one way to move the counter. He / She moves the number of steps along the board, according to the number he / she just rolled. The counter may stop on a star or on a picture:
   - If the counter stops on a star, he / she chooses a word from the word bank in the middle of the circle and makes a sentence in the Present Continuous.
   - If the counter stops on a picture, he / she needs to say what the picture is.
4. If the answer is right, the counter stays where it is, and the player needs to color a star at the bottom of the page. If the answer is wrong, the counter goes back to the starting point.
5. The first player to color all the stars is the winner.

3 In groups, answer the questions about the game.

1. Was the game easy or difficult to play?
2. What was easy? Why?
3. What was difficult? Why?
4. What did you learn from playing the game?

GRAMMAR GLOSSARY

Verb *to be* – Affirmative

Subject	Verb	Contraction
I	am	I'm
you	are	you're
he	is	he's
she	is	she's
it	is	it's
we	are	we're
they	are	they're

We use the verb *to be* to tell people our names, nationalities, and age.

I ***am*** *Lisa. I'****m*** *British. I'****m*** *13 years old.*
Petra ***is*** *Chinese. She'****s*** *14 years old.*
We ***are*** *Mexican. We'****re*** *10 years old.*
Aki and Hana ***are*** *Japanese. They'****re*** *15.*

Wh- questions

We use *What* to ask about an object or a thing.

What ***is*** *your name?*
What ***are*** *their occupations?*

The contraction of *What is* is *What's*.

*What'****s*** *your name?*

We use *Where* to ask about a place.

Where ***are*** *you from?*
Where ***is*** *she?*

The contraction of *Where is* is *Where's*.

*Where'****s*** *he from?*

Possessive Adjectives

Subject	Possessive adjective
I	my
you	your
he	his
she	her
it	its

We use *possessive adjectives* to introduce ourselves and others.

This is my best friend. ***His*** *name is Paulo.*
She is my teacher. ***Her*** *name is Wilma.*

There is / There are – Affirmative and Negative

There is / There are	
Affirmative statements	**Negative statements**
There's a bank on 7th Avenue.	**There isn't** a park in my town.
There are movie theaters in my neighborhood.	**There aren't** any trains in this city.
Contraction: There is = There's	

We use *there is / there are* to talk about things in a place.

We use a singular noun after *there is*.

There is a movie theater in my town.
There is a hospital near here.

We use a plural noun after *there are*.

We use *some* or a number after *there are*.

There are some stores on this street.
There are two shopping malls in my neighborhood.

We use *isn't / aren't* for negative sentences.

We often use *any* after *There aren't*.

There isn't a restaurant near here.
There aren't any parks near my school.

There is / There are – *Yes / No* Questions and Short Answers

There is / There are	
Yes / No questions	**Short answers**
Is there an airport in this city?	Yes, **there is.** / No, **there isn't.**
Are there any buses in front of the school?	Yes, **there are.** / No, **there aren't.**

We use *Is there* + subject to ask questions in the singular form.

Is there a park near here?
Is there a hospital?

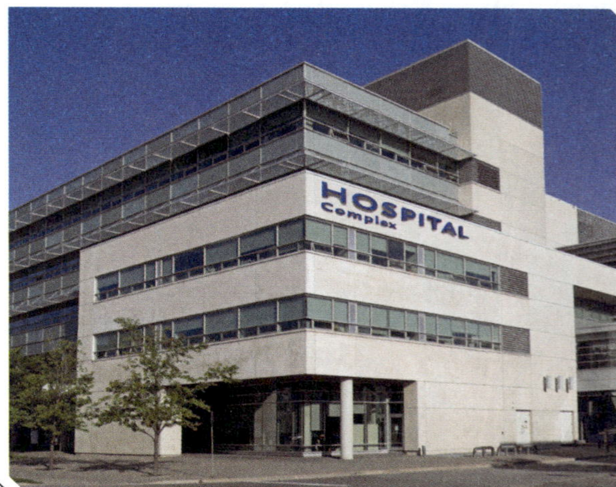

We use *Are there* + subject to ask questions in the plural form.

We often use *any* after *Are there*.

Are there any good stores in the mall?
Are there any restaurants near here?

Articles

We use *a* or *an* + singular noun.

one notebook = **a** notebook
one backpack = **a** backpack

We use *a* + word beginning with a consonant sound.

*That is **a** book.*
*There isn't **a** whiteboard in this classroom.*

We use *an* + word beginning with a vowel sound.

*This is **an** orange pen.*
*Is that **an** eraser?*

Demonstrative Pronouns

Singular	 this	 that
Plural	 these	 those

We use *this* with a singular noun and verb for objects that are close.

*This** is my pen. It's here!*

We use *these* with a plural noun and verb for objects that are close.

***These** are my favorite books. Look!*

We use *that* with a singular noun and verb for objects that are far.

***That** is our teacher. Over there!*

We use *those* with a plural noun and verb for objects that are far.

*Are **those** your friends by the bus stop?*

Possessive 's and Possessive Adjectives

Subject	Possessive adjective
I	my
you	your
he	his
she	her
it	its
we	our
they	their

We use possessive adjectives to demonstrate possession.

They are my dogs. **Their** names are Rex and Ted.
We are in the sixth grade. **Our** teacher is great.
It's my dog. **His** name is Gary.

When one thing belongs to two or more people, we use 's after the last noun that indicates the owner.

That is Pat and Jo**'s** restaurant.
Sofia and Lea**'s** books are old.

We use 's after the names of people or things to demonstrate possession.

My mom**'s** car is red.
Jeff**'s** backpack is old.

Whose

We use whose to ask about the owner of something.

Whose laptop is this?
Whose books are these?

Simple Present: Affirmative and Negative

	Affirmative	Negative
I / You / We / They	**get** up early. **take** a shower in the morning.	**don't get** up late. **don't take** a shower in the afternoon.
He / She / It	**gets** up early. **takes** a shower in the morning.	**doesn't get** up late. **doesn't take** a shower in the afternoon.

We use the Simple Present to talk about facts, routines, and things that are true.

For *he / she / it*, we add *-s* to the end of the verb.

We **go** to school every day.
Oscar **takes** a shower at night.

For negative sentences, we add *don't* before the verb for *I / you / we / they*.

For negative sentences, we add *doesn't* before the verb for *he / she / it*. We don't add *-s* to the verb in negative sentences.

I **don't go** on social media before school.
Michelle **doesn't eat** fast food.

For verbs ending in *-s*, *-ss*, *-sh*, *-ch*, *-x*, *-z*, and *-o*, we add *-es* to the end of the verb for *he / she / it*.

She **brushes** her teeth in the morning.
My brother **watches** TV at breakfast time.

For verbs ending in *-y*, we change it to *-ie* before the ending *-s* for *he / she / it*.

Fred **studies** in the afternoon.

For he / she / it, the verb *have* changes to *has*.

I **have** lunch. He **has** lunch.

Adverbs of Frequency

never → sometimes → usually → always

0% — 100%

We use adverbs of frequency to say the frequency we do something.

I **always** go to bed early.
She **never** watches TV.

We often use the adverbs of frequency between the subject and the verb, but after the verb *to be*.

Polly **always** goes on social media at night.
She is **usually** tired in the mornings.
You **never** have breakfast.
That's why you are **always** hungry before lunch!

Simple Present – *Yes / No* Questions and Short Answers

Question	Short answer
Do you live in an apartment?	Yes, I do. / No, I don't.
Do they get up early?	Yes, they do. / No, they don't.
Does he have a sister?	Yes, he does. / No, he doesn't.
Does she go to school by bike?	Yes, she does. / No, she doesn't.

We use *do / does* + subject + verb in the base form to ask questions about facts or things that are generally true in the present.

Do you **do** your homework on time?
Does your brother **live** with you?
Do those girls **exercise** every evening?
Does Alicia **sleep** a lot?

Prepositions of Place

In

On

Behind

Near

Near

Between

We use prepositions of place to say where something is.

Why is your backpack **under** the couch?
My bedroom is **between** the kitchen and the bathroom.
There is a window **behind** my bed.
His books are **on** the desk.

Can for Abilities

Affirmative statements	Negative statements	*Yes / No* questions	Short answers
I **can** play soccer.	I **can't** dance.	**Can** you swim?	Yes, I can. / No, I can't.
She **can** speak Japanese.	They **can't** spell difficult words.	**Can** he code?	Yes, he can. / No, he can't.
Contraction: cannot – *can't*			

We use *can* + the base form of a verb to talk about abilities.

We use *can't* + the base form of a verb for negative statements.

I can ***speak*** *three languages.*
Alex ***can't*** *code.*
My mom ***can't*** *sing very well!*

We use *very well* and *a little* to quantify an ability with can.

Donna can speak ***a little*** *French. =*
She knows some words, but not a lot.
I can't sing ***very well****! =*
I can sing, but I'm not very good at it.
Sam can play the piano ***very well****. =*
He's excellent at it.

We use *can* + subject + verb to ask questions about abilities.

Can *you* ***dance*** *well? = Are you able to dance?*
Can *your teacher* ***play*** *a musical instrument? =*
Is he / she able to play a musical instrument?

We also use *can* in questions to ask for permission.

Can *I* ***come*** *in? = Do you give me permission to come in?*

Imperatives

We use imperatives to give orders or say rules.

An affirmative imperative begins with a verb.

Don't comes first in a negative imperative.

We use the base form of a verb in the imperative.

Pay *attention!* ***Don't*** *talk!*
Be *careful!* ***Don't*** *walk there!*
Listen *to me!* ***Don't*** *use your cell phone!*

Wh- Questions

We use question words to ask information questions.

What do you do?
When is your birthday?
What time is it?
Who is your teacher?
Why is she angry?

We use *What* to ask about objects, qualities, etc.

What is their favorite movie?
What does she do?

We use *When* to ask about a day or date.

When is the event?
When do Americans celebrate Thanksgiving?

We use *What time* to ask about the exact time of an event / action.

What time do you get up?
What time does she start work?
What time is it?

We use *Who* to ask about people.

Who do the children live with?
Who is that woman?

We use *Why* to ask about the reason.

Why are you sad?
Why do we celebrate Christmas?

Prepositions of Time

in	on	at
months, years, *the morning*, *the afternoon*, *the evening*	specific dates, days of the week, *the weekend*	times, *night*

My birthday is **in** March. It is **on** March 2nd.
We go to the sports club **on** Saturdays.
We play soccer **in** the afternoon.
Our games start **at** 4:30 p.m.

Present Continuous – Affirmative and Negative

Present Continuous			
Affirmative		**Negative**	
I'**m**	sleep**ing** on the couch.	I'**m not**	drink**ing** water.
You'**re**		You **aren't**	
He'**s**		He **isn't**	
She'**s**		She **isn't**	
It'**s**		It **isn't**	
We'**re**		We **aren't**	
You'**re**		You **aren't**	
They'**re**		They **aren't**	

We often use the Present Continuous to talk about actions that are in progress at the moment of speaking. We often use *now*, *right now*, and *at the moment* with the Present Continuous.

*My dad **is** sing**ing** in the shower right now.*
*I'**m not** read**ing** that book now.*
*Zara **is** talk**ing** to the teacher at the moment.*

We can also use the Present Continuous to talk about temporary actions.

*I usually go to school by car, but this week I'**m** go**ing** by bus.*
*Sam doesn't usually eat fast food, but today he'**s** hav**ing** a burger for lunch.*

For verbs ending in consonant, vowel, consonant, we double the last consonant before adding *-ing*.

*We'**re** runn**ing** to class because we're late!*
*I'**m not** chatt**ing** to anyone online right now.*

For verbs ending in *-e*, we remove the *-e* before adding *-ing*.

*My sister **is** danc**ing** all around the living room.*

Present Continuous – Questions

Present Continuous – Questions			
***Yes / No* questions**		**Short answers**	
Am I	play**ing**?	Yes, I **am**.	No, I'**m not**.
Are you		Yes, you **are**.	No, you **aren't**.
Is he / she / it		Yes, he / she / it **is**.	No, he / she / it **isn't**.
Are we / you / they		Yes, you / we / they **are**.	No, we / you / they **aren't**.

Information questions
Where **are** you go**ing**?
Where'**s** he / she / it go**ing**?
Where **are** they go**ing**?

We use verb *be* + subject + verb + *-ing* to ask *Yes / No* questions in the Present Continuous.

A: ***Is*** *Ollie talk**ing** on the phone right now?*
B: *Yes, he **is**.*

We use *Wh*-question word + verb *be* + subject + verb + *-ing* to ask information questions in the Present Continuous.

A: *What **is** Ollie do**ing** now?*
B: *He'**s** talk**ing** on the phone.*

#AUDIO TRACKS

Unit	Tracks	Page	Activities
Audio Tracks			
-	01	-	-
0	02	6	1
	03	7	3
	04	10	4
1	05	12	1
	06	13	5
	07	16	4
2	08	18	4
	09/10	19	1 and 2
	11	22	4
3	12	24	1
	13/14	25	1 and 2
	15	28	4
4	16	30	1
	17	34	4
5	18	36	1
	19	40	2
	20	40	4
6	21	42	2
	22	43	3
	23	46	4
7	25 and 26	48	1 and 2
	27	52	4
8	28/29	54	1 and 2
	30	58	4

UNIT ZERO

Activity 1 02

A: Anna P: Paul J: Joseph

A: Hi. I'm Anna.

P: Hey, Anna. Nice to meet you! This is my friend Joseph

J: Nice to meet you, Anna. Where are you from?

A: I'm from Argentina. What about you?

J: We're Vietnamese. How old are you?

A: I'm 12 years old.

P: Really? We're 12 years old, too. Have a happy festival, Anna.

A: Thank you. See you later.

Activity 3 03

A: Alana M: Marie

A: Look! This is my dog Brutus. Isn't he cute?

M: Wow! Your dog is really big. And yes, he is cute.

A: It's a White Shepherd. It is a Canadian dog. My father gave it to me last year.

M: It's a baby dog! Look at his mother and all his siblings. Look at their nose!

A: Sorry. It's my mother. She is waiting for me at our home. Hello, Mom...

Activity 4 04

DI: Diving instructor Mi: Miguel Ma: Maya

DI: Good afternoon, kids! My name is Diogo. I'm from Costa Rica, and I'm a diving instructor. Nice to meet you all. Do you know how to swim, guys?

Mi: Nice to meet you, Diogo. My name is Miguel, and I'm 10 years old. I'm from Guatemala, and this is my first time here in Brazil. I'm a little nervous, but I know how to swim.

DI: Great, Miguel. Don't worry. You'll love it. The first thing to know in diving is the gestures. Maya will show you the OK gesture. It means everything is fine with you underwater.

Ma: Hi, everyone. I'm Maya. Nice to meet you. I'm 18 years old. I'm from Argentina, and I'm living in Brazil with my father. He is Brazilian. Let's learn the gestures before we go to the water. This is the OK gesture.

UNIT ONE

Activity 1 05

A: Anat P: Pablo

A: Hi. I'm Anat. I'm 16 years old, and I'm from Cairo, Egypt. I'm Egyptian. Nice to meet you. I live near a very famous tourist attraction, the Nile River. In my city, there is also the Great Pyramid of Giza, which is the oldest of the Seven Wonders of the World. Are you Peruvian? Do you know Machu Picchu?

P: Hi, Anat. Nice to meet you, too. My name is Pablo, and I'm from Santiago, Chile. In Santiago, there isn't any Wonder of the World. But in Brazil there is Christ the Redeemer.

UNIT TWO

Activities 1 and 2 09 and 10

I: Interviewer M: Mark G: Gaby F: Farid

I: Welcome to the school's radio show. Today I'll interview three students. I think everything is connected: my computer, my camera, and my microphone. Good morning! How are you today?

M, G, and F: Fine, thank you.

I: Mark, I can't see you. Can you turn on your camera?

M: Yes, of course! Sorry!

I: Can you introduce yourself?

M: I'm Mark and I'm 13 years old. I'm new to this school.

I: Oh, great! Welcome to this school. Can you talk about your study space at home?

M: Yes. At home I have a new desk. It's very big and pretty. I have a computer, but I like notebooks, too. And I have a board at home. So I have pens and markers of all colors: blue, green, pink, orange, yellow.

I: Thank you, Mark. Now, Gaby. Can you introduce yourself? Gaby, we can't hear you. Can you connect your microphone?

G: Yes! I'm Gaby, and... I'm not new to this school.

I: What's your favorite object in your study space at home?

G: Hmm... I have two favorite objects! My highlighters and my pencil case. Well, no. My highlighters and my backpack. I love my new backpack. It's big and black.

I: Very pretty. Farid, your turn.

F: I'm 13 years old, and I'm from Egypt. My favorite object is my laptop. It's here, look!

I: Very pretty. I like it. Can you talk about your study space at home?

F: I have a small, red desk, pens and pencils, and books.

I: Well, thank you very much Mark, Gaby, and Farid. This is all for today, tomorrow...

Activity 4 11

T: Teacher L: Lucas C: Carmen

T: Good morning! How are you today?

L and C: Good morning, Mr. Smith.

L: Look at my new headphones!

T: Very nice, Lucas.

C: Oh, look! I have new Post-its. They're red, pink, yellow, and orange.

T: Nice colors, Carmen. OK, open your books and notebooks, please. Lucas, how do you spell cell phone?

L: Oh, very easy. C-E-L-L-P-H-O-N-E.

T: Very good. Now Carmen, how do you spell classroom?

T: Carmen, we can't hear you. I think you're on mute.

C: Oh, yes. Sorry!

UNIT THREE

Activity 1 12

In my family, I have a sister called Bethany and a brother called Simon. My dad's name is James. That's my close family. We are very happy!

Activities 1 and 2 13 and 14

This is my favorite thing. I wear it every day. It's small and silver. There is a blue stone in it. My best friend Sarah's favorite thing is also a ring, but her ring has a pink stone. It's a sign of our friendship. What's your favorite thing?

Activity 4 15

Hello! I have a big family. We are happy together. I have four siblings, three brothers, and one sister. My brothers' names are Michael, Andrew, and Jack. My sister's name is Andrea. And I'm Liz!

UNIT FOUR

Activity 1 16

I: Interviewer S: Samia

I: Good morning! Today, we'll talk to Samia. Samia, please, introduce yourself.

S: Hello! My name's Samia, I'm 13, and I'm from Morocco.

I: What do you do on a typical day?

S: I go to school in the morning and in the afternoon. I get up at 7 or 7:10 a.m., take a shower, get dressed, have breakfast, and go to school. After class, I stay in school and do yoga or aerobics. My little twin sisters do ballet. During the weekend, I play tennis. I have a tennis class on Saturdays, and then I play with my friends. On Sundays, I go to the market with my dad. We buy food and spices.

I: Very nice! And... what do you do at home?

S: During the weekend, I play video games with my little brother. And I play chess with my mom. I like board games very much. On Fridays, I go skateboarding with my friend Adamu. On Sunday afternoons, I stay home and relax. My family and I watch a movie or series on TV. Then before going to bed, I check my notifications and post pictures of my weekend on social media. On Saturdays, I go to bed at 11 or 11:30 p.m., but on Sundays, I go to bed at 10 p.m.

I: Thank you, Samia. That's very interesting.

Activity 4 17

M: Mom A: Ayari

M: Ayari! Dad is on the phone. When do you want to have dinner with him?

A: Well, Mom, on weekdays I get home late from school because I have baseball practice, and I do homework at the school club after that. Can't we have lunch on Saturday?

M: She says lunch on Saturday. Is that OK? Oh, dear. Your dad works on Saturdays! How about Sunday?

A: Well, I usually go to the movies with my friends, but that's OK.

M: Great! She says lunch on Sunday is OK. But remember, Ayari has to go to school early in the morning, so she can't go to bed late!

UNIT FIVE

Activity 1 18

I love my home. Every day, I wake up in a different place. Sometimes, I live in the countryside. I can watch the birds and go for long walks. Sometimes, I live in the city. It's fun to see friends, go to the cinema, and museums. It's great to live on the canals and travel.

Activity 4 20

Welcome to Paradise Hotel. We work to make you happy. At our hotel, there are two restaurants, one near the beach and another inside the hotel, next to our reception desk. Our rooms are big and comfortable for families. Do you want to work? There are places to connect your laptop. There is one between the beds and another one behind the TV, in the living room. In the bedroom, there is a big balcony. On the same street as the hotel, there is a small grocery store. We are very happy to have you here.

UNIT SIX

Activity 4 23

1. I can run really fast. I'm 70, and I'll run my first marathon.
2. My father is a great soccer player, but not a professional one. He teaches me frequently, and I can play soccer very well.
3. My older brother is a master in the kitchen. He studies gastronomy, and we love it when he cooks for us. Me? Well, I can make simple meals for my family and friends.

UNIT SEVEN

Activities 1 and 2 24 and 25

T: Teacher S1: Student 1 S2: Student 2 S3: Student 3

T: Folks, pay attention. I have an announcement: This year, all the members of the Green Project will celebrate Earth Day for a whole week. This celebration will be one week before Earth Day. Can you remember when that is?

S1: That is on the 22nd of April.

T: Exactly. This year we will celebrate National Environmental Education Week! A whole week to celebrate the environment. So please, organize yourselves into three groups. Each group will choose a day from our annual environmental conservation and education calendar and work on it to present to school members.

S2: I am a vegetarian. I am going to find a day to celebrate that!

S3: And I love turtles. I hope there is a day for them on the calendar.

Activity 4 26

1. April 3rd is an annual day dedicated to aquatic animals.
2. June 8th celebrates the importance of the oceans around the world.
3. November 1st is a day to celebrate the benefits and joys of being vegan.

UNIT EIGHT

Activities 1 and 2 27 and 28

1. I love animals. This year I am spending my free time at an animal shelter. I am helping the people here to take care of abandoned dogs and cats. I feel so happy and grateful for it. The animals love me and I love them. It is a great experience.
2. My mom works at an office in the mall. Therefore, I spend my free time at the mall twice a week. Since I am there, I am responsible for buying some things for my family. I really enjoy doing that. One of my hobbies is shopping.

Activity 4 29

1. I started taking care of dogs after my aunt's surgery. Now it is my favorite hobby. I always ask my neighbors if I can walk their dogs after school.
2. During my vacations, I started to program. Now this is my new hobby. I just love it. Now I am teaching my younger brother basic codes.
3. I never thought of collecting things, but after visiting my grandfather, I started to like coins. He showed me his collection and gave me some coins so I can start my own collection.

PICTURE CREDITS

Front cover (A) Krakenimages.com/Shutterstock/Shutterstock / (B) Artistdesign29 /Shutterstock/Shutterstock / (C) Studio Harmony/Shutterstock/ Shutterstock / (D) S_L/Shutterstock/Shutterstock / (E) Maslakhatul Khasanah/ Shutterstock/Shutterstock / (F) Spasiblo/ Shutterstock/Shutterstock / (G) Macrovector/Shutterstock/Shutterstock / (H) Net Vector/ Shutterstock/Shutterstock; Page 5 (A) Jörg Carstensen/ Pearson Education Ltd/Asset Library / (B) ERIC LAFFORGUE / Alamy Stock Photo/Alamy / (C) 70sphotography. Shutterstock/Asset Library / (D) DreamSlamStudio/shutterstock/Shutterstock / (E) Belikova Oksana/shutterstock/Shutterstock / (F) T photography/shutterstock/Shutterstock; Page 6 Midori Photography/ Shutterstock/Asset Library; Page 7 (A) Paskar Alexei/shutterstock/Shutterstock / (B) Shutterstock/Asset Library / (C) ehasdemir/shutterstock/Shutterstock; Page 8 (A) Ginger Design/ shutterstock/Shutterstock / (B) Edie Layland/123rf/123RF; Page 11 Jules Selmes/ Pearson Education Ltd/Asset Library; Page 12 (A) Vitalii Nesterchuk/ Shutterstock/Asset Library / (B) Pyty/Shutterstock/Asset Library / (C) AlexAnton/Shutterstock/Asset Library / (D) Stanislav Kulesh/123rf/Asset Library / (E) Jorg Hackemann/Shutterstock/Asset Library / (F) mangostock/Shutterstock/Asset Library/; Page 14 Primorac91/Shutterstock/Asset Library; Page 15 (A) Mark Bowden/123rf/123RF / (B) Sima Hui/123rf/123RF; Page 16 AJR_photo/Shutterstock/Asset Library; Page 17(A) antoniodiaz/shutterstock/Shutterstock / (B) Coleman Yuen/ Pearson Education Asia Ltd/Asset Library / (C) valzan/Shutterstock/Asset Library / (D) PowerUp/Shutterstock/Asset Library / (E) www. BillionPhotos.com/Shutterstock/Asset Library / Asset Library / (F) RTimages/Shutterstock/Asset Library / (G) Jolypics/Shutterstock/Asset Library / (H) Sean Locke Photography/Shutterstock/Asset Library / (I) Karuka/Shutterstock/Asset Library; Page 18 (A) Monkey Business Images/shutterstock/Shutterstock / (B) Piyadanai Piyanukool/shutterstock/Shutterstock / (C) Talukdar David/shutterstock/Shutterstock; Page 19 (A) Trzykropy/shutterstock/Shutterstock / (B) Naki Photography/ Pearson Education Ltd/Asset Library / (C) Billion Photos/Shutterstock/Asset Library / (D) Gavran333/Shutterstock/Asset Library / (E) Skylines/ Shutterstock/Asset Library Page 20 (A) fizkes/123rf/123RF / (B) Motortion Films/Shutterstock/Asset Library; Page 21 Katarzyna Białasiewicz/123rf/123RF; Page 22 156268/Shutterstock/Asset Library; Page 23 (A) Melpomene. Shutterstock/Asset Library / (B) pixelheadphoto digitalskillet. Shutterstock/Asset Library / (C) Shutterstock/Asset Library; Page 25 (A) Roma Borman. Shutterstock/Asset Library / (B) Jesus Cervantes. Shutterstock/Asset Library / (C) Michael Kraus. Shutterstock/Asset Library / (D) Jane Kelly. Shutterstock/Asset Library; Page 26 (A) Sergey Eremin. Shutterstock/Asset Library / (B) Joey Chan. Pearson Education Asia Ltd/Asset Library; Page 27 Lionel Hahn/ABACAPRESS.COM/Alamy; Page 28 (A) Billion Photos. Shutterstock/Asset Library / (B) ALLA ORDATII. 123rf.com/Asset Library / (C) Littlewitz. Shutterstock/Asset Library / (D) Cheuk-king Lo. Pearson Education Asia Ltd/Asset Library / (E) Gareth Boden. Pearson Education Ltd/Asset Library / (F) Gladskikh Tatiana. Shutterstock/Asset Library; Page 29 Samuel Borges Photography. Shutterstock/Asset Library; Page 30 Shutterstock/Asset Library; Page 31 chatursunil. Shutterstock/Asset Library; Page 32 Lightspring. Shutterstock/Asset Library; Page 34 Studio 8. Pearson Education Ltd/Asset Library; Page 36 (A) pics721. Shutterstock/Asset Library / (B) Debbie Rowe. Pearson Education Ltd/Asset Library; Page 37 Photographee. eu. Shutterstock/Asset Library; Page 38 smartman. Shutterstock/Asset Library; Page 39 Khoroshunova Olga. Shutterstock/Asset Library; Page 40 (A) Andrew Lam. Shutterstock/Asset Library / (B) anekoho. Shutterstock/Asset Library / (C) AnnaTamila. Shutterstock/Asset Library/ (D) Terry Leung. Pearson Education Asia Ltd/Asset Library / (E) Room27. Shutterstock/Asset Library; Page 41 (A) Marian Fil/Shutterstock/Asset Library / (B) Rido/Shutterstock/Asset Library / (C) LightField Studios/Shutterstock/Asset Library / (D) karelnoppe/Shutterstock/Asset Library / (E) wavebreakmedia/Shutterstock/Asset Library / (F) AVAVA/ Shutterstock/Asset Library; Page 42 (A) Featureflash Photo Agency/shutterstock/Shutterstock / (B) prudencio alvarez/123rf/123RF; Page 43 (A) Samuel Borges Photography/Shutterstock/Asset Library / (B) Daisy Daisy/Shutterstock/Asset Library / (C) Voyagerix/Shutterstock/Asset Library / (D) Jon Barlow/ Pearson Education Ltd/Asset Library / (E) Andrii YURLOV/123rf/Asset Library / (F) pixelheadphoto digitalskillet/Shutterstock/Asset Library / (G) aceshot1/ Shutterstock/Asset Library / (H) dolgachov/123rf/123RF; Page 46 (A) Olesya Kuznetsova/Shutterstock/Asset Library / (B) wavebreakmedia/Shutterstock/ Asset Library / (C) Mark Bowden/123rf/123RF; Page 47 (A) Willy Barton/Shutterstock/Asset Library / (B) Andrey Kryuchkov/123rf/Asset Library / (C) Robert Crum/Shutterstock/Asset Library / (D) NadyGinzburg/Shutterstock/Asset Library / (E) IANINAS/Shutterstock/Asset Library / (F) Mega Pixel/Shutterstock/ Asset Library; Page 48 Chinch / Shutterstock/Asset Library; Page 49 (A) vanatchanan/123rf/123RF / (B) pinanatreeangle/123rf/Asset Library / (C) jemastock/123rf/Asset Library; Page 50 (A) Stewart Marsden/Shutterstock/Asset Library / (B) Jon Helgason/123rf/Asset Library / (C) Alexander Raths/123rf/ Asset Library / (D) Erin Faith Wyllie/Shutterstock/Asset Library; Page 51 Mike Flippo/Shutterstock/Asset Library; Page 53 (A) wavebreakmedia/Shutterstock/ Asset Library / (B) Pavel L Photo and Video/Shutterstock/Asset Library / (C) Warut Chinsai/123rf/Asset Library / (D) esthermm/Shutterstock/Asset Library / (E) Irina Schmidt/123rf/Asset Library; Page 54 Mirko Vitali/ 123rf/Asset Library; Page 55 insta_photos/Shutterstock/Asset Library / (B) Jules Selmes/ Pearson Education Ltd/Asset Library / (C) kedrov/Shutterstock/Asset Library / (D) Mix and Match Studio/Shutterstock/Asset Library / (E) Rawpixel.com/Shutterstock/ Asset Library; Page 57 Cheuk Kiu Mak / Alamy Stock Photo/Alamy; Page 58 StepPro/Shutterstock/Asset Library; Page 60 (A) alanadesign/shutterstock/ Shutterstock / (B) Wollertz/shutterstock/Shutterstock / (C) 19srb81/shutterstock/Shutterstock; Page 61 (A) Derek Latta/Shutterstock/Asset Library / (B) brainsil/123rf/Asset Library; Page 62(A) dolgachov/123rf/Asset Library / (B) Kumar Sriskandan / Alamy Stock Photo/Alamy / (C) Catarina Belova/shutterstock/ Shutterstock; Page 64 (A) saiko3p/123rf/123RF / (B) Intellistudies/Shutterstock/Asset Library; Page 66 mangostock. Shutterstock/Asset Library; Page 67 (A) Gareth Boden. Pearson Education Ltd/Asset Library / (B) MindStudio. Pearson Education Ltd/Asset Library / (C) Jules Selmes. Pearson Education Ltd/Asset Library / (D) SpeedKingz/shutterstock/Shutterstock / (E) Andrey_Popov/Shutterstock/Asset Library; Page 68HONGQI ZHANG/123rf/Asset Library; Page 70 (A) mauritius images GmbH / Alamy Stock Photo/Alamy / (B) Carolyn Jenkins News / Alamy Stock Photo/Alamy; Page 72 Daisy Daisy/Shutterstock/Asset Library; Page 74 (A) espies/123rf/123RF / (B) anjalig04/123rf/123RF; Page 75 (A) espies/Shutterstock/Asset Library / (B) Hafiz Ismail/123rf/Asset Library / (C) espies/Shutterstock/Asset Library; Page 76 (A) Evdoha_spb/Shutterstock/Asset Library / (B) Alexander Raths/Shutterstock/Asset Library / (C) Anastasios71/ Shutterstock/Asset Library / (D) xlt974/Shutterstock/Asset Library / (E) trattieritratti/Shutterstock/Asset Library / (F) Vasyl/123rf/Asset Library; Page 79 (A) MANDY GODBEHEAR/Shutterstock/Asset Library / (B) gt29/Shutterstock/Asset Library; Page 80 (A) andegro4ka/123rf/123RF / (B) yavuzunlu/Shutterstock/ Asset Library / (C) Granate Art/shutterstock/Shutterstock / (D) Mix3r/Shutterstock/Asset Library / (E) Sarah Maher/123rf/Asset Library / (F) curiosity/ shutterstock/Shutterstock / (G) macrovector/123rf/Asset Library; Page 81 (A) happymay/123rf/123RF / (B) MicroOne/Shutterstock/Asset Library; Page 82 (A) Jon Barlow. Pearson Education Ltd/Asset Library / (B) kurhan/Shutterstock/Asset Library / (C) Rob Byron/123rf/Asset Library / (D) Shutterstock/Asset Library / (E) Monika Wisniewska/Shutterstock/Asset Library / (F) Olga Samorodova/123rf/123RF; Page 83 limeart/shutterstock/Shutterstock; Page 84 (A) Jojje/Shutterstock/Asset Library / (B) Alona Savchuk/123rf/123RF; Page 86 (A) bryljaev/123rf/123RF / (B) Ferveez Mohideen/Shutterstock/Asset Library; Page 87denvitruk/Shutterstock; Page 99Africa Studio/shutterstock/Shutterstock; Page 100 (A) Radovancev Zarko/shutterstock/Shutterstock / (B) Spiroview Inc/shutterstock/Shutterstock; Page 101 (A) gnidkin/shutterstock/Shutterstock / (B) rvlsoft/shutterstock/Shutterstock; Page 102 (A) Ksenia Raykova/ shutterstock/Shutterstock / (B) Dmytro Zinkevych/shutterstock/Shutterstock / (C) Jure Divich/shutterstock/Shutterstock; Page 103 (A) Yuganov Konstantin/ shutterstock/Shutterstock / (B) PV productions/shutterstock/Shutterstock; Page 104 (A) Rido/shutterstock/Shutterstock / (B) Inspiring/Shutterstock/Asset Library / (C) Milan Ilic Photographer/shutterstock/Shutterstock / (D) Atstock Productions/shutterstock/Shutterstock; Page 105 Wathana/shutterstock/ Shutterstock; Page 106 (A) Ermolaev Alexander/shutterstock/Shutterstock / (B) matimix/shutterstock/Shutterstock/Shutterstock; Page 107 Olena Yakobchuk/shutterstock/Shutterstock

ROB **THOMPSON** \\ RHIANNON SARAH **BALL**

HASHTAG ENGLISH 1

STARTER

STUDENT'S BOOK

and e-book

with **Online Practice**

Pearson

MISTO
Papel | Apoiando o manejo florestal responsável
FSC® C103535

Catalogue Publication Data

Hashtag English 1 Starter. Student's Book and e-book with Online Practice

Authors: Rob Thompson, Rhiannon Sarah Ball

Pearson Educación de México, S.A. de C.V., 2023

ISBN: 978-607-32-5678-0

Area: Schools

Format: 20,5 × 24,7 cm Page count: 168

Product Vice President: Marianne Lewis ■ **ELT Director:** Marjorie Robles ■ **Product Managers:** Anita Heald, Priscila Marconi ■ **Product Developers:** Renata S. C. Victor, Carolina Andrade ■ **Editor:** Elaine Mendonça ■ **Art and Design Coordinator:** Anderson Ferreira ■ **Art and Design Editors:** Andréia A. Santa Rosa, Patricia Santos, Luiz Rubio ■ **Layout:** MRS Editorial ■ **Cover & Interior Design:** Apis Design ■ **Cover Photo:** Shutterstock ■ **Digital Development Supervisor:** Isabel Silva ■ **Digital Content and Development Editors:** Rafaela de Mendonça, Fernanda Patucci, Lara Tasso, Mirella Armentano ■ **Digital Content Authors:** 2014 Solucões Editoriais, Ohana Editorial, Bella Szyszkowska ■ **Audiovisual Coordinator:** Lucas Domingues ■ **Audiovisual Editor:** Lucas Motta ■ **R&P Coordinator:** Maiti Salla ■ **R&P team:** Maricy Queiroz, Cristiane Gameiro ■ **Content Support:** 2014 Soluções Editoriais (Editors: Carla Maurício Coelho da Silva Vianna, Fernanda Troeira Zuchini, Joyce Rocha Gomes, Marcos Carvalho Mendonça, Rebeca Pasqua de Andrade. Assistants: Cristine Zanela Monte, Elani Souza Gomes, Juliana Aga) ■ **Proofreading:** 2014 Soluções Editoriais, Silva Serviços de Educação ■ **Picture Credits:** Pearson Asset Library, Shutterstock, 123RF, Alamy Stock Photo

Contact: soporte@pearson.com

First published, 2023

ISBN PRINT BOOK: 978-607-32-5678-0

Printed in Brazil by Reproset RPSZ 221221

1 2 3 4 5 6 7 8 9 0 - 25 24 23 22

Avenida Antonio Dovalí Jaime #70
Torre B, Piso 6, Colonia Zedec Ed. Plaza Santa Fe
Delegación Álvaro Obregón, México, Ciudad de México, C. P. 01210

www.PearsonELT.com

Pearson

Pearson Hispanoamérica

Argentina ■ Belice ■ Bolivia ■ Chile ■ Colombia ■ Costa Rica ■ Cuba ■ República Dominicana ■ Ecuador ■ El Salvador ■ Guatemala ■ Honduras ■ México ■ Nicaragua ■ Panamá ■ Paraguay ■ Perú ■ Uruguay ■ Venezuela

STUDENT'S BOOK INDEX

#TABLE OF CONTENTS

SPEAKING	WRITING	PRONUNCIATION	VOCABULARY	USE OF ENGLISH	PROJECT
Asking and Answering Questions About Personal Information	Writing an E-mail Introducing Yourself to a New Friend	*What's* /s/ and /z/	Greetings Countries and Nationalities	Greetings	A Slide Presentation
Talking About Neighborhoods and Cities	Writing a Profile About You and Where you Live	Rising and Falling Intonation	Places in Town Means of Transportation	Talking About Places	A Digital Whiteboard Presentation
Talking About Objects in the Classroom	Writing About Your Classroom and School	*This* /i/ vs. *These* /iː/	Numbers and Classroom Objects Alphabet	Describing Classroom Objects	A Visual Narrative
Talking About Family	Writing a Short Text About Your Family	/ɒ/ Sounds and /æ/ Sounds	Family Members Jobs	Talking About Possessions	An Online Poster
Talking about Daily Routines	Writing a Text for a Website About Your Daily Routine	3rd Person Singular Verb Sounds /iz/ /s/ /z/	Routines	Talking About Everyday Activities	An Online Comic Strip
Asking and Answering About Home	Writing a Description of Your Home and Your Favorite Room	Stressed Syllables	Rooms in a House Furniture	Talking About a Sustainable Home	A Poster
Talking About Ability	Writing a Personal Profile About Your Abilities	/æ/ Sound in Can and Can't	General Abilities	Asking and Answering Questions Using Can	A Social Media Campaign
Asking and Answering *Wh*-question	Writing a Blog Post	*-teen* vs. *-ty* (sixteen / sixty)	Days and Months Ordinal Numbers	Asking *Wh*-questions	A Program for a Climate Action Event
Describing What People Are Wearing	Writing a Personal Profile	/ŋ/ Sound	Hobbies and Free-time Activities	Giving Opinions Using Object Pronouns	An Advertisement for a School Event

WELCOME TO HASHTAG ENGLISH!

Hashtag English is a six-level course for lower- and upper-secondary students. You are going to interact with technology to learn English through task-based learning activities, working with UNESCO's Sustainable Development Goals (SDG), Bloom's Taxonomy, and 21st century skills. *Hashtag English* aims at providing thought-provoking content that recognizes your ability to observe and make a difference to the world around you, while still retaining a light-hearted and fun approach that is age appropriate.

OPENER

Each unit starts with a picture to arouse your curiosity about the theme and to introduce the focus on the SDG.

In this unit, you will learn how to:
This shows the learning outcomes of the unit.

Say what you know:
This activates your prior knowledge of the language goals of the unit.

UNESCO'S Sustainable Development Goal

DISCOVER

The first page of this double-page section is based on a video in which two characters discuss the unit topic and the language is introduced in context. The second page introduces the vocabulary of the unit.

VIDEO **AUDIO** **FLASHCARDS**

CLARIFY

This double-page section includes one or more texts that develop the SDG and work on a reading skill, a listening text, and a writing task on the topic of the text.

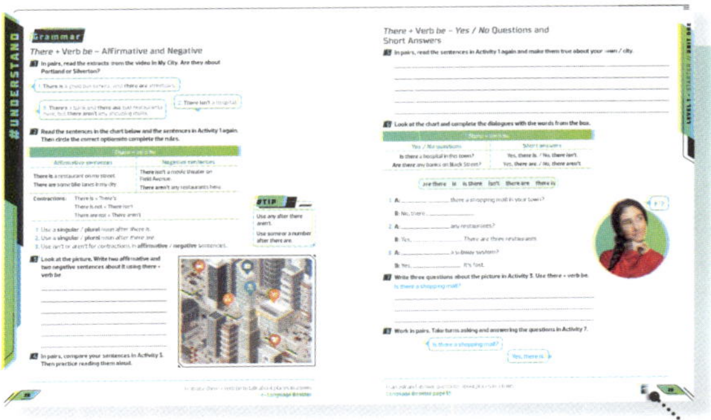

UNDERSTAND

This double-page section develops the grammar focus of the unit in an inductive manner. Grammar is presented in context and you are encouraged to work out the form for yourself.

EXAM PRACTICE

DEVELOP

The first page of this double-page section contains a listening text that develops a listening skill and sometimes a second vocabulary topic. The second page is where you develop speaking skills in natural, communicative contexts that use the grammar focus of the unit.

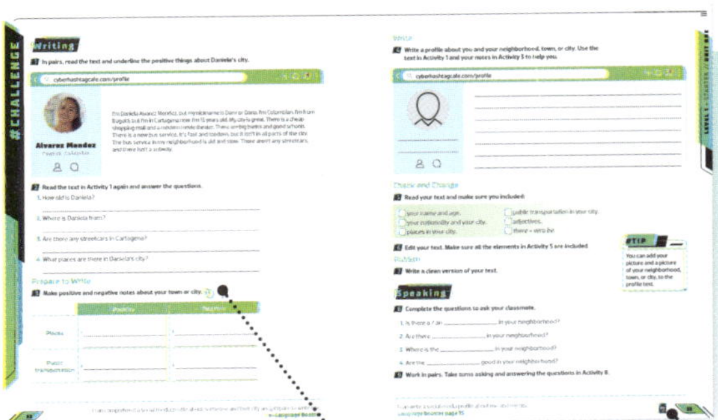

CHALLENGE

This double-page section develops your writing skills through a step-by-step writing task that puts into practice everything you have learned in the unit. The section culminates in a speaking task.

21ST CENTURY SKILL

EXAM PRACTICE

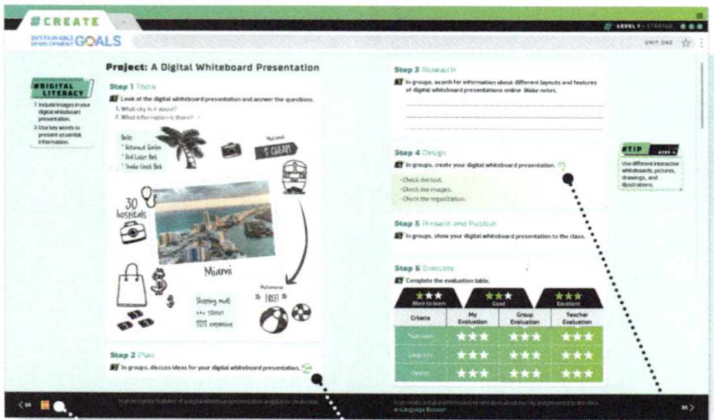

CREATE

In this section, you work collaboratively on a project to identify, critically analyze, and present a problem or potential solution related to the SDG of the unit.

21ST CENTURY SKILL

UNESCO'S SUSTAINABLE DEVELOPMENT GOAL

SELF-ASSESSMENT

This end-of-unit section presents a list of *can-do* statements related to the unit content that help you identify your progress and opportunities for improvement.

UNIT TEST

INTEGRATE

The first page of this section at the end of the book is called Learn to Learn. It aims at developing your learning skills using Bloom's Taxonomy. The second page contains new activities based on the video from the Discover section and proposes the recording of a new video to review the unit content.

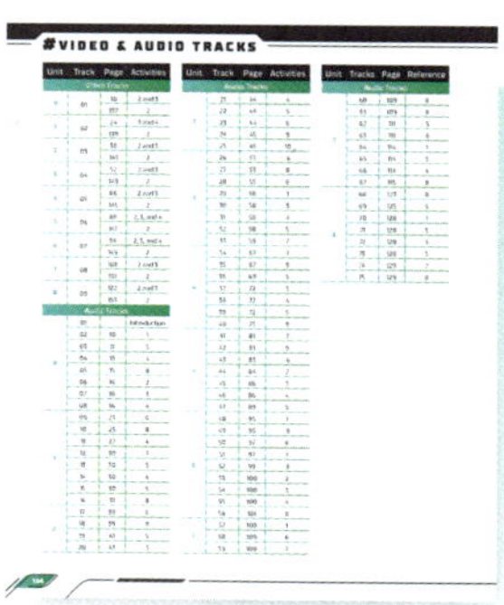

VIDEO & AUDIO TRACKS

This section at the end of the book lists the video and audio tracks from all the units.

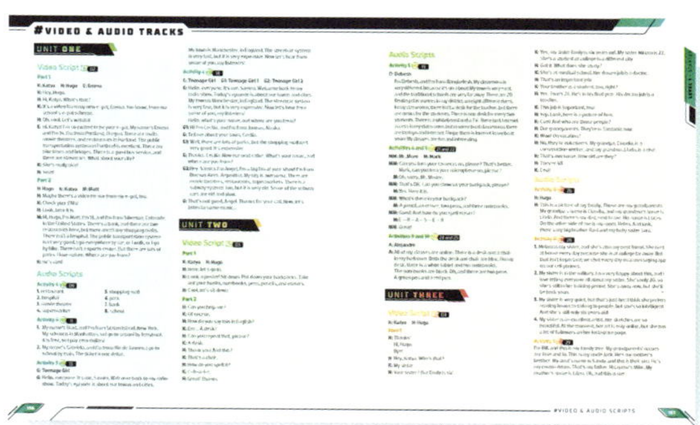

VIDEO & AUDIO SCRIPTS

This section at the end of the book contains the video and audio scripts from all the units.

UNIT ZERO 0

GETTING TO KNOW YOU

#10 REDUCED INEQUALITIES

In this unit, you will learn how to:

- Talk about countries and nationalities.
- Write an e-mail introducing yourself.
- Create a slide presentation.

Say what you know:

- Your age.
- Where you are from.
- A greeting from your country.

Video

About Myself

Before You Watch

1 Look at the ID card below. Listen and repeat. 02

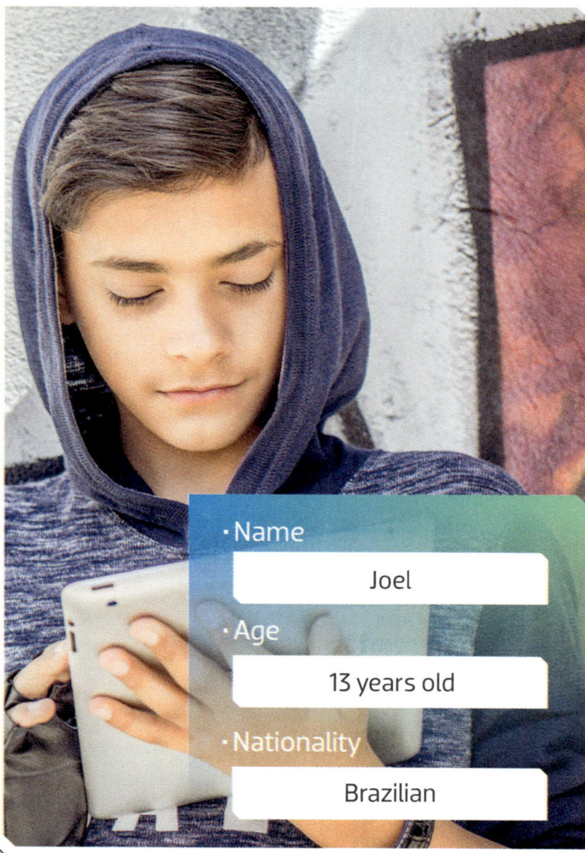

While You Watch

2 Watch Part 1 of the video and check (✓) the phrases you hear. 01

1. ☐ Hello!
2. ☐ Hey!
3. ☐ What are you called?
4. ☐ What's your name?
5. ☐ I'm 13.
6. ☐ I'm 12 years old.

3 Now watch Parts 1 and 2 of the video and complete the profiles with the words from the box. 01

12 years old	French	Hugo	Peruvian

1.

Name: Katya

Age: [1] ____________

Nationality: [2] ____________

2.

Name: [3] ____________

Age: 13 years old

Nationality: [4] ____________

After You Watch

4 Complete the ID card below with your own information.

I can greet someone and share personal information.

e-Language Booster

Vocabulary

Greetings

5 **Listen and repeat.** 03

Hello! What's your name?

Hi! My name's Raúl.

My name's Amy.

How are you, Amy?

I'm good, thanks. How are you, Raúl?

I'm good, thanks.

How old are you?

I'm 13 years old. And you?

I'm 12.

Nice to meet you, Amy.

Nice to meet you, too, Raúl.

Bye!

Goodbye!

6 **In pairs, read and practice the conversation in Activity 5 about you.**

Countries and Nationalities

7 **Label the flags with the countries from the box.**

Chile China France
Japan Mexico the United Kingdom

1. 

____

2. 

____

3. 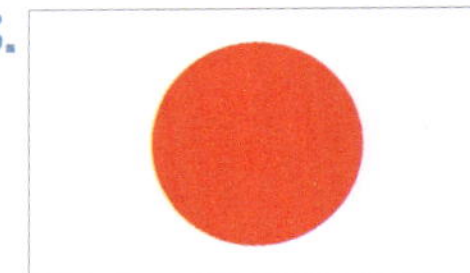

____

4. 

____

5. 

____

6. 

____

8 **Now, match the nationalities to the countries in Activity 7. Then write them in the correct column in the table. Add one more example of your own.**

☐ French ☐ British
☐ Chilean ☐ Japanese
☐ Mexican ☐ Chinese

-an	-ish / -ch	-ese
1 ______	3 ______	5 ______
2 ______	4 ______	6 ______

9 **In pairs, look at the example and take turns asking and answering.**

Where are you from?
I'm from Peru. / I'm Peruvian.

I can identify countries and nationalities.

Language Booster page 5

Reading

1 USING PRIOR KNOWLEDGE. In pairs, look at the pictures and answer the questions.

1. Where are they? ______________________
2. Are they all friends? ______________________

Jack: Hello! My name's Jack. What's your name?
Ben: My name's Ben. How are you?
Jack: I'm good, thanks. And you?
Ben: I'm OK. I'm new at this school.
Jack: Welcome! How old are you, Ben?
Ben: I'm 12 years old. How about you, Jack?
Jack: I'm 13. It's my birthday today.
Ben: Wow! Happy Birthday!
Jack: Thanks!

Jenny: Hi, Fran! This is my friend Hannah. She's a new student. Hannah, this is Fran.
Fran: Hi, Jenny! Hi, Hannah! Nice to meet you.
Hannah: Hello, Fran! Nice to meet you, too.
Fran: Where are you from?
Hannah: I'm from England.
Fran: Really? I'm from Mexico.
Jenny: It's time for class. See you later!
Hannah: Goodbye, Jenny.
Jenny: Bye, Hannah! Bye, Fran!

2 SCANNING. Read the conversations and circle the best option to complete the sentences.

1. Ben is new **at school** / **in the country**.
2. Jack is **12** / **13** years old.
3. Today is **Jack's** / **Ben's** birthday.
4. Hannah is from **England** / **Peru**.
5. Fran is **British** / **Mexican**.

I can read about greetings and introductions.

3 In pairs, ask and answer the questions about a friend.

- What is his / her name?
- How old is he / she?
- Where is he / she from?

What is her name?

Her name is Hannah.

Listening

4 Listen and write L (Lucy), M (Mike), or R (Raúl) to say who is speaking. 04

1. ☐ This is Raúl.
2. ☐ How are you?
3. ☐ I'm Brazilian.
4. ☐ Lucy is from China.
5. ☐ How old are you?
6. ☐ He's 15 years old.

Writing

5 Complete with information about you.

My name is ______________________.

I am ______________________ years old.

I'm ______________________.

I am from ______________________ in ______________________.

#TIP

You can include your information as part of your profile on a social-media app.

I can write basic information about myself.

Language Booster page 6

#UNDERSTAND

Grammar

Verb *be*

1 **Read the sentences and complete the chart.**

My name **is** Tania. I **am** 13 years old. I live in São Paulo. I'**m** Brazilian.
This **is** Martha. She'**s** 12 years old. We **are** best friends!

Subject	Verb *be*	Contraction
1 ________	am	I'm
You	3 ________	You're
He	is	6 ________
2 ________	is	She's
It	4 ________	It's
We	are	7 ________
They	5 ________	They're

2 **Complete with the correct form of *be*.**

My name 1 ________ Juan. I 2 ________ 12 years old. I live in Guadalajara. I 3 ________ Mexican. My friend 4 ________ José. He 5 ________ 13 years old. We 6 ________ best friends!

Wh- questions

3 **Read and match.**

1. What is your name?
2. Where are you from?
3. What's your teacher's name?
4. Where's your best friend from?

☐ My teacher is Consuelo Vásquez.
☐ My name is Maria.
☐ She is from Guatemala.
☐ I'm from Colombia.

4 **Check (✓) the statements that are true.**

1. ☐ We use *What* to ask about a place.
2. ☐ We use *What* to ask about a thing.
3. ☐ We use *Where* to ask about a place.
4. ☐ The short form of *What is* is *Whats*.
5. ☐ The short form of *Where is* is *Where's*.

5 **In pairs, ask and answer the questions in Activity 3.**

Where are you from?

I'm from Mexico.

I can use the verb *be* and *Wh-* questions to ask for personal information.

e-Language Booster

Possessive Adjectives

6 **Match the sentences to the pictures.**

1. **His** name is Juan.
2. She is **my** teacher.
3. What is **your** name?
4. **Its** name is Snowball.

a.

b.

c.

d.

7 **Circle the possessive adjectives in the sentences.**

1. What's your name?
2. My name's Kyle.
3. What's his name?
4. His name's Ricardo.
5. What's her name?
6. Her name is Ruth.

8 **Listen and complete the sentences.** 05

1. ________ name's Danny.
2. ________ best friend is from Chile.
3. ________ English teacher is from the United Kingdom.
4. What's ________ brother's name?
5. What is ________ nationality?
6. ________ name is Sheba.

9 **In groups, ask and answer questions about the people below using possessive adjectives.**

What's his name?

His name is Marcel Ruiz.

Marcel Ruiz
Puerto Rico

Millie Bobby Brown
Spain

Jaden Smith
the United States

I can use possessive adjectives to talk about myself and other people.

Language Booster page 7

#DEVELOP

Listening

1 Label the pictures with the countries from the box.

Brazil	Mexico	the United Kingdom

1. 
____

2. 
____

3. 
____

2 PREDICTING. Write B (Brazil), M (Mexico), or U (the United Kingdom) next to the sentences. Listen and check. 06

1. ☐ It's a small town near Guadalajara.
2. ☐ It's an island.
3. ☐ São Paulo is a big city.

3 LISTENING FOR DETAILS. Listen again and circle T (True) or F (False). 07

1. Lucas speaks Portuguese. True / False
2. Aby wants to learn French. True / False
3. Alberto is 12. True / False
4. Alberto lives in Mexico. True / False

Pronunciation

4 Listen and repeat. Then, in pairs, practice reading the question and answer aloud. Add one more sentence to each column in the chart. 08

/s/	/z/
What'**s** your name?	My name **is** Aby.
______________	______________

Speaking

5 Interview a classmate about his / her country and nationality.

Where are you from?

I'm from...

I can talk about different countries.

Use of English

6 Use the replies below to complete the dialogue.

I'm from Antigua.	I'm good, thanks.	My name's Marcus.
Where are you from?	I'm 13 years old.	And how old are you?

Teacher: Good morning, everyone! Welcome to Mexico! Are you all from Guatemala?
Students: No, Miss!
Teacher: Oh, OK. What's your name?
Marcus: [1] ______________
Teacher: Hello, Marcus. [2] ______________
Marcus: I'm from Colombia, but I live in Guatemala.
Teacher: [3] ______________
Marcus: I'm 12.
Teacher: And you, what's your name?
Gaby: I'm Gaby.
Teacher: Hello. How are you, Gaby?
Gaby: [4] ______________
Teacher: Where are you from, Gaby?
Gaby: I'm from Guatemala, but I'm not from Guatemala City, [5] ______________
Teacher: And how old are you?
Gaby: [6] ______________ I love Mexico!
Teacher: That's great news! All aboard now!

7 Read the dialogue again. Underline the question words and circle the possessive adjectives.

8 Rewrite the sentences without changing the meaning.

1. My name's Marcus.
____
2. I'm Guatemalan.
____
3. I'm very well, thanks.
____
4. I'm 13 years old.
____

9 Practice the dialogue with your own information. Then change roles.

What is your name?

My name's Lydia.

I can greet people and introduce myself.
Language Booster page 8

Writing

1 In pairs, read Nubia's text and say what her relationship with Emma is.

CANCEL SEND

TO emma123@hashtag.com

SUBJECT

Hi Emma,

How are you?

My name's Nubia. Thanks for the e-mail!

I'm 13 years old, and I'm Peruvian. I'm from a big city called Lima. Where are you from? I know you're British, but where in the U.K.? And how old are you?

Please write back soon.

Bye!

Nubia

2 Complete the information about Nubia and Emma.

1. Nubia is from ____________________.
2. Nubia's nationality is ____________________.
3. She is ________________ years old.
4. Emma is from ____________________.
5. She's ____________________.

3 Complete the sentences with the correct form of the verb *be*.

1. My name ________ Tim.
2. I ________ 12 years old.
3. I ________ French.
4. What ________ your name?
5. How old ________ you?
6. Where ________ you from?

Prepare to Write

4 Write the following personal information.

1. Your name: ____________________.
2. Your age: ____________________.
3. Where you're from: ____________________.

I can demonstrate an understanding of an e-mail with personal information and prepare to write one.

Write

5 **Write an e-mail introducing yourself to a new friend from another country.**

CANCEL SEND

TO

SUBJECT

Check and Change

6 **Read your e-mail and make sure you included:**

- ☐ your name.
- ☐ your age.
- ☐ the country you're from.
- ☐ your nationality.
- ☐ questions asking for personal information.

7 **Edit your e-mail. Make sure all the elements in Activity 6 are included.**

Publish

8 **Write a clean version of your e-mail.**

#TIP

You can create a free e-mail account through an e-mail service.

Speaking

9 **Read your classmate's e-mail and answer the questions.**

1. What is his / her name? ______________________.
2. How old is he / she? ______________________.
3. Where is he / she from? ______________________.

I can write an e-mail sharing personal information about myself and someone else.

Language Booster page 9

Project: A Slide Presentation

#DIGITAL LITERACY

1. Include headings on your presentation slides.
2. Use bullet points to present information clearly.
3. Add pictures or images to your slides.

Step 1 Think

1 Work in groups.

1. Discuss: How do you greet people in your country?
2. Read the presentation slide. What is similar or different in your country?

Greetings and Introductions
China

Chinese people bow when they greet each other. They give personal information, like...

- name.
- age.
- where they are from.

Step 2 Plan

2 In groups, complete the information about greetings and introductions in your country.

Country: ______________________

Physical greeting: ______________________

Introductions (personal information):

____

____

____

I can plan a slide presentation about greetings and introductions in different countries.

Step 3 Research

3 Research customs for greetings and introductions in different countries. Make notes like you did in Step 2.

[name of country] greetings and introductions

Step 4 Design

4 In groups, create your slide presentation.

- Check the text.
- Check the images.
- Check the organization.

#TIP STEP 4

Use different fonts and backgrounds to make your slides look interesting and attractive.

Step 5 Present and Publish

5 In groups, show your slide presentation to the class.

#TIP STEP 5

Make eye contact with your audience when presenting.

Step 6 Evaluate

6 Complete the evaluation table.

★☆☆ More to learn | ★★☆ Good | ★★★ Excellent

Criteria	My Evaluation	Group Evaluation	Teacher Evaluation
Teamwork	☆☆☆	☆☆☆	☆☆☆
Language	☆☆☆	☆☆☆	☆☆☆
Design	☆☆☆	☆☆☆	☆☆☆

I can create a slide presentation and present it to the class.

#SELF-ASSESSMENT

1 Mark the learning objectives according to the key.

★☆☆ I don't understand.	★★☆ I understand, but I need help.	★★★ I can do it!

Learning Objectives	Rating
To greet someone and share personal information.	☆☆☆
To identify countries and nationalities.	☆☆☆
To read about greetings and introductions.	☆☆☆
To write basic information about myself.	☆☆☆
To use the verb **be** and *Wh-* questions to ask for personal information.	☆☆☆
To use possessive adjectives to talk about myself and other people.	☆☆☆
To talk about different countries.	☆☆☆
To greet people and introduce myself.	☆☆☆
To demonstrate an understanding of an e-mail with personal information and prepare to write one.	☆☆☆
To write an e-mail sharing personal information about myself and someone else.	☆☆☆
To plan a slide presentation about greetings and introductions in different countries.	☆☆☆
To create a slide presentation and present it to the class.	☆☆☆

2 Work in pairs. Discuss the questions.

1. What did I find most interesting to learn? Why?
2. How did I learn it?
3. How can I use it in real life?

UT Language Booster page 10

PEOPLE AND CITIES

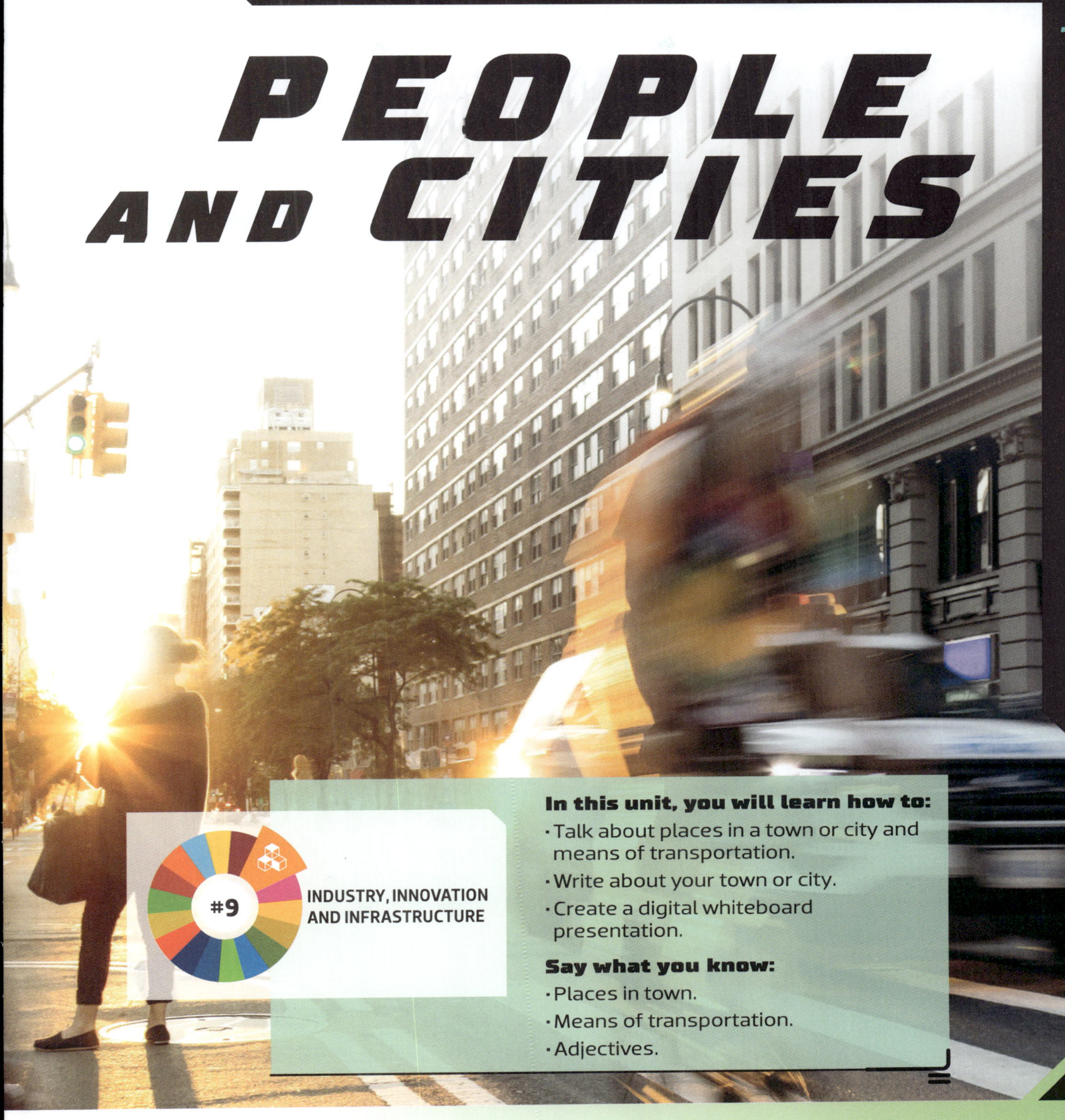

#9 INDUSTRY, INNOVATION AND INFRASTRUCTURE

In this unit, you will learn how to:

- Talk about places in a town or city and means of transportation.
- Write about your town or city.
- Create a digital whiteboard presentation.

Say what you know:

- Places in town.
- Means of transportation.
- Adjectives.

Video

In My City

Before You Watch

1 **In pairs, look at the pictures. Which of these places can you see in your town or city?**

shopping mall

movie theater

restaurant

hospital

sports center

2 **Which city is similar to your town or city? Check (✓).**

1. 
Silverton, Colorado ☐

2. 
Portland, Oregon ☐

While You Watch

3 **Watch Part 1 of the video and complete with the requested information. Then watch it a second time and check (✓) what the speaker mentions the city has.** 02

Name: [1] ____________________ Age: [2] ________

City: [3] ______________________________

Nationality: [4] ______________________________

1. ☐ bank
2. ☐ hospital
3. ☐ shopping mall
4. ☐ movie theater
5. ☐ restaurant
6. ☐ park
7. ☐ excellent public transportation system

4 **Watch Part 2 of the video and repeat the procedures in Activity 1.** 02

Name: [1] ____________________ Age: [2] ________

City: [3] ______________________________

Nationality: [4] ______________________________

1. ☐ bank
2. ☐ hospital
3. ☐ shopping mall
4. ☐ movie theater
5. ☐ restaurant
6. ☐ park
7. ☐ good public transportation system

After You Watch

5 **Now check (✓) what your town or city has and complete the sentence.**

1. ☐ bank
2. ☐ hospital
3. ☐ shopping mall
4. ☐ movie theater
5. ☐ restaurant
6. ☐ park
7. ☐ good public transportation system

My town or city has ______________________________

____.

I can interpret a conversation about somebody's city.

Vocabulary

Places in Town

6 Match the words to the pictures. Then listen and check. 09

- ☐ bank
- ☐ hospital
- ☐ movie theater
- ☐ park
- ☐ restaurant
- ☐ school
- ☐ shopping mall
- ☐ supermarket

1. 
2. 
3. 
4. 
5. 
6. 
7. 
8. 

7 Work in pairs. Which places in Activity 6 can you see near your school?

____

____

Means of Transportation

8 Listen and repeat. 10

bike

bus

car

ferryboat

subway

train

streetcar

9 Use the words from the box to label the pictures.

ferryboat subway train

1.  ____________
2.  ____________
3.  ____________

10 Read the extracts from the video and match the words in bold to the pictures.

"There is good ***bus*** service and there are ***streetcars***."

"I go everywhere by ***car*** or by ***bike***."

1.  ____________
2.  ____________
3.  ____________
4.  ____________

11 In pairs, talk about how you go to different places.

I go to the movie theater by subway.

#TIP

I go **by** bus, car, subway, etc.

I **walk**. I go **on foot**.

I can use vocabulary for places in town and transportation.

Language Booster page 11

#CLARIFY

Reading

1 USING PRIOR KNOWLEDGE. What means of transportation can you see?

1. 

2. 

3. 

4. 

2 SKIMMING. Read the text quickly. Write the means of transportation mentioned next to each city.

1. London ____________
2. Amsterdam ____________
3. Bogotá ____________

Good Public...

Good Public Transportation Is Important

Good public transportation is important because it's good for the environment.

I live in London, England. The subway system in London is very big. There are more than 200 subway stations and 11 subway lines. The subway system is very old, but there are many new subway cars.

I'm from Amsterdam, Netherlands. There are lots of special bike lanes in the city. There are bikes everywhere! They are very cheap, only ten euros per day. I usually go to school by bike, but I use the streetcars, too.

I'm from Bogotá, Colombia. There is a modern bus system in my city: *Transmilenio*. *Transmilenio* is fast. It's cheap and safe. There are special lanes for the buses. I go everywhere by bus!

3 SCANNING. Read the text again and mark the sentences T (True) or False (F).

1. ☐ The subway system in London is big.
2. ☐ There are thirteen subway lines in London.
3. ☐ There are lots of car lanes in Amsterdam.
4. ☐ The bikes in Amsterdam are ten euros per day.
5. ☐ The bus system in Bogotá isn't fast.

I can read about public transportation around the world.

e-Language Booster

Listening

4 Listen to two teenagers and complete the chart. 11

Name	Brad	Gabriela
City	1 ____________	4 ____________
Transportation	2 ____________	5 ____________
Cost	3 ____________	6 ____________

Writing

5 Complete the sentences about public transportation in your town or city.

The public transportation system in ____________ is ____________.

There is a ____________ system.

#TIP

You can include a picture of the means of transportation you use to go to school!

6 Read Brad's text. Then use the information in Activity 5 and write a similar text about yourself.

brad_
posted 3 hours ago

My name's Brad, and I'm from Staten Island, New York. My school is in Manhattan, so I go to school by ferryboat. It is free, so I pay zero dollars!

5 comments

____

____

____

____

0 comments

I can write simple information about public transportation in my town / city.

Language Booster page 12

#UNDERSTAND

Grammar

There + Verb *be* – Affirmative and Negative

1 **In pairs, read the extracts from the video *In My City*. Are they about Portland or Silverton?**

1. **There is** a good bus service, and **there are** streetcars.

2. **There isn't** a hospital.

3. **There's** a bank and **there are** two restaurants here, but **there aren't** any shopping malls.

2 **Read the sentences in the chart below and the sentences in Activity 1 again. Then circle the correct options to complete the rules.**

There + verb *be*	
Affirmative sentences	**Negative sentences**
There is a restaurant on my street. **There are** some bike lanes in my city.	**There isn't** a movie theater on Field Avenue. **There aren't** any restaurants here.
Contractions: There is = There's There is not = There isn't There are not = There aren't	

1. Use a **singular** / **plural** noun after *there is*.
2. Use a **singular** / **plural** noun after *there are*.
3. Use *isn't* or *aren't* for contractions in **affirmative** / **negative** sentences.

#TIP

Use *any* after *there aren't*.

Use *some* or a number after *there are*.

3 **Look at the picture. Write two affirmative and two negative sentences about it using *there* + verb *be*.**

____

____

____

____

____

____

4 **In pairs, compare your sentences in Activity 3. Then practice reading them aloud.**

There + Verb *be* – *Yes / No* Questions and Short Answers

5 In pairs, read the sentences in Activity 1 again and make them true about your town / city.

____

____

____

____

____

6 Look at the chart and complete the dialogues with the words from the box.

There + verb *be*	
***Yes / No* questions**	**Short answers**
Is there a hospital in this town?	Yes, **there is**. / No, **there isn't**.
Are there any banks on Black Street?	Yes, **there are**. / No, **there aren't**.

are there | is | is there | isn't | there are | there is

1. **A:** ____________ there a shopping mall in your town?
   B: No, there ____________.
2. **A:** ____________ any restaurants?
   B: Yes, ____________. There are three restaurants.
3. **A:** ____________ a subway system?
   B: Yes, ____________. It's fast.

7 Write three questions about the picture in Activity 3. Use *there* + verb *be*.

Is there a shopping mall?

____

____

____

8 Work in pairs. Take turns asking and answering the questions in Activity 7.

Is there a shopping mall?

Yes, there is.

I can ask and answer questions about places in a town.

Language Booster page 13

Listening

1 **Listen and repeat the adjectives.** 12

cheap

expensive

fast

modern

old

slow

2 **Complete the chart.**

Opposites	
fast	2 ________
1 ________	expensive
modern	3 ________

3 **USING CUES. Listen to the first part of a radio show episode and choose the best title.** 13

1. ☐ My city is great.
2. ☐ My city: the good and the bad.
3. ☐ My city is terrible.

4 **LISTENING FOR DETAILS. Listen to the whole episode and mark the sentences T (True) or F (False).** 14

1. ☐ The streetcars in Manchester aren't cheap.
2. ☐ There is a shopping mall in Juneau.
3. ☐ There aren't any restaurants in Buenos Aires.
4. ☐ Some of the subway cars are slow in Buenos Aires.

Pronunciation

5 **Listen to the dialogues. Pay attention to the rising and falling intonations.** 15

1.
A: Is the subway cheap?
B: Yes, it is.

2.
A: Is the bus fast?
B: No, it isn't.

Speaking

6 **Work in pairs. Role play the dialogues in Activity 5 using the correct intonation.**

I can demonstrate an understanding of a radio show episode about towns and cities.

e-Language Booster

Use of English

7 **Work in pairs. Say if there are places like these in your town / city and where they are.**

bank hospitals
shopping mall supermarkets

There is a bank in my town. It's on Ocean Street.
There aren't any hospitals in my town.

#TIP
Use *on* + ________ Street / Avenue

8 **Order the sentences and form dialogues. Then listen and check.** 16

Dialogue 1
- ☐ You're welcome.
- ☐ Excuse me, is there a supermarket in this neighborhood?
- ☐ Thanks!
- ☐ Yes, there is. It's on Lime Street.

Dialogue 2
- ☐ Yes, there are. They're on Beach Street.
- ☐ Are there any restaurants near here?
- ☐ Great, thanks.

Dialogue 3
- ☐ Excuse me, is there a shopping mall on this avenue?
- ☐ Oh, no!
- ☐ Yes, there is. But it's very expensive.

9 **Complete the neighborhood map with different places.**

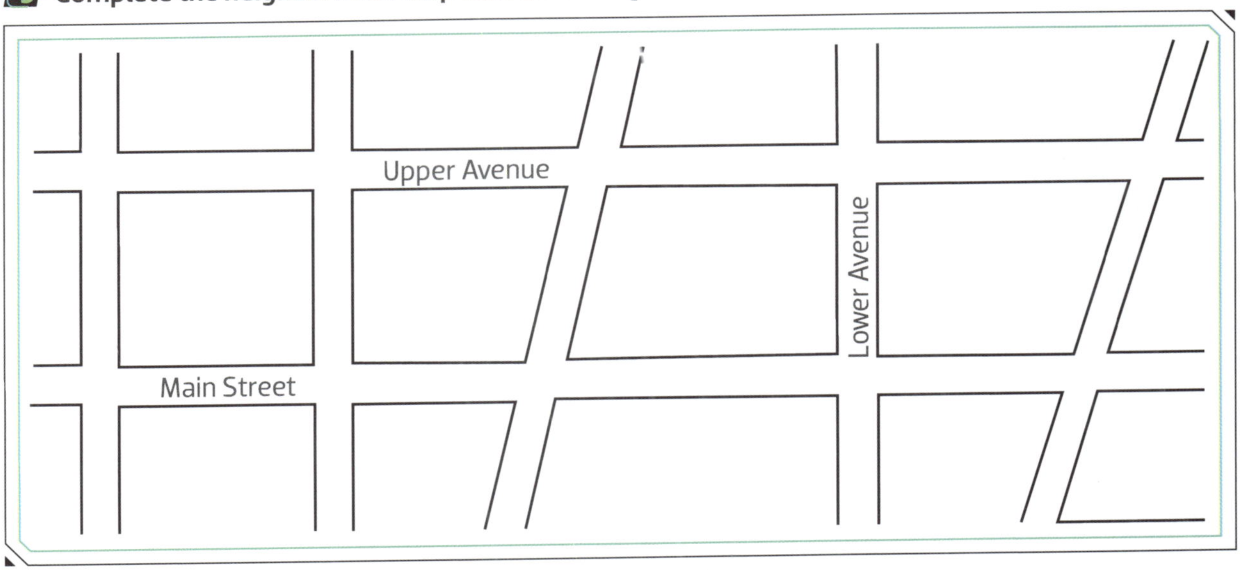

10 **Work in pairs. Take turns asking and answering questions about each other's maps.**

Is there a bank in your neighborhood?

Yes, there is. It's on Main Street.

I can ask and answer questions about places in a city.
Language Booster page 14

Writing

1 **In pairs, read the text and underline the positive things about Daniela's city.**

cyberhashtagcafe.com/profile

Alvarez Mendez

Bogotá, Colombia

I'm Daniela Alvarez Mendez, but my nickname is Dany or Dana. I'm Colombian. I'm from Bogotá, but I'm in Cartagena now. I'm 13 years old. My city is great. There is a cheap shopping mall and a modern movie theater. There are big banks and good schools. There is a new bus service. It's fast and modern, but it isn't in all parts of the city. The bus service in my neighborhood is old and slow. There aren't any streetcars, and there isn't a subway.

2 **Read the text in Activity 1 again and answer the questions.**

1. How old is Daniela?

____

2. Where is Daniela from?

____

3. Are there any streetcars in Cartagena?

____

4. What places are there in Daniela's city?

____

Prepare to Write

3 **Make positive and negative notes about your town or city.**

	Positive	Negative
Places	1 ___________ ___________	3 ___________ ___________
Public transportation	2 ___________ ___________	4 ___________ ___________

I can comprehend a social media profile about someone and their city and prepare to write one.

e-Language Booster

Write

4 **Write a profile about you and your neighborhood, town, or city. Use the text in Activity 1 and your notes in Activity 3 to help you.**

cyberhashtagcafe.com/profile

____

____

____

____

____

____

____

Check and Change

5 **Read your text and make sure you included:**

- ☐ your name and age.
- ☐ your nationality and your city.
- ☐ places in your city.
- ☐ public transportation in your city.
- ☐ adjectives.
- ☐ *there* + verb *be*.

6 **Edit your text. Make sure all the elements in Activity 5 are included.**

Publish

7 **Write a clean version of your text.**

#TIP

You can add your picture and a picture of your neighborhood, town, or city, to the profile text.

Speaking

8 **Complete the questions to ask your classmate.**

1. Is there a / an ______________ in your neighborhood?
2. Are there ______________ in your neighborhood?
3. Where is the ______________ in your neighborhood?
4. Are the ______________ good in your neighborhood?

9 **Work in pairs. Take turns asking and answering the questions in Activity 8.**

I can write a social media profile about me and my city.

Language Booster page 15

Project: A Digital Whiteboard Presentation

#DIGITAL LITERACY

1. Include images in your digital whiteboard presentation.
2. Use key words to present essential information.

Step 1 Think

1 Look at the digital whiteboard presentation and answer the questions.

1. What city is it about?
2. What information is there?

Step 2 Plan

2 In groups, discuss ideas for your digital whiteboard presentation.

I can recognize features of a digital whiteboard presentation and plan to create one.

Step 3 Research

3 In groups, search for information about different layouts and features of digital whiteboard presentations online. Make notes.

____

____

____

Step 4 Design

4 In groups, create your digital whiteboard presentation.

- Check the text.
- Check the images.
- Check the organization.

#TIP STEP 4

Use different interactive whiteboards, pictures, drawings, and illustrations.

Step 5 Present and Publish

5 In groups, show your digital whiteboard presentation to the class.

Step 6 Evaluate

6 Complete the evaluation table.

★☆☆ More to learn | ★★☆ Good | ★★★ Excellent

Criteria	My Evaluation	Group Evaluation	Teacher Evaluation
Teamwork	☆☆☆	☆☆☆	☆☆☆
Language	☆☆☆	☆☆☆	☆☆☆
Design	☆☆☆	☆☆☆	☆☆☆

I can create a digital whiteboard presentation about my city and present it to the class.

#SELF-ASSESSMENT

1 Mark the learning objectives according to the key.

★☆☆ I don't understand.	★★☆ I understand, but I need help.	★★★ I can do it!

Learning Objectives	Rating
To interpret a conversation about somebody's city.	☆☆☆
To use vocabulary for places in town and transportation.	☆☆☆
To read about public transportation around the world.	☆☆☆
To write simple information about public transportation in my town / city.	☆☆☆
To use *there* + verb *be* to talk about places in a town.	☆☆☆
To ask and answer questions about places in a town.	☆☆☆
To demonstrate an understanding of a radio show episode about towns and cities.	☆☆☆
To ask and answer questions about places in a city.	☆☆☆
To comprehend a social media profile about someone and their city and write one.	☆☆☆
To write a social media profile about me and my city.	☆☆☆
To recognize features of a digital whiteboard presentation and plan to create one.	☆☆☆
To create a digital whiteboard presentation about my city and present it to the class.	☆☆☆

2 Work in pairs. Discuss the questions.

1. What did I find most interesting to learn? Why?
2. How did I learn it?
3. How can I use it in real life?

UT Language Booster page 16

MY CLASSROOM

#4 QUALITY EDUCATION

In this unit, you will learn how to:
- Talk about different classrooms.
- Write about your classroom and school.
- Create a visual narrative.

Say what you know:
- Objects in the classroom.
- Colors.
- Numbers from 0 to 100.

#DISCOVER

Video

In the Library

Before You Watch

1 **Label the classroom objects with the words from the box.**

book	chair	desk	eraser	notebook	pencil

1. 
____

2. 
____

3. 
____

4. 
____

5. 
____

6. 

____

While You Watch

2 **Watch Part 1 of the video. Which words from Activity 1 can you hear? Check (✓).** 03

3 **Watch Part 2 of the video and check (✓) the questions you hear.** 03

1. ☐ Can you help me?
2. ☐ Can I have a pen?
3. ☐ Can I go to the restroom?
4. ☐ How do you say this in English?
5. ☐ How do you spell it?
6. ☐ Can you repeat that, please?

After You Watch

4 **Match the answers to the questions from Activity 3. Write them down.**

1. ______________________
Of course.

2. ______________________
It's a whiteboard.

3. ______________________
W-H-I-T-E-B-O-A-R-D.

4. ______________________
Sure. W-H-I-T-E-B-O-A-R-D.

5. ______________________
Yes. Blue or black?

6. ______________________
Yes, but be quick, please.

5 **Role play the short dialogues and record them.**

I can ask and answer common classroom questions.

Vocabulary

Numbers and Classroom Objects

6 Listen and repeat the numbers. 17

0 zero
1 one
2 two
3 three
4 four
5 five
6 six
7 seven
8 eight
9 nine
10 ten
11 eleven
12 twelve
13 thirteen
14 fourteen
15 fifteen
16 sixteen
17 seventeen
18 eighteen
19 nineteen
20 twenty
21 twenty-one
22 twenty-two
23 twenty-three
30 thirty
40 forty
50 fifty
60 sixty
70 seventy
80 eighty
90 ninety
100 one hundred

7 Look at the pictures. Count and answer.

1. How many chairs are there? ____________

2. How many books are there? ____________

3. How many pens are there? ____________

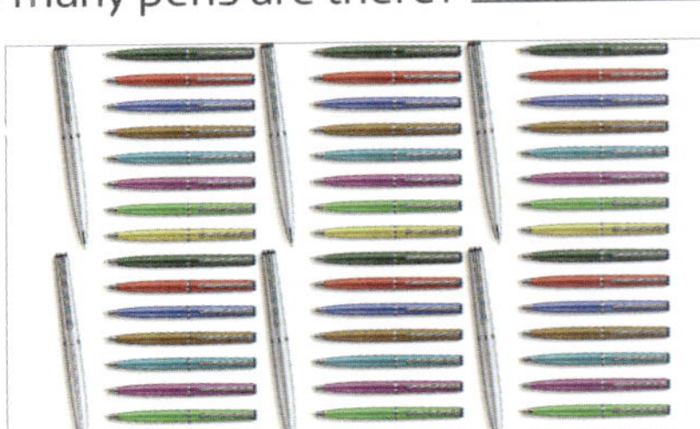

8 Match the classroom objects to their names.

1. 
2. 
3. 
4. 
5. 
6. 
7. 
8. 
9. 
10. 

- ☐ backpack
- ☐ bulletin board
- ☐ chair
- ☐ clock
- ☐ desk
- ☐ laptop
- ☐ marker
- ☐ notebook
- ☐ pen
- ☐ whiteboard

Alphabet

9 Listen and say the alphabet. 18

A B C D E F G H I J K L M N
O P Q R S T U V W X Y Z

10 In pairs, take turns asking about the objects in Activity 8.

How do you spell backpack?

B-a-c-k-p-a-c-k.

How many backpacks are there?

There are 35 backpacks.

I can identify and talk about classroom objects.

Language Booster page 17

#CLARIFY

Reading

1 USING PRIOR KNOWLEDGE. Look at the pictures. What is there in each classroom?

a.

b.

2 The texts below describe the classrooms in Activity 1. Read and number the pictures accordingly.

1.

Mr. Silva

I'm a teacher in an elementary school. The school is new, so the classrooms are very modern. There is Internet access and an interactive whiteboard in every classroom. The classes are small – there are 20 students in my class. There are four tables in my classroom, and students work in groups. There is a tablet for each group. Students use the tablet to look online for information for their projects. Their projects are on the bulletin board.

2.

Ms. Garcia

My classroom is traditional. It's a small classroom, but there are 30 students in my class. The desks are small, and there is one desk for each student. There is a whiteboard, but there isn't Internet or a projector. There are two big bulletin boards with students' projects. There isn't a lot of technology in our school, but there are lots of books. Students have a book for each subject, and there is a huge library with a nice reading corner. I think books are important to learn new things.

3 MONITORING COMPREHENSION. Read the texts again and write *Ms. Garcia* or *Mr. Silva*.

1. The classroom isn't old. ______________
2. There is new technology in the classroom. ______________
3. There are twenty students in the classroom. ______________
4. There are thirty desks in the classroom. ______________
5. There are lots of books. ______________

4 Work in pairs. Answer the questions.

1. Which classroom is your favorite?
2. Which classroom is like your classroom?

I can read about different classrooms.

e-Language Booster

Listening

5 **Listen to Debesh and circle the correct answers.** 19

1. Debesh's classroom is on a **boat** / **bus**.
2. There are **twelve** / **twenty** floating classrooms in his district.
3. There **are** / **aren't** desks for the students.
4. There isn't a **whiteboard** / **laptop** in Debesh's classroom.
5. There **is** / **isn't** Internet in some floating classrooms.
6. Debesh's classes are **big** / **interesting**.

Writing

6 **Write sentences about your classroom. Use the prompts given.**

In my classroom, there is ______________________________.

There isn't ______________________________.

There are ______________________________.

There aren't ______________________________.

I can write simple sentences about my classroom.

Language Booster page 18

Grammar

Articles

1 **Complete the school supplies list with *a* or *an*.**

1. _____ notebook	**4.** _____ eraser	**7.** _____ pink marker
2. _____ black pen	**5.** _____ new backpack	**8.** _____ whiteboard
3. _____ blue pen	**6.** _____ orange marker	**9.** _____ class

2 **Circle the options to complete the rules.**

1. We use *a* or *an* + **singular** / **plural** noun.
2. We use **a** / **an** + word beginning with a consonant sound.
3. We use **a** / **an** + word beginning with a vowel sound.

3 **Work in pairs. Make the sentences true about your classroom.**

There is a clock in my classroom.

There aren't five books on the teacher's desk.

1. There is a clock in my classroom.
2. There are five books on the teacher's desk.
3. There is a door at the back of the class.
4. There is an eraser on the floor.
5. There isn't a backpack on the floor.

Plural Nouns

4 **In pairs, ask and answer about the objects in your classroom.**

How many books are there?

There are eight books.

How many backpacks are there?

There are ten backpacks.

I can identify and use *a* and *an*.
e-Language Booster

Demonstrative Pronouns

5 **Listen. Pay attention to the words in bold in the text.** 20

A: What's **that**, Mel?
B: This is a picture of a floating school. Look, **this** is the teacher, and **these** are the desks.
A: What are **those** at the back?
B: **Those** are the books! And **that** is the whiteboard.

6 **Underline the correct option. Use the dialogue in Activity 5 to help you.**

1. **This** / **These** is a book.
2. **Those** / **That** are pencils.
3. **That** / **Those** are pens.
4. What is **that** / **these**?
5. What are **this** / **those**?

7 **Complete the chart with *this*, *these*, *that*, and *those*.**

Singular	 1 ______________	 3 ______________
Plural	 2 ______________	 4 ______________

8 **In pairs, role play the conversation. Replace the words in bold with different objects.**

What is this?

It's a **pen**.

What are those?

They are **books**.

I can ask about objects in the classroom.
Language Booster page 19

Listening

1 Match the words to the pictures.

camera chat box microphone

1. 

2. 

3. 

2 Read and write T (Teacher) and /or S (Student) to say who usually says these in class.

1. ☐ ☐ How do you spell it?
2. ☐ ☐ Can you turn on your microphone, please?
3. ☐ ☐ Can I borrow a pen?
4. ☐ ☐ Listen, please.
5. ☐ ☐ How do you say this in English?
6. ☐ ☐ Can you turn on your camera, please?
7. ☐ ☐ Type your answer in the chat box.
8. ☐ ☐ Can you help me?
9. ☐ ☐ Can I go to the restroom?
10. ☐ ☐ Can you type that in the chat box, please?

3 Look at Activity 2 again. Which options are more common in online classes? Check (✓).

4 LISTENING FOR GIST. Listen. Is it a face-to-face or online class? 21

____

5 LISTENING FOR DETAILS. Number the sentences and form a dialogue. Then listen again and check. 22

☐ A pencil, an eraser, two pens, and three notebooks.
☐ Can you turn your cameras on, please? [pause] That's better. Mark, can you turn your microphone on, please?
☐ E – R – A – S – E – R.
☐ Good! [pause] And how do you spell eraser?
☐ Great!
☐ Oh, sorry, Mr. Moore.
☐ That's OK. Can you show us your backpack, please?
☐ What's there in your backpack?
☐ Yes. Here it is.

Pronunciation

6 Listen and pay attention to these sounds. Then listen and repeat. 23

this /i/	these /iː/
This is it.	**These** three, please.

Speaking

7 In pairs, role play the dialogue in Activity 5 asking to spell different words.

Use of English

8 **Look and match the words to the colors in the color wheel.**

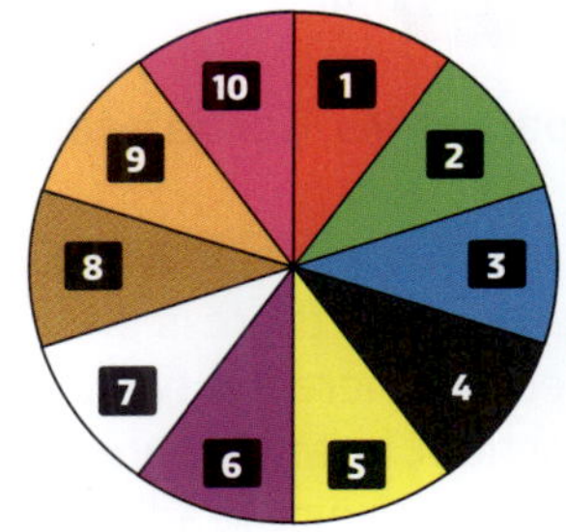

- ☐ black
- ☐ blue
- ☐ brown
- ☐ green
- ☐ orange
- ☐ pink
- ☐ purple
- ☐ red
- ☐ white
- ☐ yellow

9 **Listen to Alejandro and circle the objects in his study place.** 24

10 **Listen again and list the colors and the objects.** 25

- *blue desk*
- ____________
- ____________
- ____________
- ____________
- ____________

11 **Match the questions to the answers.**

1. Are your classes face-to-face or online?
2. Is there a desk in your bedroom?
3. What is there in your backpack?
4. What colors are your markers?
5. What color is your notebook?

- ☐ They're pink and yellow.
- ☐ It's blue.
- ☐ There are two notebooks, an eraser, and two pens.
- ☐ They're online.
- ☐ Yes, there is.

12 **Work in pairs. Take turns asking and answering the questions in Activity 11.**

I can describe a study place.

Language Booster page 20

#CHALLENGE

Writing

1 **Read part of Ms. Garcia's text and underline the adjectives.**

My classroom is traditional. It's a small classroom, but there are 30 students in my class. The desks are small, and there is one desk for each student. There is a whiteboard, but there isn't Internet or a projector. There are two big bulletin boards with students' projects. There isn't a lot of technology in our school, but there are lots of books. Students have a book for each subject, and there is a huge library with a nice reading corner. I think books are important to learn new things.

2 **Read the text again and match the adjectives to the objects or places.**

1. big
2. huge
3. important
4. nice
5. small
6. traditional

a. 

b. 

c. 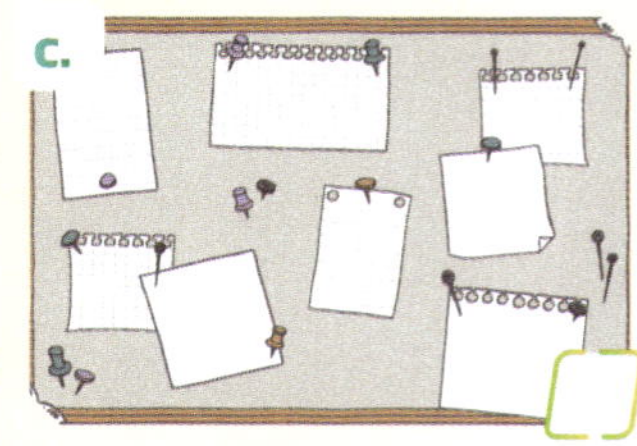

d. 

e. 

f. 

Prepare to Write

3 **Write about your classroom and school. Use true information.**

Classroom

Technology

Classroom objects

School places

I can demonstrate an understanding of a description of a classroom and prepare to write one.

Write

4 **Write about your classroom and school. Use the text in Activity 1 as a model and the words/expressions/phrases from the circles.**

Check and Change

5 **Read your text and make sure you included:**

- ☐ one or two adjectives that describe your classroom.
- ☐ the number of students in class.
- ☐ two or three objects in the classroom.
- ☐ different adjectives to describe the objects.
- ☐ a place that you like at school.
- ☐ an adjective that describes this place.

6 **Edit your text. Make sure all the elements in Activity 5 are included.**

Publish

7 **Write a clean version of your text. Then draw a picture of your classroom.**

#TIP

Use online drawing apps to make your drawing.

Speaking

8 **Present your classroom drawing to a classmate.**

This is my drawing. My classroom is big and modern. There are 25 students in my class. The desks are big. There is a whiteboard and a projector. There is Internet, too. There is one big bulletin board with students' projects. There is a lot of technology in my school. Technology is important to learn new things.

I can write about my classroom and school.

Language Booster page 21

Project: A Visual Narrative

#DIGITAL LITERACY

1. Prepare what to say before you present it to the audience.
2. Decide on visuals to represent the events of your narrative.
3. Add movement to still images.

Step 1 Think

1 Work in groups.

1. Discuss: What is there in your classroom? What isn't there?
2. Look at the image: Does it give support to tell a story?

My Ideal Classroom

CLASSROOM DESCRIPTION

- big
- huge
- modern
- small
- traditional

CLASSROOM OBJECTS

- backpack
- book
- bulletin board
- chair
- clock
- computer
- desk
- interactive whiteboard
- laptop
- notebook
- pen
- pencil
- projector

OBJECT DESCRIPTION

- black
- blue
- green
- huge
- important
- interesting
- new
- nice
- old

QUANTITY

- a lot of
- lots of
- thirty

STRUCTURE

15 students

I can recognize the features of a visual narrative about an ideal classroom.

Step 2 Plan

2 In groups of three, list the words you want to use in each category.

Structure | Classroom objects | Quantity | Object description

Step 3 Research

3 In groups, look for examples of classrooms online. Add more ideas to Step 2.

ideal classrooms

Step 4 Design

4 Still in groups, create your visual narrative.

- Check the events.
- Check the visuals.
- Check the organization.

#TIP STEP 4

Visual narratives can be static or dynamic. In a static narrative, viewers can determine the viewing order. In a dynamic narrative, actors determine the order of the events.

Step 5 Present and Publish

5 Present your narrative to the class. Then publish it.

Step 6 Evaluate

6 Complete the evaluation table.

★☆☆ More to learn | ★★☆ Good | ★★★ Excellent

Criteria	My Evaluation	Group Evaluation	Teacher Evaluation
Teamwork	☆☆☆	☆☆☆	☆☆☆
Language	☆☆☆	☆☆☆	☆☆☆
Design	☆☆☆	☆☆☆	☆☆☆

I can create a visual narrative and present it to the class.

#SELF-ASSESSMENT

1 Mark the learning objectives according to the key.

★☆☆ I don't understand.	★★☆ I understand, but I need help.	★★★ I can do it!

Learning Objectives	Rating
To ask and answer common classroom questions.	☆☆☆
To identify and talk about classroom objects.	☆☆☆
To read about different classrooms.	☆☆☆
To write simple sentences about my classroom.	☆☆☆
To identify and use *a* and *an*.	☆☆☆
To ask about objects in the classroom.	☆☆☆
To use language for face-to-face and online classes.	☆☆☆
To describe a study place.	☆☆☆
To demonstrate an understanding of a description of a classroom and prepare to write one.	☆☆☆
To write about my classroom and school.	☆☆☆
To recognize the features of a visual narrative about an ideal classroom.	☆☆☆
To create a visual narrative and present it to the class.	☆☆☆

2 Work in pairs. Discuss the questions.

1. What did I find most interesting to learn? Why?
2. How did I learn it?
3. How can I use it in real life?

UT Language Booster page 22

FAMILY IS SPECIAL

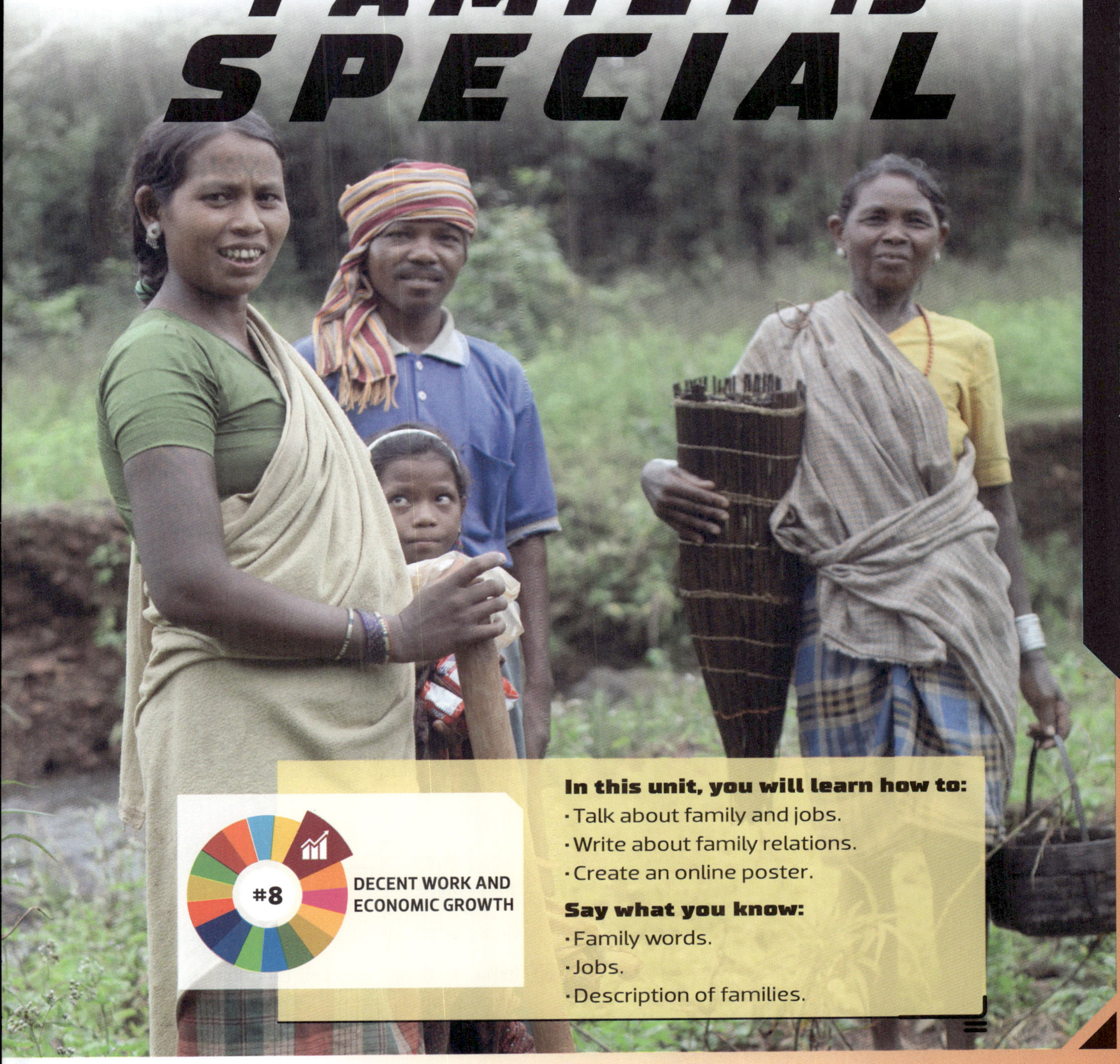

#8 DECENT WORK AND ECONOMIC GROWTH

In this unit, you will learn how to:

- Talk about family and jobs.
- Write about family relations.
- Create an online poster.

Say what you know:

- Family words.
- Jobs.
- Description of families.

Video

My Family

Before You Watch

1 **In pairs, use the jobs from the box to label the pictures. Which job do you prefer?**

chef construction worker doctor
fashion designer nurse teacher

1. 
____

2. 
____

3. 
____

4. 
____

5. 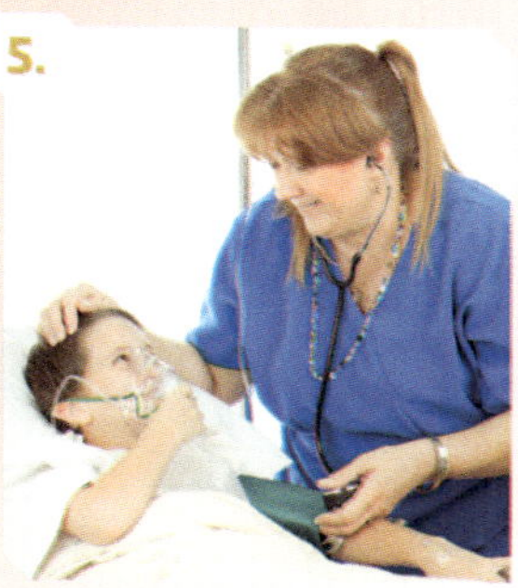
____

6. 
____

While You Watch

2 **Watch the video and complete the sentences with the jobs from Activity 1.** ▷ 04

1. Claudio is a ______________.
2. Linda is a ______________.
3. Hugo's dream job is a ______________.
4. Miriam's dream job is a ______________.

3 **Watch again and answer the questions with the correct options from the box.** ▷ 04

Claudio Emily Katya
Linda Miriam Hugo

1. Who is six years old? ______________.
2. Who is at college in a different city? ______________.
3. Who is Emily and Miriam's sister? ______________.
4. Who is Tom's brother? ______________.
5. Who is in a different country? ______________ and ______________.

After You Watch

4 **Choose a member of Hugo's family and complete the sentences below about him / her.**

1. He / She is Hugo's ______________.
2. His / Her name is ______________.
3. He's / She's ______________ years old.
4. He's / She's a / an ______________.

5 **In pairs, record yourself talking about Hugo's family.**

I can demonstrate an understanding of a conversation about different family members.

e-Language Booster

Vocabulary

Family Members

6 Listen and complete Hugo's family tree. 26

1 ____________ grandpa

2 ____________ grandma

3 ____________ mom

____________ me

4 ____________ dad

5 ____________ brother

6 ____________ sister

7 Work in pairs. Talk about Hugo's family.

Claudio is Hugo's grandpa.

#TIP

Lucas is Sara'**s** dad.

Hugo is Raul'**s** brother.

Jobs

8 Read the jobs in the box, listen, and repeat. Then look at the pictures and complete the text. 27

chef **construction worker** **delivery driver** **engineer** **pilot** **police officer** **store assistant**

My dream job is a  1 ____________, and my sister's dream job is a  2 ____________. But we are still students! My brother is at college, and his dream job is a teacher. On the weekends, he is a 

3 ____________ at the local mall. Our mom is an  4 ____________, and our dad is a  5 ____________. Our grandparents are volunteers. Grandma is a  6 ____________, and Grandpa is a  7 ____________.

9 In pairs, take turns miming and guessing the jobs from Activity 8.

Are you a chef?

No, I'm not.

Are you a pilot?

Yes, I am.

I can identify family members and jobs.

Language Booster page 23

#CLARIFY

Reading

1 **USING PRIOR KNOWLEDGE. In pairs, describe the pictures. Can you identify their jobs?**

1. 
2. 
3. 

2 **GENERATING QUESTIONS. Read the texts. How is your family similar to or different from Tania's and Danny's families?**

3 **SCANNING. Read the texts again and complete the sentences.**

My family tree is complicated. We are all over the world! My grandma is Chinese, and my grandpa is Brazilian, so my dad is Chinese-Brazilian. My mom is Brazilian, but her mom and dad are Argentinian. They are teachers in Brazil. My parents live in the United States, and my brother and I are American! My mom's a computer engineer at a big company here. I love my international family.

Tania

My family is from Mexico, except for my grandpa Kim. He's Japanese. My brother and sister are 30 years old – they're twins. My brother is a nurse, and my sister and mom are dentists. I'm a store assistant at my uncle and aunt's clothing store.

Danny

1. Tania's grandma is from ______________.
2. Danny's grandpa is from ______________.
3. Danny's mom is a ______________.
4. Tania's mom is in ______________.
5. Danny's brother is a ______________.
6. Tania's brother is ______________.

4 **MONITORING COMPREHENSION. Read the text and answer the questions.**

1. Where are Tania's family members from?

____

2. How old are Danny's brother and sister?

____

5 **Work in groups. Take turns asking and answering about each other's dream job.**

What is your dream job?

My dream job is a / an ...

I can read descriptions of people's families and their jobs.

e-Language Booster

Listening

6 **Listen and number the sentences according to the speaker. There are two extra options.** 28

- [ ] My sister is very quiet.
- [ ] My sister's job is important.
- [ ] My sister is a fan of Harry Potter.
- [ ] My sister is creative.
- [ ] My sister is my best friend, too.
- [ ] My sister is at home right now.

7 **Relate the picture to one of the speakers in Activity 6.**

Speaker ______

Writing

8 **Choose a member of your family and write a short paragraph about his / her job.**

My grandma is a garbage collector. It's an important job for the community.

#TIP

You can use an online dictionary to look up your family member's job. Create a vocabulary bank.

I can write about my family members' jobs.

Language Booster page 24

#UNDERSTAND

Grammar

Possessive 's and Possessive Adjectives

1 Work in pairs. Do you know this family? Complete the sentences with the words from the box.

brother dad mom sister

1. The girl's name is Lisa. Her ______________'s name is Homer.
2. The boy's name is Bart. His baby ______________'s name is Maggie.
3. Bart is Lisa and Maggie's ______________.
4. The woman's name is Marge. She's Lisa and Maggie's ______________.

2 Complete the text with the missing words.

[1]__________ name is Angela. I'm from Manta, in Ecuador. This is my family's ceviche restaurant. [2]__________ ceviche is delicious! It's my grandpa's restaurant. That's [3]__________ fishing boat on the beach. Is [4]__________ favorite food ceviche? Visit us!

The other restaurant is big. [5]__________ name is Garcia Restaurant. The chef is my parents' friend. [6]__________ name is Rosa.

3 Look at the sentences extracted from Activities 1 and 2 and underline the correct options to complete the statements.

This is my family**'s** ceviche restaurant.
The chef is my parents**'** friend.
The woman's name is Marge. She**'s** Lisa and Maggie**'s** mom.

1. We use **is** / **'s** after the names of people or things to show **quantity** / **possession**.
2. Plural nouns that **end** / **don't end** in -s only get an apostrophe.
3. Use 's after **the first** / **the last** noun that indicates the owner of two things.

4 Rewrite the sentences using 's.

1. That's his laptop. (Jimmy)
   ____
2. Her cell phone is old. (Rachel)
   ____
3. Its ball isn't red. (The dog)
   ____
4. Their dad is a pilot. (Anya and Teresa)
   ____

I can use possessive 's and possessive adjectives correctly.
e-Language Booster

5 **Look at the Brown family tree and write four sentences using the possessive 's.**

Terrence is William and Jessica's son.

____

____

____

____

____

____

____

____

____

Whose

6 **In pairs, answer the questions according to the pictures.**

1. 

A: Whose family is this? (Renan)

B: It's ______________ family.

2. 

A: Whose mother is this? (Leon and Kelly)

B: She's ______________ mother.

3. 

A: Whose video game is that? (her boyfriend)

B: It's ______________ video game.

7 **Read the questions and answers in Activity 6 again, pay attention to the word in bold, and complete the statements.**

1. We use ______________ to ask about ______________.
2. We can answer questions with *whose* using ______________ or a ______________.

8 **Work in pairs. Take turns asking and answering questions about the people in Activity 5.**

I can ask questions with whose and answer them with the possessive 's or possessive adjectives.

Language Booster page 25

Listening

1 LISTENING FOR DETAILS. Listen and complete the family tree with the names from the box. 29

Adam Jack Jane Jo Lilian Mike Sandy

2 Read and complete the sentences.

1. Your mom's brother is your ________________.
2. Your dad's sister is your ________________.
3. Your aunt and uncle's child is your ________________.
4. Your mom's son is your ________________.
5. Your dad's daughter is your ________________.

3 LOCATING SPECIFIC INFORMATION. Listen and answer. What is Lidia's mom's name? 30

____

4 LISTENING FOR DETAILS. Listen again and mark the sentences T (True) or F (False). 31

1. ☐ Lidia is in high school.
2. ☐ Aunt Genny is Melanie's mom's sister.
3. ☐ Lidia's favorite thing is a car.
4. ☐ The sunglasses are a gift from Linda.

Pronunciation

5 Listen and repeat. Then listen again and underline the /ɒ/ sounds and circle the /æ/ sounds in bold. 32

My **da**d's **mo**m is a **do**ctor.
She's my gr**a**ndma.

Speaking

6 Choose three family members and make sentences about them. Then work in pairs. Your classmate has to guess the family relations.

She's my aunt's daughter. Her favorite thing is her cell phone.

Your cousin!

I can talk about extended family members.

e-Language Booster

Use of English

7 **Order the words to make statements and questions. Then listen and check.** 33

1. Whose / these / are / sunglasses / ?
2. her / Yes, / sunglasses / they're / .
3. is / case / Whose / laptop / this / ?
4. Lucy's / That's / skateboard / .
5. think / it's / my / case / I / laptop / .

8 **Read the conversation and answer.**
Whose headphones are they?

Mom: Whose headphones are these?
Ben: I think they're Peter's.
Peter: No, they aren't. My headphones are blue. These are black and green. Are they Wilma's?
Wilma: My headphones are here. They are his headphones, Mom.
Mom: Whose headphones?
Wilma: Ben's!
Ben: Let me see. You're right. Sorry.

9 **Work in groups of three. Write a conversation similar to the one in Activity 8. Use the possessive 's, possessive adjectives, and whose.**

10 **Role play your conversation.**

I can ask and answer about things and identify who they belong to.

Language Booster page 26

#CHALLENGE

Writing

1 **Read about Mark's family and answer the questions.**

My name is Mark. I have two brothers and a sister. My sister's name is Lisa, and she's 16. She's a student in high school, but on the weekend she's a waitress at a local restaurant. My brother's name is Rick. He's 19. He's at college, and he's a delivery driver in the evenings. My mom is a teacher at the local school, and my dad is an engineer. I'm at my grandparents' house now. My grandma and grandpa are nurses.

1. How old is Mark's sister?

___

2. Whose house is Mark at now?

___

3. What's grandma and grandpa's job?

___

4. Where is Mark's mother a teacher?

___

#TIP

Research online for family tree templates.

Prepare to Write

2 **Make notes about your family – their names, ages, and jobs.**

3 **Use the information in Activity 2 to create a family tree. Use the family trees in this unit as models.**

I can plan and create a family tree.

e-Language Booster

Write

4 Write a short text about your family. Use the text in Activity 1 and your family tree in Activity 3 to help you.

Check and Change

5 Read your text and make sure you included:

- [ ] family words.
- [ ] jobs.
- [ ] the possessive 's.
- [ ] possessive adjectives.

6 Edit your text. Make sure all the elements in Activity 5 are included.

Publish

7 Write a clean version of your text.

Speaking

8 Show a picture of your family to your classmate. Answer your classmate's questions about your family members.

Who's he?	He's my cousin.
What's his name?	His name's Leo.
How old is he?	He's seven.
What's Leo's dream job?	His dream job is a pilot!

I can write about my family.

Language Booster page 27

#DIGITAL LITERACY

1. Use fonts in different sizes, for example large font for important information.
2. Use different colors.
3. Save your poster as a PDF file.

Project: An Online Poster

Step 1 Think

1 **Read about the Youth Jobs Fair and discuss in groups.**

Youth Jobs Fair

- Delivery driver assistant
- Youth medical assistant
- Graphic design apprentice
- Construction worker assistant

1. Which youth job do you think is interesting?
2. Are these youth jobs important for students at your school? Why?

2 **Now read the poster advertising a youth job.**

#TIP STEP 1

Look closely at the poster. Does it get your attention? Why? Think about the colors, fonts, text size, and picture.

I can recognize the features of an online poster about a youth job.

Step 2 Plan

3 In groups, choose one of the jobs in Activity 1 and write ideas about what you can include in your poster for the youth jobs fair.

___

Step 3 Research

4 Discuss the characteristics that a person needs for the youth job of your choice. Use an online dictionary to look up the words. Make notes.

___

5 Search for a good picture to include in your poster.

Step 4 Design

6 In groups, use the information from the previous activities to create your poster.

- Check the text.
- Check the picture.
- Check the organization.

Step 5 Present and Publish

7 Present your poster to the class.

Step 6 Evaluate

8 Complete the evaluation table.

★☆☆ More to learn | ★★☆ Good | ★★★ Excellent

Criteria	My Evaluation	Group Evaluation	Teacher Evaluation
Teamwork	★★★	★★★	★★★
Language	★★★	★★★	★★★
Design	★★★	★★★	★★★

#TIP STEP 4

Make sure to choose pictures that attract the readers' attention.

#TIP STEP 5

Point to the pictures and the highlighted information on the poster while presenting.

I can create an online poster and present it to the class.

#SELF-ASSESSMENT

1 Mark the learning objectives according to the key.

★☆☆ I don't understand.	★★☆ I understand, but I need help.	★★★ I can do it!

Learning Objectives	Rating
To demonstrate an understanding of a conversation about different family members.	☆☆☆
To identify family members and jobs.	☆☆☆
To read descriptions of people's families and their jobs.	☆☆☆
To write about my family members' jobs.	☆☆☆
To use possessive 's and possessive adjectives correctly.	☆☆☆
To ask questions with *whose* and answer them with the possessive 's or possessive adjectives.	☆☆☆
To talk about extended family members.	☆☆☆
To ask and answer about possessions and identify who they belong to.	☆☆☆
To plan and create a family tree.	☆☆☆
To write about my family.	☆☆☆
To recognize the features of an online poster about a youth job.	☆☆☆
To create an online poster and present it to the class.	☆☆☆

2 Work in pairs. Discuss the questions.

1. What did I find most interesting to learn? Why?
2. How did I learn it?
3. How can I use it in real life?

UT Language Booster page 28

UNIT FOUR 4

MY DAILY ROUTINE

In this unit, you will learn how to:

- Talk about your daily routine and different parts of the day.
- Write about someone else's routine.
- Create an online comic strip.

#3 GOOD HEALTH AND WELL-BEING

Say what you know:

- Parts of the day.
- Things you do every day.
- Things a family member does every day.

Video

Daily Routines

Before You Watch

1 **In pairs, match the pictures to the sentences.**

- ☐ I brush my teeth.
- ☐ I go to school.
- ☐ I get dressed.
- ☐ I take a shower.
- ☐ I have breakfast.
- ☐ I play video games.

While You Watch

2 **Watch the video and choose the correct alternatives from the box to complete the sentences.** ▷ 05

> Katya's / Hugo's
> in the morning / in the evening
> watch a movie / go to school
> is / isn't

1. Becca is ______________________ friend.
2. Katya and Becca chat ______________________.
3. Katya and Hugo ______________________ together.
4. In Hugo's opinion, breakfast ________ important.

3 **Watch the video again and circle the correct options about Katya.** ▷ 05

> Every day,...

1. I **watch** / **don't watch** movies late at night.
2. I **sleep** / **don't sleep** much.
3. I **go** / **don't go** on social media in the morning.
4. I **have** / **don't have** breakfast.
5. I **go** / **don't go** to school with Becca.

After You Watch

4 **Work in pairs. Is Katya's routine healthy? Justify your answer using parts of the text.**

____

____

____

5 **Make the sentences in Activity 3 true for you.**

1. ____
2. ____
3. ____
4. ____
5. ____

6 **In pairs, think about your healthy and unhealthy habits and complete the chart. You can use the information in Activity 5.**

Healthy habits	Unhealthy habits

I can interpret a conversation about daily routines.
e-Language Booster

Vocabulary

Routines

7 **Label the pictures with the routine actions from the box. Then listen and repeat.** 34

do homework	get up	go to bed	have breakfast / have lunch / have dinner

1. 

2. 

3. 

4. 

1. ______________ 2. ______________ 3. ______________ 4. ______________

8 **Think about when you do the routine actions in Activity 7. Complete the sentences with *in the morning*, *in the afternoon*, *in the evening*, or *at night*.**

1. I do homework ______________.
2. I get up ______________.
3. I have breakfast ______________.
4. I have lunch ______________.
5. I have dinner ______________.
6. I go to sleep ______________.

9 **Listen to Jon and number his routine actions in the correct order.** 35

☐ have a snack	☐ go home	☐ get dressed
☐ do homework	☐ take a shower	☐ get up
☐ have lunch	☐ brush my teeth	☐ go to school

10 **Work in pairs. Tell each other about your routine using the information in Activities 8 and 9.**

I get up in the morning. I take a shower...

I can talk about routines.

Language Booster page 29

#CLARIFY

Reading

1 USING PRIOR KNOWLEDGE. In pairs, answer the questions.

1. What countries do the flags represent?

____

2. Do you think you have the same routine as teenagers in these countries? Why?

____

2 Take a quick look at the text. Is it a blog post or a comic strip?

3 MONITORING COMPREHENSION USING DETAILS. Read the text and complete the sentences with *Fernando*, *Zoe*, or *Omar*.

My Daily Routine +

omarfrenchteenblog.net

Teen Blog

Omar
France

My Daily Routine

Writen by Omar, 04/30/2021

I have family all over the world. I have two cousins. They are 13. We have different daily routines. My cousin Fernando is from Brazil, and he goes to school in the morning. He goes home at lunchtime. My cousin Zoe is from Switzerland. She has classes in the morning and in the afternoon, but she has lunch at home.

I live in Paris, and I go to a very special school. I start my day like my cousins: I get up, take a shower, get dressed, and go to school by bus. I don't go to bed late because I get up early in the morning.

At my school, we don't eat fast food. We have lunch with fresh ingredients. I do my homework every day!

1. ____________ goes to school in the morning.
2. ____________ and ____________ go to school in the morning and in the afternoon.
3. ____________ isn't at home at lunchtime.
4. ____________ goes to school by bus.
5. ____________ does homework every day.
6. ____________ and ____________ have classes in a regular school.

4 In your notebook, write two routine actions that you and Omar have in common.

I get up early in the morning, too.

Listening

5 Listen and complete the chart. 36

1. Johanna	 Finland	**Age:** [1] ______
		School: in the [2] ______
		Lunch: at [3] ______
		Homework: No
2. Gabriel	 The Philippines	**Age:** [4] ______
		School: in the [5] ______
		Lunch: at [6] ______
		Homework: [7] ______

Writing

6 Research into a school in a different country and complete the chart below.

	School: [1] ______
	Lunch: [2] ______
	Homework: [3] ______

7 Work in pairs. Compare your charts in Activity 6. Make notes about your classmate's chart.

______

______

______

#TIP

To carry out your research, use key words like *school day in (country)*.

I can write about school routines around the world.

Language Booster page 30

#UNDERSTAND

Grammar

Simple Present – Affirmative and Negative

1 **Work in pairs. Tell your classmate three things you do every day.**

I brush my teeth.
I have lunch.
I go on social media.

2 **Read the text and label the pictures *Darren* or *Leon*. Then underline the verbs in the affirmative and negative forms.**

Hi, Leon here! I live in the United States. In the morning, I get up early and I go to school. I don't have breakfast, but I have a snack at school. My cousin Darren lives in England. He gets up early too, and he gets dressed in his school uniform. I don't have a school uniform. Darren has breakfast and lunch at school because his mom goes to work early. He doesn't do his homework at home; he does it at school in the afternoon. We both go to bed early.

1.

2.

3 **Read the text in Activity 2 again and circle the correct words to complete the statements about the Simple Present.**

1. We use the Simple Present to talk about facts, **possibilities** / **routines**, and things that are true.
2. For negative sentences, we use **don't** / **doesn't** before the verb for *I*, *you*, *we*, and *they*.
3. For negative sentences, we use **don't** / **doesn't** before the verb for *he*, *she*, and *it*.
4. In the affirmative form, we add *-s* to the verb for **I, you, we, and they** / **he, she, and it**.
5. We add *-es* to some verbs like **brush and go** / **be and have**, for example, in the third person singular.
6. The third person singular form of *have* is **haves** / **has**.

4 **Complete the chart. Use the text in Activity 2 and the rules in Activity 3 to help you.**

	Affirmative	Negative
I / You / We / They	do	5 ____________
	1 ____________	don't go
	have	6 ____________
	2 ____________	don't brush
He / She / It	3 ____________	doesn't do
	goes	7 ____________
	4 ____________	doesn't have
	brushes	8 ____________

5 **Complete the sentences with the correct form of the verbs in parentheses.**

1. Marc and I ____________ (go) to school by bus.
2. The students ____________ (have) lunch at school.
3. My mom ____________ (have) a snack in the afternoon.
4. Jennifer ____________ (go) to bed late.
5. You ____________ (take) a shower in the morning.
6. Luke ____________ (get) dressed very fast.
7. I ____________ (brush) my teeth before and after breakfast.

I can use the Simple Present in the affirmative and negative forms.
e-Language Booster

6 Work in pairs. Change the sentences in Activity 5 into the negative form.

1. ______________________________
2. ______________________________
3. ______________________________
4. ______________________________
5. ______________________________
6. ______________________________
7. ______________________________

7 Use the prompts to write quiz statements in the Simple Present. Then take the quiz in pairs. Circle your classmate's answers.

Quiz Do You Have A Healthy Routine?

1. have / breakfast / every day

   You ______________________________. Yes No

2. have / fast food / for lunch

   You ______________________________. Yes No

3. not feel / tired / morning

   You ______________________________. Yes No

4. not do / homework / late at night

   You ______________________________. Yes No

5. go to bed / early

   You ______________________________. Yes No

6. go on / social media / when / get up

   You ______________________________. Yes No

8 Work in groups. Talk about your classmate's answers to the quiz. Does he / she have a healthy daily routine?

Tomás doesn't have breakfast every day.

I can talk about someone else's daily routine in the Simple Present.

Language Booster page 31

Listening

1 **Label the pictures with the routine actions from the box.**

chat with friends | exercise | go on social media | sleep | watch a movie / series

1.  ______________

2.  ______________

3.  ______________

4.  ______________

5.  ______________

2 **Look at the chart and complete the sentences.**

●●●	always
●●○	usually
●○○	sometimes
○○○	never

1. ●●● I ______________ go on social media.
2. ●○○ I ______________ chat online with my family.
3. ●●○ I ______________ watch movies on my laptop.
4. ○○○ I ______________ sleep ten hours a night.
5. ●●● I ______________ exercise.

3 **LISTENING FOR DETAILS. Listen to Part 1 of a podcast and write *Gabriela* or *Samuel*.** 37

1. ______________ doesn't always watch series.
2. ______________ does homework in the evening.
3. ______________ sleeps nine hours every night.
4. ______________ goes to school in the morning and in the afternoon.

4 **LISTENING FOR DETAILS. Listen to Part 2 of the podcast and mark the sentences T (True) or F (False).** 38

1. ☐ Daniel never goes on social media.
2. ☐ Daniel sometimes exercises.
3. ☐ Daniel always chats with his family at dinnertime.

Pronunciation

5 **Complete the chart with the verbs *does*, *has*, *sleeps*, and *watches*. Then listen and check.** 39

/iz/	/s/	/z/
brushes	gets	goes

Speaking

6 **Work in pairs. Look at the sentences in Activity 2 and make them true for you. Use *always*, *usually*, *sometimes*, or *never*.**

I can interpret a podcast about teenagers' well-being.

Use of English

7 **Complete the conversation with verbs in the Simple Present. Then discuss in pairs: Does Alice have a healthy routine?**

Sarah

Today

Sarah:
Alice, you're online! You never [1] _______ on social media.

Me:
I sometimes [2] _______ with my friends here, Sarah.

Sarah:
I always go on social media. But I always [3] _______ my homework, too.

Me:
Me too. I do homework after school. I [4] _______ it late at night.

Sarah:
Me neither.

Sarah

Me:
Because I go to bed early.

Sarah:
Oh, I don't go to bed early. I usually [5] _______ series in bed!

Me:
Yeah...

Sarah:
But it's OK because I go to school in the afternoon!

Me:
Don't worry about it. I'm not your mom!!

8 **Read the text in Activity 7 again and underline the adverbs of frequency.**

9 **Match the statements to the responses. Then listen and check.** 40

1. I don't go on social media in the morning.
2. I have lunch at school.

☐ Me too.
☐ Me neither.

10 **Circle the correct option. Use the sentences in Activities 7 and 9 to help you.**

1. We use *me too* to agree with **an affirmative** / **a negative** statement.
2. We use *me neither* to agree with **an affirmative** / **a negative** statement.

11 **In pairs, role play the dialogue in Activity 7.**

12 **Work in groups. Try to find at least two things in common with each classmate about your daily routine.**

I go to bed late.

Me too!

#TIP

Use *me too* and *me neither* in your informal conversations.

I can compare my daily routines to my classmates'.

Language Booster page 32

#CHALLENGE

Writing

1 **Read the text and complete the chart with the activities in the correct columns.**

Hi, everyone! I'm Petra and I'm from Australia. In the morning, I get up, take a shower, and get dressed. I have breakfast with my mom and my brother. Then I go to school. I have lunch at school. In the afternoon, I have a snack and I do my homework. Then I watch series and have dinner in the evening.

My brother is five years old. He goes to school in the morning and goes back home at 1 p.m. He has lunch at home. He doesn't do homework!

	In the morning	In the afternoon	In the evening
Petra	*gets up*		
Petra's brother			

2 **Look at Genna's notes. Write sentences using *then* to indicate what happens next.**

1. get up – brush teeth
   I get up. Then I brush my teeth.
2. have lunch – go on social media and watch a movie
   ____
   ____
3. exercise – have a snack
   ____
4. take a shower – go to bed
   ____

3 **Write about Genna's routine. Use the information in Activity 2.**

1. She ______________________.
   Then she ______________________.
2. ______________________
   ____
3. ______________________
   ____
4. ______________________
   ____

I can read about someone else's routines.

e-Language Booster

Prepare to Write

4 You are going to write for a website about your daily routine in order to make friends. Complete the table with the information you want to include in your text. Use the table in Activity 1 as a model.

In the morning	In the afternoon	In the evening	At night

Write

5 Write a text for a website about your daily routine. Use the text in Activity 1 and your notes in Activity 4 as models.

#TIP

Add a picture of your country's flag to show where you are from.

Check and Change

6 Read your text and make sure you included:

- [ ] personal information.
- [ ] information about your routine in the morning, afternoon, evening, and at night.
- [ ] verbs in the Simple Present.
- [ ] *then* to indicate what happens next.

7 Edit your text. Make sure all the items in Activity 6 are included. Then choose an avatar to add to your text.

Publish

8 Write a clean version of your text.

Speaking

9 Work in groups. Read a classmate's text, and then talk about his / her daily routine.

Ted doesn't get up late because he goes to school in the morning. He gets up early. Then he has breakfast and gets dressed. Then he walks to school...

I can write a text about my daily routine.

Language Booster page 33

Project: An Online Comic Strip

#DIGITAL LITERACY

You can create your comic strip online using a comic strip generator.

Step 1 Think

1 Work in groups.

1. Do you like to read comic strips? Why?
2. Read the comic strip below. Who are the characters? What verb tense is used?
3. Do comic strips make us think? What does the comic strip below make you think?

Step 2 Plan

2 In groups, discuss ideas for a comic strip about healthy routines. Make notes.

Think about:

- The number of frames for your comic strip (4 or 6).
- Your main character.
- His / Her healthy routine.

____

____

____

____

____

I can read a comic strip and discuss ideas to create one.

Step 3 Research

3 In groups, do some research online about healthy routine habits. Make notes.

___

___

___

Step 4 Design

4 In groups, create your comic strip about healthy routines. Use the information from your research and the previous activities.

- Check the text.
- Check the purpose.
- Check the organization.

#TIP STEP 4

Choose a teenage character.

Write captions at the bottom of each frame.

Represent a daily routine that is good for teenagers' well-being.

Consider using a color scheme in your comic strip.

Step 5 Present and Publish

5 In groups, present your comic strip to the class.

#TIP STEP 5

Look at the audience and say the captions. Don't read them from the screen.

Step 6 Evaluate

6 Complete the evaluation table.

★☆☆ More to learn | ★★☆ Good | ★★★ Excellent

Criteria	My Evaluation	Group Evaluation	Teacher Evaluation
Teamwork	☆☆☆	☆☆☆	☆☆☆
Language	☆☆☆	☆☆☆	☆☆☆
Design	☆☆☆	☆☆☆	☆☆☆

I can create a comic strip about healthy routines.

#SELF-ASSESSMENT

1 Mark the learning objectives according to the key.

★☆☆ I don't understand.	★★☆ I understand, but I need help.	★★★ I can do it!

Learning Objectives	Rating
To interpret a conversation about daily routines.	☆☆☆
To talk about routines.	☆☆☆
To read descriptions of people's routines.	☆☆☆
To write about school routines around the world.	☆☆☆
To use the Simple Present in the affirmative and negative forms.	☆☆☆
To talk about someone else's daily routine in the Simple Present.	☆☆☆
To interpret a podcast about teenagers' well-being.	☆☆☆
To compare my daily routines to my classmates'.	☆☆☆
To read about someone else's routines.	☆☆☆
To write a text about my daily routine.	☆☆☆
To read a comic strip and discuss ideas to create one.	☆☆☆
To create a comic strip about healthy routines.	☆☆☆

2 Work in pairs. Discuss the questions.

1. What did I find most interesting to learn? Why?
2. How did I learn it?
3. How can I use it in real life?

MT UT Language Booster page 34

DIFFERENT HOMES

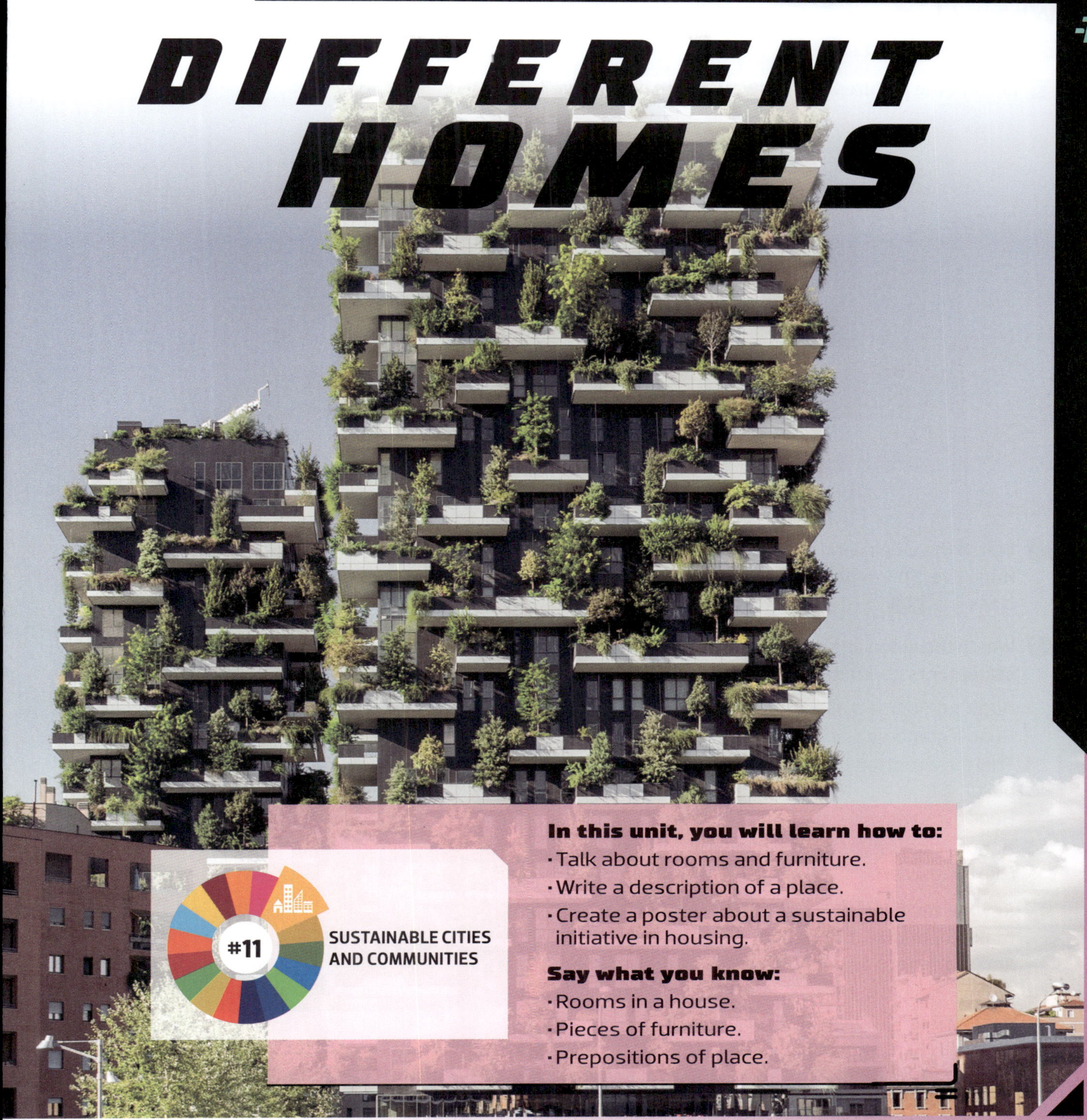

#11 SUSTAINABLE CITIES AND COMMUNITIES

In this unit, you will learn how to:

- Talk about rooms and furniture.
- Write a description of a place.
- Create a poster about a sustainable initiative in housing.

Say what you know:

- Rooms in a house.
- Pieces of furniture.
- Prepositions of place.

#DISCOVER

Video

Where I Live

Before You Watch

1 **Look at the pictures and answer. Where do you live?**

I live in a / an...

1\. 

apartment [ ]

2\. 

house [ ]

While You Watch

2 **Watch the video. Find out where Katya and Hugo live. Share the answers with the whole class.** ▷ 06

3 **Watch the video again and underline the false statements about it.** ▷ 06

1. Hugo's grandma's apartment is big.
2. Hugo's grandma's apartment is noisy.
3. There is a rooftop garden in his grandma's building.
4. Hugo lives with his grandma.
5. Hugo needs Katya's help with his grandma's rooftop garden.

4 **Rewrite the false statements from Activity 3 to make them true. Then watch the video again and check your answers.** ▷ 06

____

____

____

After You Watch

5 **In pairs, discuss the questions.**

1. Do you think the rooftop garden in Hugo's grandma's apartment building is a good idea? Why?
2. Are there any gardens like this in your neighborhood? If so, how do they work? If not, why not?

6 **Go online and search for a picture of a rooftop garden. Then complete the caption.**

This is a rooftop garden in __________________.

I can interpret a conversation between two friends.

Vocabulary

Rooms in a House

7 **Listen and repeat the words below. Then label the pictures.** 41

bathroom bedroom kitchen
laundry room living room yard

1. 
______

2. 
______

3. 
______

4. 
______

5. 
______

6. 
______

8 **Work in pairs. Take turns talking about the rooms in your house / apartment.**

There is a bathroom, a kitchen, and a living room in my house. There are three bedrooms.

Furniture

9 **Match the words to the pictures. Then listen and repeat.** 42

1. bed
2. closet
3. couch
4. refrigerator
5. shower
6. stove

a.  ☐

b.  ☐

c.  ☐

d.  ☐

e.  ☐

f.  ☐

10 **Read and complete Hugo's description of his grandma's apartment. Use the words from the box.**

bathroom bed bedroom couch kitchen shower

My grandma's apartment is small. There are two bedrooms, a kitchen, a living room, and a [1] ______. There is a sink, a toilet, and a [2] ______ in the bathroom. There is a [3] ______ in the living room. There is a table and two chairs in the [4] ______. There is one [5] ______ and one closet in each bedroom. There is also a small desk and a chair in my [6] ______.

11 **In pairs, take turns describing the rooms in Activity 7.**

There is a refrigerator in the kitchen.

I can describe rooms in a house.

Language Booster page 35

#CLARIFY

Reading

1 **In pairs, look at the pictures and answer the questions.**

1. What is different about the houses below?
2. Where do you think they are located?
3. What rooms and furniture do you think they have?

a.

____

b.

____

c.

____

2 **SCANNING. The texts below describe different types of houses. Read them and label the pictures in Activity 1 with the correct countries.**

Houses Around the World

Fales are traditional houses in Tonga. [1] ______________________ ______________________ There is one large room. There are no walls – only mats from palm tree leaves.

The Dai people are an ethnic group in China. They live in bamboo houses. There are two rooms – a large room to make dinner and a bedroom to sleep in. [2] ______________________ ______________________ ______________________

A *riad* is a traditional house in Morocco. [3] ______________________ ______________________ Riads have large gardens in the center. Most windows and doors open to the garden. There are bedrooms, living rooms, and a large kitchen.

3 **Complete the texts in Activity 2 with the sentences below.**

1. It is a community, so everybody in the village helps to build their neighbors' houses.
2. They have an oval or circular shape.
3. *Riad* means *garden* in Arabic.

4 **GENERATING QUESTIONS. In groups, discuss the types of houses in Activities 1 and 2: How is your house / apartment similar to or different from them?**

I can read about homes from around the world.

Listening

5 **MAKING PREDICTIONS. Look at the picture. What type of house do you think the audio is about? What rooms does it have? What are the pieces of furniture in it? Make notes.**

6 **CONFIRMING PREDICTIONS. Listen to Lauren describe her narrowboat and circle the correct options to complete the sentences.** 43

1. Lauren lives in the **U.K.** / **United States**.
2. She lives with her **mom** / **aunt** on a narrowboat.
3. They move the boat every **five** / **two** weeks.
4. There isn't a **big couch** / **big refrigerator** on the boat.
5. She prefers a narrowboat to **an apartment** / **a house**.

Writing

7 **Research into a traditional house or building in your country. Make notes to complete the mind map below.**

8 **Use your notes from Activity 7. Write a short paragraph about a traditional house or building in your country.**

____

____

____

____

____

____

#TIP

Research your topic and make notes before you start writing.

I can write about a traditional house or building in my country.

Language Booster page 36

#UNDERSTAND

Grammar

Simple Present – Questions and Short Answers

1 **Read the dialogues and complete the following questions and answers.**

Sarah: **Do** you **live** with your grandma?
Ross: **No**, I **don't**.

Ross: **Does** you grandma **live** in an apartment?
Sarah: **No**, she **doesn't**.

Sarah: **Do** you **have** a vegetable garden, too?
Ross: **Yes**, I **do**.

1. **A:** [1] ____________ you live in a house?
   B: Yes, [2] ____________. / No, [3] ____________.
2. **A:** [4] ____________ they live on a boat?
   B: [5] ____________ / [6] ____________
3. **A:** [7] ____________ he have a big yard?
   B: Yes, [8] ____________. / No, [9] ____________
4. **A:** [10] ____________ she have a balcony?
   B: [11] ____________ / [12] ____________

2 **Listen and complete the dialogues.** 44

Part 1

Kate: [1] ____________ Miguel [2] ____________ on a narrowboat?
Oli: [3] ____________, he [4] ____________. [5] ____________ you [6] ____________ in an apartment?
Kate: [7] ____________, I [8] ____________.

Part 2

Sally: [9] ____________ you [10] ____________ with your grandparents?
Ted: [11] ____________, I [12] ____________.
Sally: [13] ____________ you [14] ____________ in a house?
Ted: [15] ____________, we [16] ____________. We live in an apartment.

3 **In pairs, role play the dialogues in Activity 2.**

4 **Where do you do the daily routine actions below?**

1. do homework: *I do my homework at home.*
2. get dressed: ____________
3. have breakfast: ____________
4. brush my teeth: ____________
5. chat with my family: ____________

5 **In pairs, ask and answer questions about the actions in Activity 4.**

Where do you brush your teeth?

I brush my teeth in the kitchen!

I can ask and answer questions in the Simple Present.

e-Language Booster

Prepositions of Place

6 **Read the text. Check (✓) the picture that shows Nick's bedroom.**

Hi, I'm Nick and this is my bedroom. There are small pictures **on** the wall, **next to** the map. And there's my bed **under** the window. There are big boxes **on** the floor, **between** the bed and the desk, and there is a lamp **behind** the blue boxes. **On** the desk, there are pens and pencils **in** the pencil holders. There is a white chair and there are lots of pictures **on** the wall.

1. 

2. 

7 **There is a mouse in Nick's kitchen. But where is it? Label the pictures with the prepositions in bold in Activity 6.**

1. 
______

2. 
______

3. 
______

4. 
______

5. 
______

6. 
______

8 **Write a short paragraph describing picture number 1 in Activity 6. Use *there is / there are* and prepositions of place.**

______
______
______
______
______
______

#TIP

Use *between* with *and*.

It is ***between*** *the bed* ***and*** *the desk.*

9 **In pairs, take turns reading your descriptions. Are your paragraphs similar?**

I can describe rooms in a house.

Language Booster page 37

Listening

1 **Look at the pictures. In pairs, say where these pieces of furniture are in a house / apartment. Then write.**

1. 
sink
____

2. 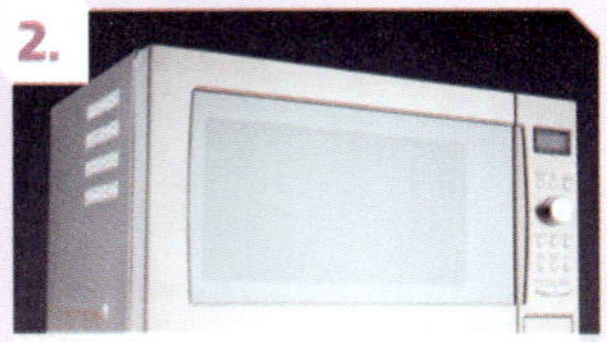
microwave oven
____

3. 
washing machine
____

4. 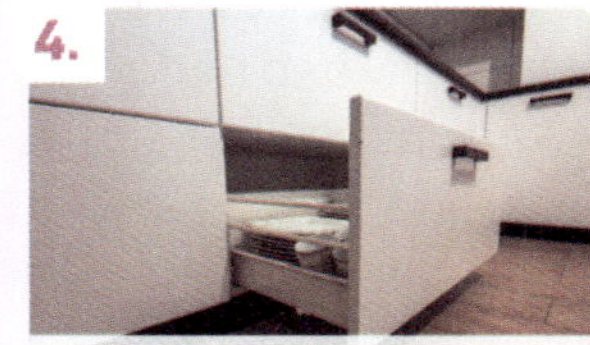
cabinet
____

2 **MAKING PREDICTIONS. Look at the picture and guess the answers to the questions below.**

1. How many people live in this house?
____
2. What rooms does it have?
____
3. What furniture does it have?
____
4. Does Ana like her house?
____

3 **CHECKING PREDICTIONS. Listen to Ana's interview about her experience living in a tiny house. Check your predictions in Activity 2.** 45

4 **Listen again and mark the sentences below T (True) or F (False).** 46

1. ☐ There is a sink in the bathroom.
2. ☐ There are four bedrooms in the tiny house.
3. ☐ Ana sleeps under a window.
4. ☐ The furniture in Ana's house transforms into other objects.
5. ☐ There is an old washing machine in her house.

Pronunciation

5 **Listen and underline the stressed syllable in the words. Then practice saying the words aloud.** 47

1. bathroom	3. closet	5. shower
2. bedroom	4. kitchen	6. window

Speaking

6 **Work in pairs. Use the questions below to interview your classmate.**

1. Do you live in a house or an apartment?
2. What rooms are there in your home?
3. What furniture do you have in each room?

Use of English

7 Read the text and circle the prepositions of place.

A Sustainable Neighborhood

This is a sustainable house in a sustainable neighborhood. There are **solar panels** on the roof of the house. There is a yard behind the house with a **vegetable garden**. There are **recycling cans** next to the kitchen. The Mendes family lives in this house. They go everywhere by bus because there is a **bus stop** on their street. There are some **streetlamps** on their street. The streetlamps use energy-saving light bulbs. There are many **green spaces** here.

8 Draw a picture of the house in Activity 7 and label the words in bold in your drawing.

9 Match the sentence halves to make questions.

1. Does your house have solar panels on
2. Is there a bus stop next to
3. Do you have a recycling can in
4. Is your home next to
5. Are there plants on

- ☐ your desk?
- ☐ your laundry room?
- ☐ your home?
- ☐ the roof?
- ☐ green spaces?

10 What are the answers to the questions in Activity 9?

- ☐ No, it isn't.
- ☐ Yes, there are.
- ☐ Yes, it does.
- ☐ No, I don't.
- ☐ Yes there is.

11 In pairs, take turns answering the questions in Activity 9 about yourselves. Use question words (who, what, where, how) to expand the conversation about each other's home.

Who do you live with?

I live with my mom, dad, and sister.

I can talk about a sustainable home.

Language Booster page 38

Writing

1 **Read the text. What is Isabel's favorite room in her apartment?**

____

I live in an apartment with my dad and my two brothers. Our apartment is big. There is a kitchen, a living room, and a laundry room. There are three bedrooms and two bathrooms. I share a bathroom with my brothers, and my dad has a bathroom in his room. My favorite room is my bedroom. In my room, there is a bed, a desk, and a closet. There are posters and lamps on the wall. There is a window next to the desk.

2 **Read the text again and find the requested information.**

1. Three different prepositions of place: ______________________.
2. Five rooms in a house: ______________________.
3. Three pieces of furniture: ______________________.

3 **In pairs, discuss the questions below.**

1. What is your favorite room in your house?
2. What is there in this room?

Prepare to Write

4 **You are going to write a description of your home. Complete the chart with the information you want to include in your text.**

Rooms	Furniture

I can read about someone's home and prepare to write about mine.

e-Language Booster

Write

5 **Write a description of your home, including information about your favorite room. Use the text in Activity 1 and your notes in Activity 4 to help you.**

Check and Change

6 **Read your text and make sure you included:**

- ☐ rooms.
- ☐ furniture.
- ☐ information about your favorite room.
- ☐ prepositions of place.
- ☐ *there is / there are.*

7 **Edit your text. Make sure all the elements in Activity 6 are included.**

Publish

8 **Write a clean version of your text.**

#TIP

You can draw and label a picture of your favorite room before Activity 5. This will help you write the description.

Speaking

9 **Work in pairs. Describe your favorite room to your classmate. Then listen to your classmate's description and draw his / her favorite room.**

I can write a description of my home and my favorite room.

Language Booster page 39

Project: A Poster

#DIGITAL LITERACY

You can use the image tab of different search engines online to find images. Some images have a watermark because they are not free to use. Improve your search by using more specific key words.

Step 1 Think

1 Work in groups.

1. Are sustainable initiatives in housing important?
2. Read the notice from a local newspaper. Why does the city council want to build tiny homes?

Notice

Houses and apartments are very expensive in our city. Many people don't have decent places to live. We need an alternative. Send us your ideas for a new sustainable neighborhood to citycouncil@citycouncil.com. We need tiny homes for individuals and families. Help us create a clean, safe, and environmentally friendly neighborhood.

2 Now imagine you live in a tiny home. What things (rooms and furniture) would you have? Check out Angelica's poster about her tiny home.

My Tiny Home

My tiny home is for two people. There is a table and there are two chairs. There is a couch that transforms into a bed. There is a window next to the couch. There is a sink between the refrigerator and the stove. There is a small bathroom with a toilet and a shower. On the second floor, there is a bedroom. In the bedroom, there is a desk and a bed. The bed is behind the curtains. My home is sustainable, comfortable, and cheap.

I can read a poster about sustainable housing.

Step 2 Plan

3 **In groups, discuss ideas for a poster about a tiny home. Make notes in your notebook.**

1. Rooms
2. Furniture
3. Furniture that transforms into other furniture
4. Ideas to be environmentally friendly

Step 3 Research

4 **In groups, look for pictures of tiny houses online. Add more ideas to Step 2.**

Step 4 Design

5 **In groups, create a poster about a tiny home. Use the information from your research and the previous activities.**

• Check the text. • Check the purpouse. • Check the organization.

Step 5 Present and Publish

6 **In groups, present your poster to the class. Remember to say why you think tiny homes are important to the environment.**

Step 6 Evaluate

7 **Complete the evaluation table.**

★★★ More to learn | ★★★ Good | ★★★ Excellent

Criteria	My Evaluation	Group Evaluation	Teacher Evaluation
Teamwork	★★★	★★★	★★★
Language	★★★	★★★	★★★
Design	★★★	★★★	★★★

#TIP STEP 4

Draw a floor plan of your tiny home.

Draw and label pictures of furniture that transforms into other furniture.

#TIP STEP 5

Speak clearly and slowly.

I can create a poster about a sustainable housing solution and present it to the class.

e-Language Booster

#SELF-ASSESSMENT

1 Mark the learning objectives according to the key.

★☆☆ I don't understand.	★★☆ I understand, but I need help.	★★★ I can do it!

Learning Objectives	Rating
To interpret a conversation between two friends.	☆☆☆
To describe rooms in a house.	☆☆☆
To read about homes from around the world.	☆☆☆
To write about a traditional house or building in my country.	☆☆☆
To ask and answer questions in the Simple Present.	☆☆☆
To describe rooms in a house.	☆☆☆
To demonstrate an understanding of an interview about a tiny house.	☆☆☆
To talk about a sustainable home.	☆☆☆
To read about sustainable housing.	☆☆☆
To create a poster about a sustainable housing solution and present it to the class.	☆☆☆

2 **Work in pairs. Discuss the questions.**

1. What did I find most interesting to learn? Why?
2. How did I learn it?
3. How can I use it in real life?

UT Language Booster page 40

ABILITIES AND TALENTS

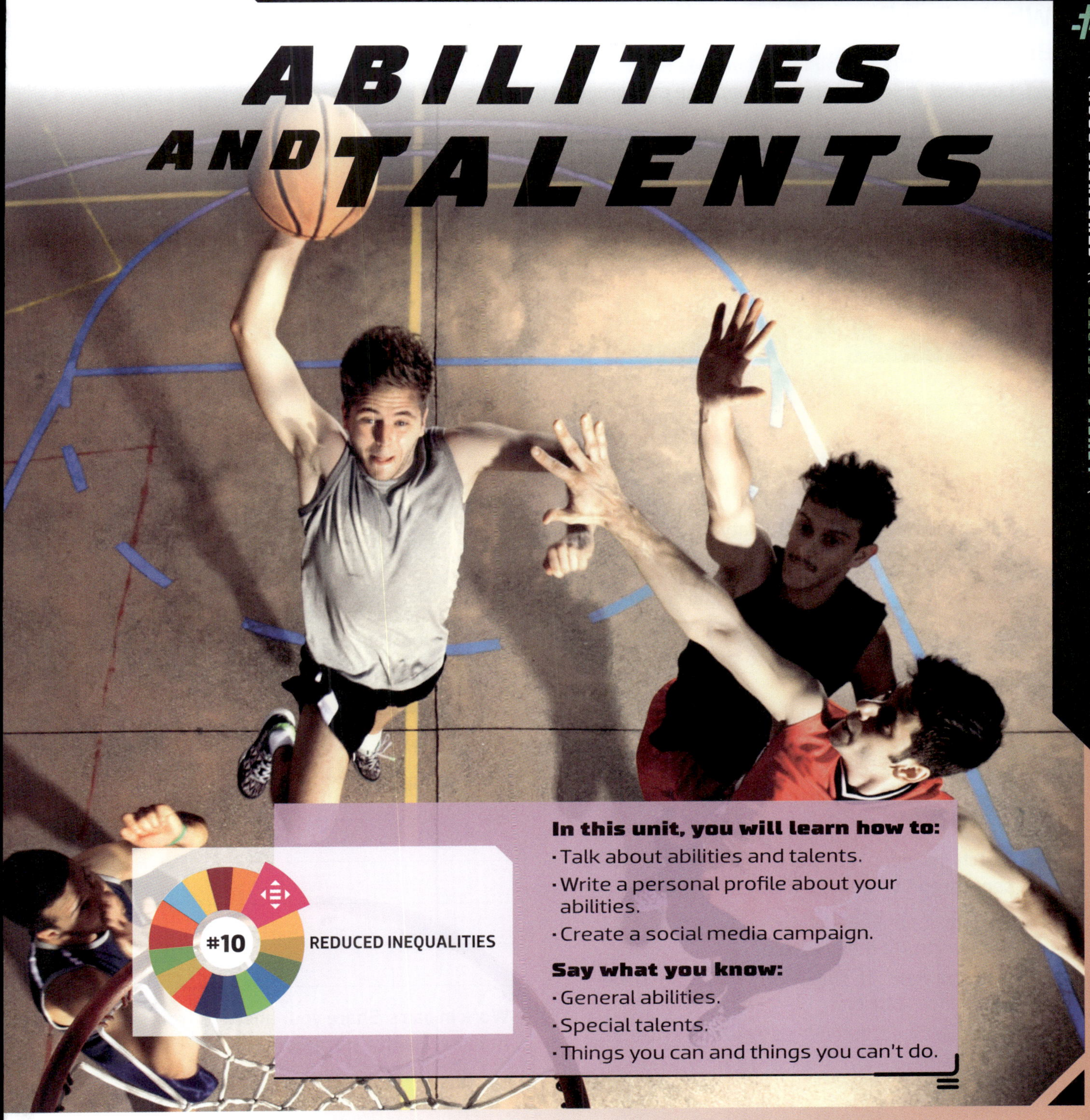

In this unit, you will learn how to:

- Talk about abilities and talents.
- Write a personal profile about your abilities.
- Create a social media campaign.

Say what you know:

- General abilities.
- Special talents.
- Things you can and things you can't do.

#10 REDUCED INEQUALITIES

Video

What I Can Do

Before You Watch

1 **Look at the pictures and complete the captions with the verbs from the box.**

draw	play	sing	swim

1. 
I can ______________.

2. 
I can ______________.

3. 
I can ______________.

4. 
I can ______________ a musical instrument.

While You Watch

2 **Watch the video and write K (Katya), H (Hugo), or B (both) for the pictures in Activity 1.** ▷ 07

3 **Watch the video again and circle the correct option to complete the sentences.** ▷ 07

1. Hugo **wants** / **doesn't want** to show his drawing to the teacher.
2. **Katya** / **Hugo** thinks that the drawings are good.
3. **Katya** / **Katya's sister** can dance tango.
4. Katya is on the school's **soccer** / **swim** team.
5. Katya and Hugo decide to go to a **dance party** / **karaoke party**.

4 **Watch the video one more time and mark the sentences T (True) or F (False).** ▷ 07

1. ☐ Hugo is confident about showing his drawings to other people.
2. ☐ Katya wants to show Hugo's drawing to the science teacher.
3. ☐ Katya thinks that her sister is more talented than her.
4. ☐ Katya can't sing.
5. ☐ It's Hugo's brother's birthday party on Saturday.

After You Watch

5 **Rewrite the sentences in Activity 1 so they are true for you. Use *can* / *can't*.**

1. ______________________________
____
2. ______________________________
____
3. ______________________________
____
4. ______________________________
____

6 **Work in pairs. Share your answers from Activity 5 with a classmate.**

I can interpret a conversation about abilities.
e-Language Booster

Vocabulary

General Abilities

7 **Match the verbs from the box to the pictures. Listen and check.** 48

code	cook	dance	play	speak	use

1. 

_____________ a foreign language

2. 

_____________ sign language

3. 

____

4. 

_____________ sports

5. 

____

6. 

____

8 **Write the abilities in Activity 7 from 1 (I can't do it) to 6 (I can do it) according to how easy they are for you. Compare your answers with your classmate.**

1
2
3
4
5
6

9 **Listen to five people talk about their abilities. Circle the correct option to complete the sentences.** 49

1. She can't **dance** / **cook**.
2. He can't **swim** / **sing**.
3. He can **use sign language** / **speak a foreign language**.
4. She can't **play soccer** / **dance**.
5. She can **code** / **sing**.

10 **Work in pairs. Look at your list of abilities in Activity 8 and talk about them. Use can and can't.**

*I **can** swim.* *I **can't** dance.*

I can talk about general abilities.

Language Booster page 41

Reading

1 **Work in pairs. Write two sentences with each verb below.**

I can see the whiteboard.

1. see

____

____

2. touch

____

____

3. hear

____

____

2 **ACTIVATING PRIOR KNOWLEDGE. In pairs, discuss the topics below. Then read the title of the text and check (✓) what you think it is about.**

1. ☐ Routines and free-time activities.
2. ☐ Special skills and abilities.
3. ☐ School rules.

3 **Read the text and mark the sentences T (True) or F (False).**

1. ☐ Keith uses a special app to communicate his needs and emotions.
2. ☐ Joe's favorite sport is tennis.
3. ☐ Joe uses his arms to swim.
4. ☐ Ellie doesn't know how to play the piano very well.
5. ☐ Ellie can play the piano because she reads music in braille.

4 **Write two examples of abilities that are different from or similar to yours and Keith's, Joe's, and Ellie's abilities.**

Keith and I can use a tablet. Ellie can play the piano, but I can't.

1. ______________________________

____

2. ______________________________

____

5 **Read your sentences in Activity 4 to a classmate and listen to his / hers. What can you do? What can't you do?**

We Can Practically Do the Same Things!

Many children and young people have disabilities. They can't do some things in the same way as people without disabilities can, but that doesn't mean that they can't do them at all. Here are some special ways that design and technology make things easy for them.

Keith is nonverbal. He's six years old and he is in preschool. He uses a special app to communicate. He can touch a picture to show his parents and teachers what he wants or how he feels. For example, he can click on the food button when he is hungry. His mom and dad can ask him what he wants to eat. Keith clicks on a specific food item, and his mom and dad can make what he wants to eat.

Joe loves the water. He uses a wheelchair because he can't walk, but that doesn't stop him from doing his favorite sport. He can swim very well using only his arms. He's the best swimmer on his team.

Music is Ellie's passion. She can play the piano very well. She reads music in braille. Ellie touches the points and learns the music composition. Then she plays it on her piano! Ellie touches the piano keys and remembers the different sounds they make because she is blind.

Listening

6 LISTENING FOR GIST. Listen and check (✓) what the texts are about. 50

1. ☐ Two famous nonverbal actresses. They use sign language in movies.
2. ☐ A blind actress and a deaf athlete. They have incredible skills.
3. ☐ Two people with different disabilities. They can do amazing things.

7 Listen and complete the fact files. 51

1.

Name: Millicent Simmonds

Age: [1] ______________

Nationality: [2] ______________

Job: [3] ______________

She can't [4] **hear / see**.

She can [5] **speak a foreign language / use sign language**.

2.

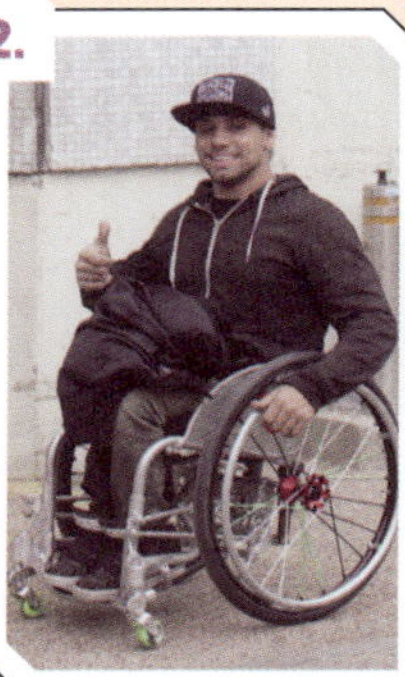

Name: Aaron Fotheringham

Age: [6] ______________

Nationality: [7] ______________

Job: [8] ______________

He can't [9] **walk / speak**.

He can do wheelchair tricks that are similar to [10] **BMX bike tricks / gymnastics**.

Writing

8 Research someone with a physical disability in your country who has a special talent. Write a short paragraph about this person.

#TIP

Search for information about Paralympic athletes from your country.

I can write about the achievements of someone with a physical disability.

Language Booster page 42

#UNDERSTAND

Grammar

Can / Can't for Abilities

1 **Read an extract from the video in #Discover and pay attention to the parts in bold. Then complete the chart.**

Katya: Well, I think they are amazing. I **can't** draw! [...]
Hugo: But you **can** swim! You're on the school team, and you **can** play the violin, too.
Katya: Yeah, I guess.
Hugo: **Can** you sing well?
Katya: Yes, I **can**. Why?

Affirmative	I [1] ______ play the piano.	She [6] ______ speak French.
Negative	I [2] ______ swim.	They [7] ______ code.
Yes / No Questions	[3] ______ you dance?	[8] ______ he sing?
Short Answers	Yes, I [4] ______. / No, I [5] ______.	Yes, he [9] ______. / No, he [10] ______.
Contraction	*cannot = can't*	

2 **Look at the dialogue in Activity 1 again. Use the words from the box to complete the rules.**

abilities	before	can
can't	negative	questions

1. Use [1] ______________ + the base form of a verb to talk about a person's [2] ______________.
2. Use [3] ______________ + the base form of a verb for [4] ______________ statements.
3. To make [5] ______________, use *can* [6] ______________ the subject.

3 **Complete the dialogues with can or can't.**

1. **A:** My mom is blind, so she [1] ______________ see.
B: [2] ______________ she read braille?
A: Yes, she [3] ________. I [4] ________ read braille, too.
B: Cool!

2. **A:** [5] ______________ your sister swim?
B: No, she [6] ______________. I often take her to the swimming pool.
A: [7] ______________ you swim?
B: Yes, I [8] ______________. I help my sister.

4 **Order the words to form questions.**

1. you / use / Can / sign language / ?
____
2. brother / speak Japanese / Can / your / ?
____
3. Can / a / tricks / wheelchair / he / do / on / ?
____
4. she / special app / Can / use / a / ?
____

5 **Use can / can't to complete the sentences. Then write a sentence about an ability you have.**

1. My classmates ______________ speak Japanese.
2. My mom __________ play a musical instrument.
3. My grandpa ______________ cook very well.
4. My best friend ______________ code.
5. ______________________________

6 **Compare your sentences in Activity 5 to a classmate's. What do you have in common?**

I can use *can / can't* to talk about abilities.
e-Language Booster

Imperatives

7 **Read two sentences from the video and pay attention to the parts in bold. Then circle the options to complete the statements.**

Show Mrs. Ramirez your drawing.

Don't touch my book!

1. Both sentences express **abilities** / **commands**. They are in the imperative form.
2. **An affirmative** / **A negative** imperative begins with a verb.
3. *Don't* comes first in an **affirmative** / a **negative** imperative.
4. Use **the base form of a verb** / **can or can't** to form the imperative form.

8 **Listen and check (✓) or cross (✗) the sentences according to the use of affirmative or negative imperatives.** 52

1. 

2. 

3. 

4. 

5. 

9 **Read the notice on a school website. Circle the correct option to complete the sentences.**

Section VI

Section VI: Making the School an Inclusive Space

Follow these tips to be thoughtful toward your classmates with disabilities:

1. **Open** / **Don't open** doors for classmates.
2. **Be** / **Don't be** respectful if you have a question about your classmate's disability.
3. **Offer** / **Don't offer** to carry a classmate's books if he / she uses a walking aid.
4. **Be** / **Don't be** patient with your classmates.
5. **Exclude** / **Don't exclude** your classmates.
6. **Feel** / **Don't feel** afraid to talk to a nonverbal classmate.
7. **Touch** / **Don't touch** a classmate's wheelchair without permission.
8. **Act** / **Don't act** respectfully inside and outside the classroom!

10 **Work in groups. Write a list of six Dos and Don'ts for your school so that everyone can study in a respectful environment.**

1. ______________________
2. ______________________
3. ______________________
4. ______________________
5. ______________________
6. ______________________

I can use imperatives.

Language Booster page 43

Listening

1 **Talk in pairs. Which of the activities below can you do?**

1. 

play chess ☐

2. 

run fast ☐

3. 

speak many languages ☐

4. 

spell difficult words ☐

2 **LISTENING FOR GIST. Listen to a news report about talented teens. Go back to Activity 1 and mark a cross (✕) next to the activity that isn't mentioned.** 53

3 **LISTENING FOR DETAILS. Listen again and mark the sentences T (True) or F (False).** 54

1. ☐ Angela can run 100 meters in 20 seconds.
2. ☐ Students at La Cruz High School study foreign languages.
3. ☐ Henrique can speak three languages.
4. ☐ Henrique watches movies without subtitles.
5. ☐ Patty participates in Spelling Bee competitions.
6. ☐ Patty can't remember words very well.

Pronunciation

4 **Listen and repeat.** 55

/æ/
A: Can you dance? **B:** Yes, I **can**.
A: Can you act? **B:** No, I **can't**.

5 **Work in pairs. Practice the dialogues in Activity 4. Pay attention to the /æ/ sound in *can* and *can't*.**

Speaking

6 **Circle the options to make the sentences true for you.**

1. I **can** / **can't** understand movies or TV series in English.
2. I **can** / **can't** understand English songs.
3. I **can** / **can't** read social media posts in English.
4. I **can** / **can't** understand the teacher well.
5. I **can** / **can't** spell words easily in English.
6. I **can** / **can't** concentrate on my homework and watch TV at the same time.

7 **In pairs, share your answers in Activity 6.**

I can interpret a news report about talented teens.

e-Language Booster

Use of English

8 Listen to the dialogues. Underline the imperative sentences. 56

1. **A:** Can I come in your room?
   B: Of course. Come in.
   A: I'm so confused. Please, help me with my homework!
   B: Sure. Show it to me.

2. **A:** Can you dance?
   B: Of course!
   A: Then show me how to do the new social media dance.
   B: I'm sorry, I can't. I'm busy.

9 Complete the table with the questions with can from the dialogues in Activity 8.

Ability	Permission

10 Work in pairs. Practice the dialogues in Activity 8.

11 Add two new questions to each column in Activity 9.

12 Work in pairs. Take turns asking and answering each other's questions in the table in Activity 9. Use short answers.

Can I use your cell phone?

Yes, you can!

I can ask and answer questions using *can*.

Language Booster page 44

#CHALLENGE

Writing

1 **Discuss the questions in pairs.**

1. Do you read blogs?
2. What is your favorite blog? What is it about?

2 **Read the personal profile published on a blog and complete the table.**

Michelle
Guatemala

Hello, everyone!

Welcome to my blog! My name's Michelle. I'm 13 and I'm from Guatemala. My mom is from Guatemala and my dad is from Senegal, so I can speak French and Spanish. My grandma lives in Senegal, and she can speak French and Wolof. Wolof is the national language in Senegal. I can understand **a little** Wolof, but I can't speak it **very well**.

I love books! I can read a book in two days. I have a YouTube channel about books. I talk about books and give my opinion about them. I'm good at computing, and I can code **very well**. I'm not very sporty. I can't play soccer or run very fast. My sister is good at sports. She can swim fast and play volleyball **well**, too.

This blog is all about me and my life. I hope you enjoy it!

Name	1 ________
Age	13
Nationality	2 ________
Family	3 ________ (Guatemala), 4 ________ (Senegal), 5 ________
Abilities	can speak 6 ________, can understand a little Wolof, can read a book in 7 ________

3 **Complete with the words in bold from the text in Activity 2.**

Abilities	
✗✗✗ can't	✗ can't... 1 ________
✓ can... 2 ________	✓✓✓ can... 3 ________

Prepare to Write

4 **You are going to write a personal profile about your abilities for a blog. Make notes about the information you want to include in your text.**

1. Personal information
____
2. My family
____
3. Things I can do
____
4. Things I can't do
____

I can read a personal profile on a blog and prepare to write one.

e-Language Booster

Write

5 Write a personal profile about your abilities for a blog. Use your notes in Activity 4 and the text in Activity 2 to help you.

Check and Change

6 Read your text and make sure you included:

- [ ] your personal information.
- [ ] information about your family.
- [ ] things you can do.
- [ ] things you can't do.

#TIP

Choose a headshot to include as your profile picture.

7 Edit your text. Make sure all the elements in Activity 6 are included.

Publish

8 Write a clean version of your text.

Speaking

9 Work in pairs. Take turns asking and answering about the abilities from the box.

cook dance hip-hop read a book in one day sing opera speak three languages

I can write a personal profile about my abilities.

Language Booster page 45

Project: A Social Media Campaign

#DIGITAL LITERACY

Effective social media campaigns use a mixture of real photos and illustrations.

Step 1 Think

1 **Work in groups. Look at the social media campaign and discuss the questions below.**

1. What is the campaign for?
2. What do the students want?

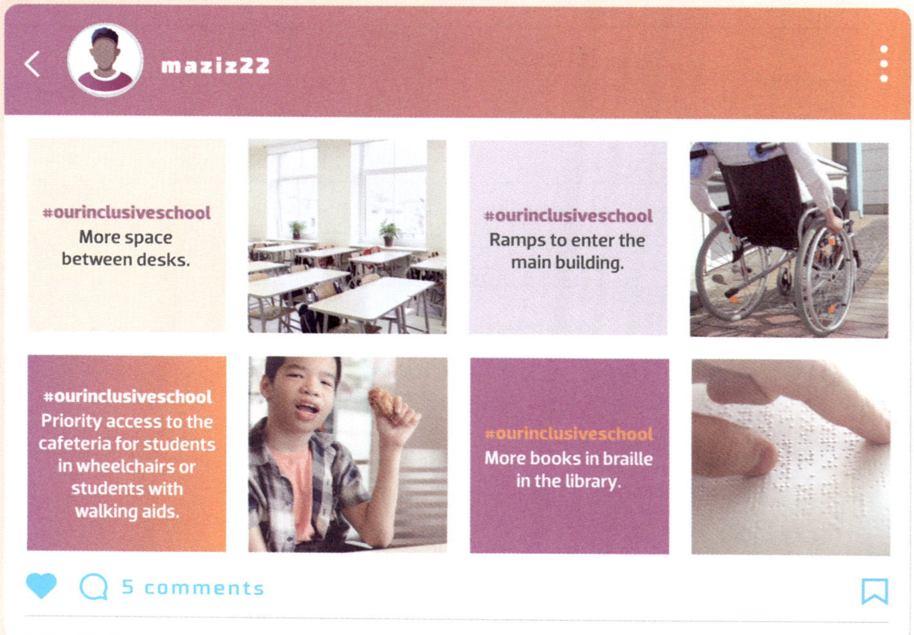

2 **Work in groups. How does your school deal with inclusion issues? Make notes.**

____

____

____

____

____

____

I can recognize the features and the aim of a social media campaign.

Step 2 Plan

3 Work in groups. You are going to create a social media campaign. Make a list of the key points you would like to use in your campaign.

____

____

Step 3 Research

4 Go online and research into what kinds of inequalities there are in schools and how they can be fixed. Make notes in your notebook, if necessary. Choose pictures to add to your campaign.

Step 4 Design

5 Work in groups. Create your social media campaign. Include the hashtag #ourinclusiveschool.

• Check the text. • Check the pictures. • Check the organization.

Step 5 Present and Publish

6 In groups, present your social media campaign to the class.

Step 6 Evaluate

7 Complete the evaluation table.

★☆☆ More to learn | ★★☆ Good | ★★★ Excellent

Criteria	My Evaluation	Group Evaluation	Teacher Evaluation
Teamwork	☆☆☆	☆☆☆	☆☆☆
Language	☆☆☆	☆☆☆	☆☆☆
Design	☆☆☆	☆☆☆	☆☆☆

#TIP STEP 4

1. Choose a color scheme to make your campaign coherent and attractive.
2. Use short sentences.
3. Use capital letters for important words.

#TIP STEP 5

Remember to explain the results you want from the campaign and say why it is important.

I can create and present a social media campaign about inclusion at my school.

#SELF-ASSESSMENT

1 Mark the learning objectives according to the key.

★☆☆ I don't understand.	★★☆ I understand, but I need help.	★★★ I can do it!

Learning Objectives	Rating
To interpret a conversation about abilities.	☆☆☆
To talk about general abilities.	☆☆☆
To read about how design and technology can help people with disabilities.	☆☆☆
To write about the achievements of someone with a physical disability.	☆☆☆
To use *can / can't* to talk about abilities.	☆☆☆
To use imperatives.	☆☆☆
To interpret a news reports about talented teens.	☆☆☆
To ask and answer questions using *can*.	☆☆☆
To read a personal profile on a blog and prepare to write one.	☆☆☆
To write a personal profile about my abilities.	☆☆☆
To recognize features and the aim of a social media campaign.	☆☆☆
To create and present a social media campaign about inclusion in my school.	☆☆☆

2 Work in pairs. Discuss the questions.

1. What did I find most interesting to learn? Why?
2. How did I learn it?
3. How can I use it in real life?

UT Language Booster page 46

SPECIAL DATES

#13 CLIMATE ACTION

In this unit, you will learn how to:

- Talk about special dates.
- Write a blog post.
- Create a program for a climate action event.

Say what you know:

- Special dates.
- Days, months, years.
- Earth climate.

#DISCOVER

Video

When Is Earth Day Again?

Before You Watch

1 **Label the pictures. Use the words from the box. Then listen and check.** 57

disposable tableware	plastic bag
plastic straw	reusable water bottle

1. 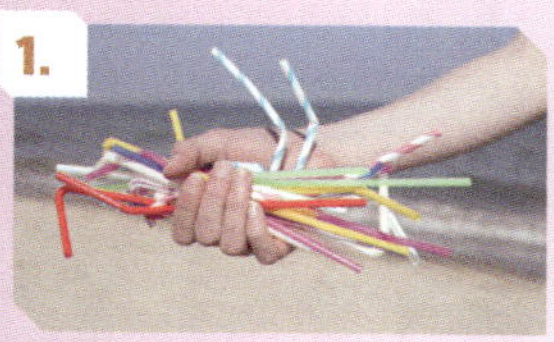

____

2. 

____

3. 

____

4. 

____

While You Watch

2 **Watch the video and answer.** 08

1. When is Earth Day?

2. What time is it?

3 **Watch the video again. Check (✓) the options that Katya and Hugo mention.** 08

1. ☐ Don't use plastic bags.
2. ☐ Use cotton or fabric bags.
3. ☐ Don't use plastic straws.
4. ☐ Take a metal straw with you when you go to restaurants and cafés.
5. ☐ Drive electric cars.
6. ☐ Take public transportation.
7. ☐ Ride your bike or walk to school.
8. ☐ Don't use disposable tableware.
9. ☐ Take a reusable bottle of water to school.
10. ☐ Don't buy plastic bottles of water or soda.

After You Watch

4 **Work in pairs. Which of the habits in Activity 3 are common in your community?**

____

____

____

5 **Choose one of the habits that isn't common in your community. In your notebook, create a sticker to promote this habit.**

I can demonstrate an understanding of a conversation about Earth Day.

e-Language Booster

Vocabulary

Days and Months

6 Complete the calendar with the days of the week from the box in the correct order. Then listen, repeat, and check. 58

Friday Monday Saturday Sunday Thursday Tuesday Wednesday

1	2	3	4	5	6	7
		1	2	3	4	5
6	7	8	9	10	11	12
13	14	15	16	17	18	19
20	21	22	23	24	25	26
27	28	29	30			

7 Write the missing months. Then listen and check. 59

August December July March May

1. January
2. February
3. ______
4. April
5. ______
6. June
7. ______
8. ______
9. September
10. October
11. November
12. ______

Ordinal Numbers

8 Listen and repeat the ordinal numbers. 60

1st – first	13th – thirteenth
2nd – second	14th – fourteenth
3rd – third	15th – fifteenth
4th – fourth	16th – sixteenth
5th – fifth	17th – seventeenth
6th – sixth	18th – eighteenth
7th – seventh	19th – nineteenth
8th – eighth	20th – twentieth
9th – ninth	21st – twenty-first
10th – tenth	22nd – twenty-second
11th – eleventh	23rd – twenty-third
12th – twelfth	30th – thirtieth

9 Look and write the dates. Then listen and check. 61

APRIL 16 — 04/16 April sixteenth

FEBRUARY 02 — 1. 02/02 ______

AUGUST 30 — 2. 08/30 ______

JULY 19 — 3. 07/19 ______

JANUARY 11 — 4. 01/11 ______

10 In pairs, practice saying the dates in Activity 9. Then take turns saying the date of your birthday.

When's your birthday?

It's on November 5th.

I can talk about days of the week and months of the year.

Language Booster page 47

#CLARIFY

Reading

1 In pairs, look at the posters. Answer the questions.

1. What is each poster about?
2. What do the three posters have in common?
3. How do you think people celebrate these dates?

a.

b.

c.

2 **MAKING PREDICTIONS.** Read the title and the first paragraph of the blog post. What is the text about?

____

____

3 **CONFIRMING PREDICTIONS.** Read the whole text and check your predictions.

Green Holidays

Green Holidays

Earth Day isn't the only day that celebrates planet Earth. Here are some other holidays that are about protecting our planet and the people on it.

World Water Day

On March 22, the United Nations organizes World Water Day. Fresh water is very important. We use it to drink, to prepare food, to shower, and to wash our clothes. Sometimes we forget that fresh water isn't unlimited. For World Water Day, experts suggest how we can use water responsibly.

World Nature Conservation Day

World Nature Conservation Day takes place every year on July 28. The message of this day is to live in harmony with nature. People share messages on social media to protect nature and natural resources.

International Clean Air Day

A clean blue sky is beautiful and good for our health. Chemicals from cars, trucks, and factories pollute the air. This is bad for our health and for ecosystems. On September 7, International Clean Air Day, people are educated about air pollution. There's a special hashtag #HealthyAirHealthyPlanet.

4 **SUMMARIZING AND EVALUATING DETAILS.** In pairs, read the text in Activity 3 again and summarize it. Then talk about the special date mentioned in the text you find the most important to celebrate.

____

____

____

I can interpret a blog post about green holidays.

e-Language Booster

Listening

5 Listen to Hugo and Liz. Which event from the text in Activity 3 is their school celebrating? 62

____

6 Listen to people talk about special days in the United States. Then number the pictures accordingly. 63

a.

b.
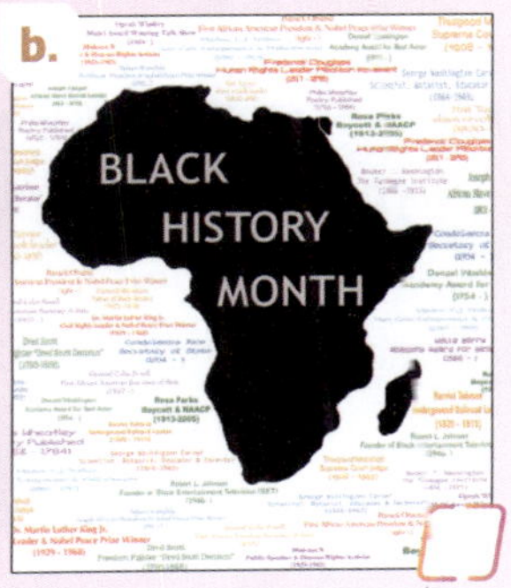

c.

Writing

7 Work in groups. Choose a special day from Activity 6. Do some research and make notes of the most relevant information.

____

____

____

____

____

#TIP

Make notes of the most relevant information. Write down key facts avoiding the details.

8 Write a paragraph about the special day you chose. Use the information in Activity 7.

____

____

____

____

____

____

I can write about special dates.

Language Booster page 48

Grammar

Wh- question Words

1 **Read the dialogue and underline the question words.**

Jada: When is Earth Day?
Lee: It's on the 22nd of April.
Jada: What does it celebrate?
Lee: It celebrates the planet Earth.
Jada: Who celebrates it?
Lee: Everyone at school.
Jada: Why do they celebrate it?
Lee: Because it's important to protect our planet!
Jada: What time does the celebration start this year?
Lee: It starts at 10 o'clock.

2 **Look at the grammar chart and the dialogue in Activity 1. Complete the rules.**

Questions with *be*	Questions with other verbs
Who is that man?	**Who** do you live with?
When is her birthday?	**When** does he take a shower?
What is your brother's name?	**What** do they do on the weekend?
What time is it?	**What time** does Lisa go to school?
Where are you?	**Where** do they live?
Why are they here?	**Why** does he need help?

1. Use ____________ to ask about days or dates.
2. Use ____________ to ask about the exact time.
3. Use ____________ to ask about people.
4. Use ____________ to ask about actions, objects, qualities, etc.
5. Use ____________ to ask about reasons.
6. Use ____________ to ask about places.

3 **Unscramble the words to make questions.**

1. you / Where / do / live / ?
____
2. class / When's / next / our / English / ?
____
3. What's / name / mom's / your / ?
____
4. your / When's / birthday / dad's / ?
____
5. actor / is / your / favorite / Who / ?
____
6. do / you / What / use / social media apps / ?
____

4 **Answer the questions in Activity 3. Then take turns asking and answering them in pairs.**

1. ____________________________
2. ____________________________
3. ____________________________
4. ____________________________
5. ____________________________
6. ____________________________

I can use Wh-question words.
e-Language Booster

Wh- questions and Prepositions of Time

5 **Read the dialogues and complete the rules.**

When's Lucy's birthday?
In August.

When's the event?
On March 3rd.

What time's the party?
At 8:00.

1. Use the preposition __________ with dates and days of the week.
2. Use the preposition __________ with time.
3. Use the preposition __________ with months of the year.

6 **Write questions about the underlined parts of the sentences.**

When's Valentine's Day?
Valentine's Day is on February 14th.

1. ______________________________
Volleyball practice is at 3:00.
2. ______________________________
The party is on Friday.
3. ______________________________
Winter vacation is in December.

7 **Complete the questions with ONE word in each blank.**

1. __________ is World Water Day?
2. __________ activities are there?
3. __________ does the event start and finish?
4. __________ is the event?

8 **Work in pairs. Ask and answer the questions in Activity 7 about the special dates in the posts.**

r_livie

r_livie Join us for our International Polar Bear Day event! Feb. 27 at Maxwell County Hall from 10 a.m. to 2 p.m. Activities include polar bear face painting, educational videos about polar bears, and a polar bear quiz. Post your pictures using #savethepolarbears.

r_livie

r_livie Get involved in World Planting Day! March 22 at Steinwald 8 – 11 a.m. Plant a tree to save the planet! Post your pictures with #worldplantingday.

I can use *Wh-* questions and prepositions of time.
Language Booster page 49

Listening

1 **Listen and repeat the times.** 64

1.

Eight o'clock

2.

Eight oh five

3.

Eight ten **or** Ten after / past eight

4.

Eight fifteen **or** A quarter after / past eight

5.

Eight twenty **or** Twenty after / past eight

6.

Eight thirty **or** Half past eight

7.

Eight forty **or** Twenty to nine

8.

Eight forty-five **or** A quarter to nine

9.

Eight fifty **or** Ten to nine

2 **Work in pairs. Take turns asking and answering the questions.**

1. What time is it now?
2. What time is your English class?
3. What time does school start?
4. What time does school finish?

#TIP

Don't use *o'clock* with a.m. / p.m.
9 a.m. = in the morning
4 p.m. = in the afternoon
8 p.m. = in the evening
12:00 = noon
00:00 = midnight

3 **LISTENING FOR DETAILS. Listen and complete with the missing information.** 65

Stephanie

Christmas Eve

help my [1] __________ prepare food
go home at [2] __________
take a shower and change my clothes
go to my aunt's house at [3] __________
eat and open presents at midnight
visit neighbors

Christmas Day

get up late
go to the beach

Pronunciation

4 **Listen and circle the correct options.** 66

1. 16 / 60
2. 19 / 90
3. 15 / 50
4. 14 / 40
5. 13 / 30

Speaking

5 **In pairs, take turns asking and answering the questions.**

1. What time do you usually get up?
2. What time do you get up on Christmas Day?
3. What time do you usually go to bed?
4. What time do you go to bed on Christmas Eve?

I can tell the time.

Use of English

6 **Work in pairs. Take turns asking questions about the special dates below. Use *Wh-* question words.**

1\.

Christmas Eve / Christmas Day

2\.

Halloween

3\.

Independence Day

4\.

New Year's Eve

5\.

Carnival

When's Christmas Eve?

It's on December 24th.

Where do you go on Christmas Eve?

I stay home with my family.

What do you do?

We celebrate the special date with delicious food and presents.

7 **Match the activities to the special dates in Activity 6. You can use the same activity for more than one date.**

1. Visit my family.

____

2. Watch fireworks.

____

3. Wear special clothes.

____

4. Eat traditional food.

____

8 **Read the dialogue. Then listen and repeat.** 67

Max: When is New Year in your country, Li?
Li: It's different every year, but the Chinese New Year is usually in February.
Max: What do you do on New Year's Eve?
Li: I usually wear special clothes and visit my family. We eat delicious food. And you? What do you do?
Max: I go to a party with my friends.

9 **In pairs, practice reading the dialogue in Activity 8.**

10 **Still in pairs, role play the dialogue in Activity 8 about your traditions.**

I can ask Wh-questions.
Language Booster page 50

#CHALLENGE

Writing

1 Work in pairs. What do you know about Thanksgiving? Make notes.

____

____

____

____

____

____

2 Read Kaylie's blog post and check your answers in Activity 1.

Kaylie's blog

My favorite special date is Thanksgiving. It is a big holiday here in the United States. Thanksgiving is on a different date every year because it falls on the third Thursday in November. This year it is on November 25. On Thanksgiving Day, we give thanks for everything we have. I spend Thanksgiving with my family. In the morning, my sister and I help my parents before our grandparents, aunts, uncles, and cousins come to visit. We eat a special lunch. After lunch, everyone says something they are thankful for. Then we play games. It is always a special day.

3 Look at the schedule. Complete the sentences with *before* or *after*.

Sandy's Thanksgiving Schedule	
10:00	clean my bedroom
12:00	take a shower
12:30	get dressed in special clothes
13:30	go to grandma's house
14:00	have lunch
16:00	play games with family
20:00	watch fireworks

1. Sandy takes a shower ____________ she cleans her bedroom.
2. She goes to her grandma's house ____________ she gets dressed in special clothes.
3. She has lunch ____________ she plays games with her family.
4. She plays games ____________ she watches the fireworks.

I can interpret a schedule.

e-Language Booster

Prepare to Write

4 **You are going to write about a special date that you and your family celebrate in your country. Answer these questions about the special date.**

1. What special date is it?

____

2. What does it celebrate?

____

3. When is it?

____

4. What do you like to do on this date?

____

5. Who do you celebrate the date with?

____

6. Where do you celebrate the date?

____

Write

5 **Write a blog post about your special date. Use your answers in Activity 4 and the text in Activity 2 as a model.**

DRAFT

____

____

____

____

____

____

____

____

____

____

____

____

#TIP

A blog post must be visually appealing. Therefore, make sure to include pictures to make your post more appealing to your audience.

Check and Change

6 **Read your text and make sure you included:**

- [ ] the name of the special date / day.
- [ ] what is celebrated.
- [ ] how you celebrate it.

7 **Edit your text. Make sure you included all the items in Activity 6. Then choose a picture to illustrate your post.**

Publish

8 **Write a clean version of your blog post.**

BLOG POST

____

____

____

____

____

____

____

Speaking

9 **Work in pairs. Take turns telling each other about your favorite special date.**

I can write a blog post.

Language Booster page 51

Project: A Program for a Climate Action Event

#DIGITAL LITERACY

Think carefully about the layout. Is it easy to find practical information about dates, times, and names of events in the event program? How is the information organized?

Step 1 Think

1 Discuss in groups.

1. What is an event program?
2. What information do we expect to find in an event program?

2 Read the program below and underline the information about dates, times, and activities.

World Bee Day

May 20 – Hashtag High School

Event program

2:00 - 3:00 p.m. Opening Ceremony. Interactive presentation on the importance of bees to our ecosystem by Dr. Susan Jenkins, a bee expert. Main Hall

3:00 - 4:00 p.m. Bee Experience. Experience the daily life of a bee through this amazing virtual reality experience. Classroom 1

3:00 - 4:00 p.m. Honey Tasting. Learn how honey is made and sample some local honey products. Classroom 2

2:30 – 4:00 p.m. Bake Sale. Purchase cakes and other sweet treats. All money raised goes to the Save the Bees Foundation. Main Hall

4:00 – 5:00 p.m. Bee Dance. Interpretive dance by the Hashtag High School dance group about the role of bees in nature and the dangers of bee extinction. Main Hall

#WorldBeeDay #Savethebees

Step 2 Plan

3 In groups, choose one of these climate action special dates. Discuss what activities you can do to promote this date in an event at your school.

Earth Day **World Turtle Day** **World Water Day** **Zero Emissions Day**

I can recognize the features of an event program and plan to create one.

Step 3 Research

4 In groups, research more information about your climate action special date. Look for more ideas of possible activities for the event.

____

____

____

____

____

Step 4 Design

5 In groups, create a program for your event. Use the information from your research and the previous activities.

• Check the text. • Check the purpose. • Check the organization.

#TIP STEP 4

Do not forget to indicate:

1. the name, place, and date of your event.
2. a schedule of the day's activities.

Step 5 Present and Publish

6 Work in groups. Present your program to the class.

Step 6 Evaluate

7 Complete the evaluation table.

★☆☆ More to learn ★★☆ Good ★★★ Excellent

Criteria	My Evaluation	Group Evaluation	Teacher Evaluation
Teamwork	☆☆☆	☆☆☆	☆☆☆
Language	☆☆☆	☆☆☆	☆☆☆
Design	☆☆☆	☆☆☆	☆☆☆

#TIP STEP 6

1. Practice the presentation and video record it.
2. Don't read out the descriptions.
3. Speak slowly and fluently.

I can create an event program and present it to the class.

#SELF-ASSESSMENT

1 Mark the learning objectives according to the key.

★☆☆ I don't understand.	★★☆ I understand, but I need help.	★★★ I can do it!

Learning Objectives	Rating
To demonstrate an understanding of a conversation about Earth Day.	☆☆☆
To talk about days of the week and months of the year.	☆☆☆
To interpret a blog post about green holidays.	☆☆☆
To write about special dates.	☆☆☆
To use *Wh*-question words.	☆☆☆
To use *Wh*-questions and prepositions of time.	☆☆☆
To tell the time.	☆☆☆
To ask *Wh*-questions.	☆☆☆
To interpret a schedule.	☆☆☆
To write a blog post.	☆☆☆
To recognize the features of an event program and plan to create one.	☆☆☆
To create an event program and present it to the class.	☆☆☆

2 Work in pairs. Discuss the questions.

1. What did I find most interesting to learn? Why?
2. How did I learn it?
3. How can I use it in real life?

HOBBIES

#12 RESPONSIBLE CONSUMPTION AND PRODUCTION

In this unit, you will learn how to:

- Talk about hobbies and free-time activities.
- Write a personal profile.
- Create an online advertisement for a school event.

Say what you know:

- Favorite free-time activities.
- Items of clothing.
- Activities happening at the moment.

Video

An Adventure Field Trip

Before You Watch

1 **Look at the pictures and discuss the questions in pairs.**

1. Which of these activities do you do?
2. Which of these activities would you like to do?

1. 
horseback riding

2. 
climbing

3. 
kayaking

While You Watch

2 **Watch the video and mark the sentences T (True) or F (False).** 09

1. ☐ Katya is talking to Hugo on a video chat.
2. ☐ Katya isn't having a good time in her group.
3. ☐ Katya is having lunch at the moment.
4. ☐ Katya is eating a chicken quiche and chips.
5. ☐ The vegetables and the chips are leftovers from the day before.
6. ☐ Katya likes the food there.
7. ☐ Katya's T-shirt is made of recycled cotton.
8. ☐ Hugo is watching a movie.

3 **Watch the video again and write the activity each group is doing.** 09

1. Group 1: ______________________
2. Group 2: ______________________
3. Group 3: ______________________
4. Group 4: ______________________

After You Watch

4 **Katya's lunch is made with leftovers. This reduces food waste. In pairs, look at the picture and say which actions you do.**

1. Don't buy food in large quantities.
2. Use leftovers to make something new.
3. Donate excess food.
4. Use less water.

5 **In pairs, research two more ways to reduce food waste.**

____

I can demonstrate an understanding of a conversation about a field trip.

e-Language Booster

Vocabulary

Hobbies and Free-time Activities

6 Complete the mind map with the hobbies from the box.

gardening | going to the beach | hanging out with friends | hiking | making videos | playing video games | reading books | shopping | taking pictures

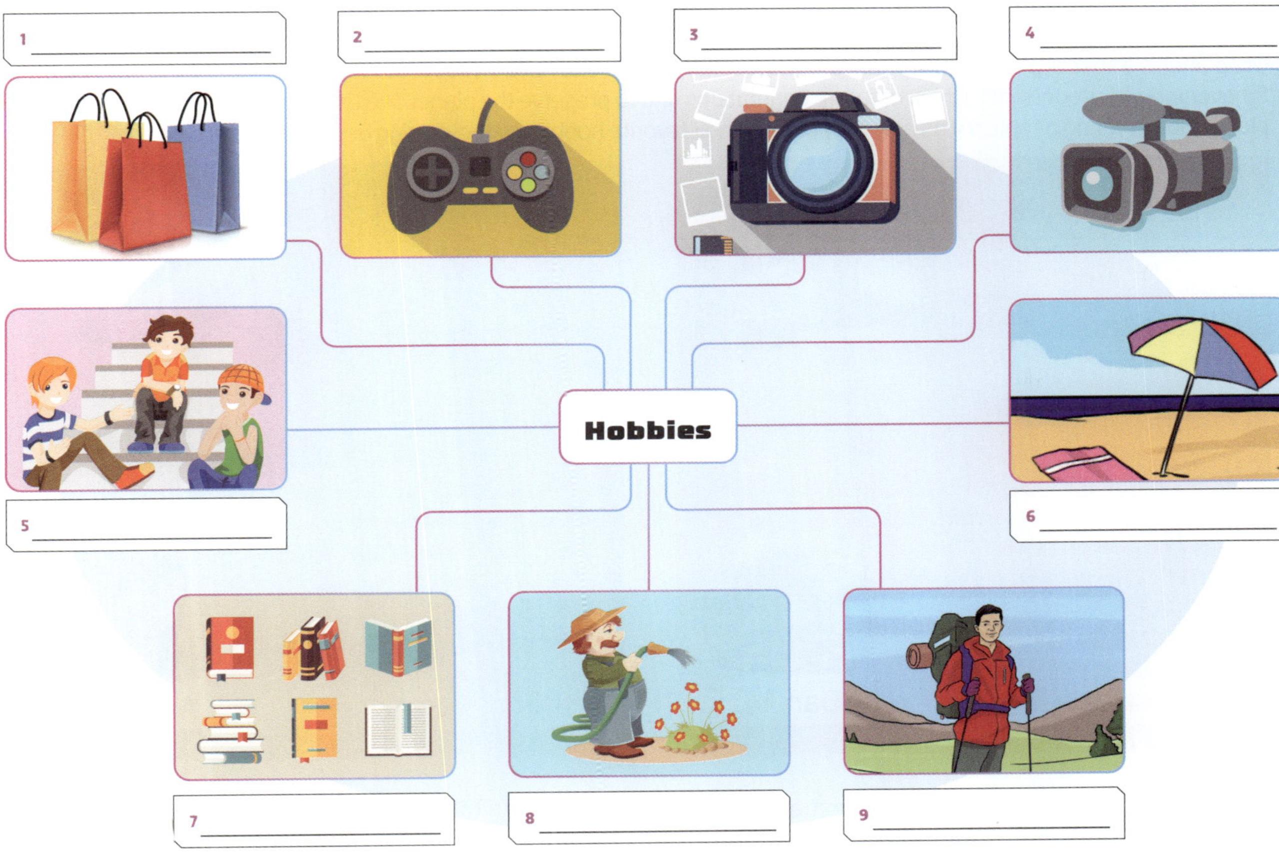

7 Add three more hobbies to the mind map in Activity 6.

____

____

8 Listen and complete the sentences with the correct hobbies. 68

1. **Francisco:** I like ______________.
2. **Genny:** I love reading ______________.
3. **Kevin:** I don't like ______________.
4. **Hannah:** I like ______________.

9 Work in pairs. Take turns talking about the hobbies in Activity 6.

I love shopping.

I don't like dancing.

I like playing video games.

I can talk about hobbies and free-time activities.

Language Booster page 53

#CLARIFY

Reading

1 Discuss the questions in pairs.

1. What's your favorite hobby?
2. When do you do it?

2 SCANNING. Read the text quickly. What is each person's hobby?

1. Dan: ____________________
2. Ana: ____________________

My Hobbies

Our planet is a special place and we must take care of it. We must use natural resources carefully so that there's enough for everyone. It's important to think of future generations and to preserve the planet. We can minimize our impact on the planet. Some young people tell us how they pursue their favorite hobbies without using or wasting too much.

I'm crazy about gardening! My aunt and uncle have a huge garden, and I love to help them. I go to their house every weekend. I have a vegetable garden there. My mom saves vegetable peels and eggshells for me. I use them as compost for my vegetables. That helps them grow. I plant flowers and herbs in old plastic soda bottles and milk cartons. The birds like to eat my vegetables. My dad has lots of old CDs, and I put them on sticks around the vegetable garden. The birds don't like the light from the CDs, so they stay away! I don't throw many things in the trash because they might be useful in the garden!

Dan, 14

I love fashion, but I don't like to go shopping. There are many stores with cheap clothes, but they aren't of good quality. Many of my classmates buy clothes online every month so they can take pictures for social media. They don't wear the clothes often. I don't do that – I make my own clothes! My family lives near a factory. Every month I go to the factory and collect old fabric scraps. I use them to make my dresses, skirts, and T-shirts. Everyone always asks where my new clothes come from. I answer: they aren't new, they're old!

Ana, 14

3 MAKING INFERENCES. Read the text again and mark the sentences T (True) or F (False).

1. ☐ Dan likes helping people.
2. ☐ Ana likes good quality clothes.
3. ☐ Ana likes old clothes.
4. ☐ Dan likes it when birds eat his vegetables.
5. ☐ Ana acts sustainably.

4 Complete the following sentences about Dan and Ana.

1. Dan uses eggshells and vegetable peels to help ____________________ his plants.
2. Ana makes her clothes out of fabric ____________________.
3. Dan uses old CDs to scare the ____________________ away.
4. Ana's classmates like to take ____________________ for social media.
5. Both Dan and Ana have sustainable ____________________.

Listening

5 Complete the tips with the words from the box. Then listen and check. 69

listen	local	long	quantity	read

Tips to Be a Conscious Consumer

1. Quality, not ______________ — buy a low number of good things.
2. Keep things for a ______________ time — do you really need something new?
3. Support ______________ companies to help your community.
4. Understand the problems with consumption. ______________ books or ______________ to podcasts.

Writing

6 Match the pictures to their descriptions.

1. This can be a nice hobby for the whole family. You can create useful and beautiful things from objects that are usually discarded. For example, you can put flowers or plants in plastic bottles and display them in your garden.
2. Participating in an outdoor activity is great. You can see a variety of bird species. It also makes you more open and active in the fight to protect birds and their habitats.
3. Volunteering helps you maintain your health and improve your self-esteem. You can help people in need, clean up a street, volunteer with local environmental organizations, plant trees, and more.
4. Cycling is a great sport that benefits not only your health, but also the environment. If you ride a bike, you don't need public transportation or a car. Both of them have a negative impact on the environment.

a. 

b. 

c. 

d. 

7 In your notebook, write a paragraph about an eco-friendly hobby. Do some research and use the texts in Activity 6 as models.

I can write about an eco-friendly hobby.

Language Booster page 54

#UNDERSTAND

Grammar

Present Continuous – Affirmative and Negative

1 Read the text and look at the chart. Then underline the verbs in the Present Continuous.

I have a big family! We are all at home right now. My dad is cooking in the kitchen. My brother isn't helping – he is eating the ingredients! My grandma and grandpa aren't watching TV. They are singing karaoke! It's a little annoying because I'm studying. I have a big test at school. I'm using my cell phone, but I'm not looking at social media. My friends and I are studying together.

Present Continuous

Affirmative		Negative	
I'm	reading	I'm **not**	singing
You'**re**		You **aren't**	
He'**s**		He **isn't**	
She'**s**		She **isn't**	
		It **isn't**	
You'**re**		You **aren't**	
We'**re**		We **aren't**	
They'**re**		They **aren't**	

Spelling of *-ing* verbs

watch – watch**ing**
play – play**ing**
run – run**ning**
dance – danc**ing**

2 Use the chart and the text in Activity 1 to complete the rules.

1. Use the Present Continuous for ____________ happening at the time of speaking.
2. Use ________ or ________ + verb *-ing* with *I*.
3. Use ________ or ________ + verb *-ing* with *he*, *she*, and *it*.
4. Use ________ or ________ + verb *-ing* with *we*, *you*, and *they*.

3 Rewrite the sentences with the correct form of the Present Continuous.

1. Miguel are watching TV.
____
2. Petra and I is chatting online.
____
3. The teacher doesn't talk at the moment.
____
4. My brothers play in the park.
____
5. You aren't listen to me!
____

4 Work in pairs. What are the people doing?

1. 
Maria ____________________.

2. 
Ana ____________________.

3. 
André ____________________.

4. 
The children ____________________.

5. 
Max ____________________.

I can use the Present Continuous in the affirmative and negative forms.

e-Language Booster

Present Continuous – Questions

5 **Look at the chart and circle the correct options to complete the sentences.**

Present Continuous – Questions			
Yes / No questions		Short answers	
Am I **Are** you **Is** he / she / it **Are** you / we / they	sing**ing**?	Yes, I **am**. Yes, you **are**. Yes, he / she / it **is**. Yes, you / we / they **are**.	No, I'**m not**. No, you **aren't**. No, he / she / it **isn't**. No, you / we / they **aren't**.

Wh- questions

What **are** you do**ing**?
What**'s** he / she / it do**ing**?
What **are** they do**ing**?

1. In *Yes / No* questions, ***the question word*** / ***verb be*** comes before the subject.
2. In *Wh-* questions, the ***question word*** / ***verb be*** comes first.

6 **Write questions in the Present Continuous.**

1. Dan – listen to – Selena Gomez
____
2. Liliana – hang out – with her friends
____
3. you – send a message to – that influencer
____
4. the girls – wait to – see – you
____
5. you – watch – a horror movie
____
6. they - buy - tickets to the theater
____

7 **Complete the short answers to the questions in Activity 6.**

1. Yes, he ________.
2. No, she ________.
3. No, I ________.
4. Yes, they ________.
5. Yes, I ________.
6. No, they ________.

Object Pronouns

8 **Read the dialogue and the chart. Then circle the correct option in the sentence below.**

A: Are you reading your new book?
B: Yes! I like **it** a lot.
A: Can you lend **it** to **me** afterwards?
B: Yes, of course.

Subject pronouns	Object pronouns	Subject pronouns	Object pronouns
I	me	it	it
you	you	we	us
he	him	you	you
she	her	they	them

Object pronouns go ***before*** / ***after*** a verb or a preposition.

9 **Read the questions in Activity 6 and complete the answers.**

1. Yes, he really likes ________.
2. No, she's chatting with ________ online.
3. Of course not! I don't like ________.
4. Yes, they are waiting to see ________.
5. Yes, but I'm not enjoying ________.
6. No, they are selling ________.

10 **Look at the pictures in Activity 4 again. In pairs, take turns asking and answering questions.**

A: Is Maria swimming?
B: No, she isn't.
A: What is Maria doing?
B: She's riding a bike.

I can ask questions in the Present Continuous and use object pronouns.

Language Booster page 55

Listening

1 Listen and repeat the items of clothing. 70

1. 
jacket

2. 
dress

3. 
pants

4. 
shorts

5. 
skirt

6. 
sneakers

7. 
sweater

8. 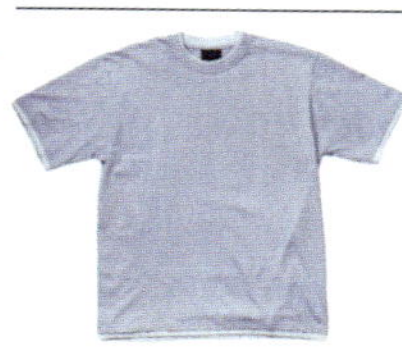
T-shirt

9. 
socks

10. 
sandals

2 **Work in pairs. Describe what you are wearing. Use as many words from Activity 1 as possible.**

I'm wearing blue pants and a white T-shirt.

3 **LISTENING FOR DETAILS. Listen and check (✓). What does Elena buy?** 71

1.  [ ]
2.  [ ]
3.  [ ]

4 **Listen again and circle the correct options to complete the sentences.** 72

1. The girls go to **the mall** / **a thrift store**.
2. Elena thinks the clothes are **expensive** / **cheap**.
3. Elena wants to buy a **dress** / **jacket**.
4. Elena doesn't buy the clothes because she doesn't **want** / **need** them.
5. Elena spends **fifteen** / **fifty** cents.

Pronunciation

5 **Listen and repeat. Pay attention to the / ŋ / sound.** 73

1. This thi**ng** looks like a skirt.
2. The boat is sinki**ng**.
3. I am practici**ng** my E**ng**lish.
4. I like walki**ng** to school.

Speaking

6 **Work in pairs. Take turns describing what the people in the picture are wearing.**

The short girl is wearing a green dress.

Use of English

7 **Listen to the dialogues. Underline the questions used to ask about opinion.** 74

What do you think about superhero movies?

I love them!

What do you think of this dress?

To be honest, I don't really like it.

8 **Match the questions to the answers. Then listen and check.** 75

1. What do you think about her cooking?
2. What do you think about these sneakers?
3. What do you think about this influencer?
4. What do you think of Noah Centineo?

- [ ] I **can't stand** her.
- [ ] I **love** it!
- [ ] I **like** him.
- [ ] I **don't like** them.

9 **Label the pictures with the words in bold in Activity 8.**

1.  ______________
2.  ______________
3.  don't mind
4.  ______________
5.  ______________

10 **Complete the table with one example for each category. Add a category of your own.**

1. A creative hobby	______________
2. A sports team	______________
3. A music artist or group from your country	______________
4. ______________	______________

11 **Work in pairs. Take turns asking and answering questions about the items in Activity 10.**

What do you think of Will Smith?

I can't stand him!

I can give opinions using object pronouns.

Language Booster page 56

#CHALLENGE

Writing

1 **Read the texts. Which profile do you have the most in common with?**

Bruno, 14

Add Chat

Hi! I'm using this app because I want to practice my English. I love being outdoors. My favorite hobbies are swimming, kayaking, and playing sports. I can't stand playing video games. I don't mind reading books, but I don't like comic books.

Emilia, 14

Add Chat

Hello everyone! I'm creating this profile because I want to meet other Harry Potter fans! I love everything that's to do with the Harry Potter universe. I read the books, watch the movies, make the toys, and wear the costumes. One of my hobbies is making videos about Harry Potter for social media – check them out! Sorry, no Marvel fans allowed – I can't stand superhero movies.

Alex, 14

Add Chat

Hello. I live in the countryside and I'm on this app because I want to have more friends! I have many different hobbies: I like playing the piano, making funny videos, playing video games, and reading comics. I love to walk in the forest near my house. I don't really like drawing or painting.

2 **Read the texts again. Why is each person using the app?**

1. Bruno: ______________________________
2. Emilia: ______________________________
3. Alex: ______________________________

3 **Work in pairs. Check (✓) the correct options. What should you include in a personal profile?**

1. ☐ Your address
2. ☐ Your hobbies
3. ☐ Your job
4. ☐ How much money you earn
5. ☐ Your personality

I can interpret personal profiles for a friendship app.

e-Language Booster

4 **Match the sentences. Rewrite them using *because*.**

*I'm running in the park **because** I want to lose some weight.*

1. I'm watching a nature series.
____
2. I'm listening to Dua Lipa.
____
3. I'm eating lunch.
____
4. I'm using my laptop.
____

☐ My classes are online. ☐ I love animals. ☐ It's 12 o'clock. ☐ She's my favorite singer.

Prepare to Write

5 **Make notes about yourself.**

1. My hobbies: ______________________
2. Things I love: ______________________
3. Things I like: ______________________
4. Things I don't like: ______________________
5. Things I can't stand: ______________________

Write

6 **Write your profile for a friendship app in your notebook. Review the features in Activity 3. Use the texts in Activity 1 as models.**

Check and Change

7 **Read your personal profile for a friendship app and make sure you included:**

☐ Your hobbies.
☐ Likes and dislikes.
☐ The reason why you are using the app.

8 **Edit your text. Make sure all the items in Activity 7 are included.**

Publish

9 **Write a clean version of your personal profile.**

Speaking

10 **Work in groups. Read your classmates' personal profiles. Then give your opinion about them. How can they improve their profiles?**

#TIP

1. Focus on your positive attributes rather than your flaws.
2. Don't go over everything. Pick a few points to concentrate on.
3. Leave your contact details off the list. It's possible that you'll get unsolicited texts.
4. Before you write anything, double-check your spelling and grammar.
5. When making jokes, you can use emojis.

I can write a personal profile.

Language Booster page 57

Project: An Advertisement for a School Event

#DIGITAL LITERACY

While browsing the Internet:

1. Look for established institutions. The Internet is full of websites that are not reliable.
2. Look for websites with expertise.
3. Stay away from websites with a lot of ads.

Step 1 Think

1 **Work in pairs. Read the text and answer the questions.**

Buying Smart

Before you buy something new, think. Buying a lot of new things isn't good for the environment. It creates more trash and uses up natural resources like water, for example. Try a preloved item – an item that a person doesn't want any longer. You can buy it cheap or maybe even trade it in for an item that you don't want any longer, either.

Come to our thrift store! Here you can get anything, from socks to umbrellas, for up to 50% of the original price!

1. Where can you get preloved items?

____

2. What preloved items can you get?

____

3. How much do they usually cost?

____

Step 2 Plan

2 **Work in groups. Plan a conscious consumption event at your school. Answer the questions below with your ideas.**

1. What type of event is it going to be? Is it a swap event or a preloved sale?

____

2. What items are available? _______________________
3. Where is the event? _______________________
4. When is the event? _______________________

I can read an advertisement and plan to create one.

Step 3 Research

3 In groups, look for examples of online websites and events for preloved items. Make notes.

websites and events for preloved items

Step 4 Design

4 In groups, create an advertisement for your event. Use the information from Steps 2 and 3 for help and the advertisement in Step 1 as a model.

- Check the text.
- Check the purpose.
- Check the organization.

Step 5 Present and Publish

5 In groups, present your advertisement to your classmates.

Step 6 Evaluate

6 Complete the evaluation table.

★☆☆ More to learn ★★☆ Good ★★★ Excellent

Criteria	My Evaluation	Group Evaluation	Teacher Evaluation
Teamwork	☆☆☆	☆☆☆	☆☆☆
Language	☆☆☆	☆☆☆	☆☆☆
Design	☆☆☆	☆☆☆	☆☆☆

#TIP STEP 4

Think about the *what*, *where*, *when*, *who*, and *why*.
If possible, include these important pieces of information in your advertisement.

#TIP STEP 5

1. Practice the presentation and video record it.
2. Don't read out the information.
3. Speak slowly and fluently.

I can create an advertisement for an event and present it to the class.

#SELF-ASSESSMENT

1 **Mark the learning objectives according to the key.**

★☆☆ I don't understand.	★★☆ I understand, but I need help.	★★★ I can do it!

Learning Objectives	Rating
To demonstrate an understanding of a conversation about a field trip.	☆☆☆
To talk about hobbies and free-time activities.	☆☆☆
To interpret a magazine article about sustainable actions.	☆☆☆
To write about an eco-friendly hobby.	☆☆☆
To use the Present Continuous in the affirmative and negative forms.	☆☆☆
To ask questions in the Present Continuous and use object pronouns.	☆☆☆
To describe what people are wearing.	☆☆☆
To give opinions using object pronouns.	☆☆☆
To interpret personal profiles for a friendship app.	☆☆☆
To write a personal profile.	☆☆☆
To read an advertisement and plan to create one.	
To create an advertisement for an event and present it to the class.	☆☆☆

2 **Work in pairs. Discuss the questions.**

1. What did I find most interesting to learn? Why?
2. How did I learn it?
3. How can I use it in real life?

UT FT Language Booster page 58

INTEGRATE

Learn to Learn

Bloom's Taxonomy

1 **Read the verbs in the pyramid below. How can you relate them to the sections in the book?**

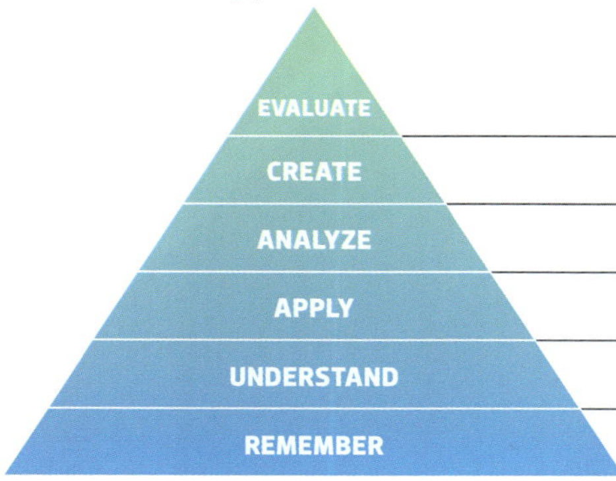

2 **Read the definition below. What conclusions can you draw from it? Write your ideas.**

Bloom's Taxonomy explains the ***proccess*** *of learning. It is a tool to develop learning objectives.*

3 **Go back to page 9. Identify the learning objectives and write them down.**

4 **Analyze the learning objectives in Activity 3. Where did you reach them during Unit 0, according to Bloom's Taxonomy?**

5 **Evaluate your learning progress by reviewing the Self-assessment box on page 22.**

6 **How do you usually memorize information? Check (✓).**

- ☐ Drawing
- ☐ Highlighting information in a text
- ☐ Reading aloud
- ☐ Taking notes
- ☐ Watching videos
- ☐ Writing examples

7 **Create a board with your study habits.**

Video

About Myself

Before You Watch

1 What do you remember from the video in the #Discover section? Make notes and share them with a classmate.

Wh- questions	Personal information
1 ________	4 ________
2 ________	5 ________
3 ________	6 ________

While You Watch

2 Watch the video and check your notes in Activity 1. ▷ 01

3 Complete these sentences.

1. Oh, hi! ________? My name's Katya.
2. ________, Katya. I'm Hugo.
3. **A:** How old ________?
   B: ________.
4. **A:** ________ in Peru.
   B: Where are you from, Hugo?
   ________.

While You Watch

4 Work in groups. You are going to make a video showing people greeting each other and introducing themselves. Make notes before you begin.

5 Use the checklist to review your video script.

Our dialogue includes...
- [ ] questions to ask for information.
- [ ] possessive adjectives for giving personal information.
- [ ] information about name, age, country, and / or nationality.

6 In groups, make your video and share it with your classmates.

7 In groups, provide feedback to your classmates about their video.

Language	
Presentation	
Layout	

Learn to Learn

In the Neighborhood

1 What places in town do you remember?

1.

2.

3.

4.

5.

2 Can you give examples of the places in the pictures in your neighborhood?

____

____

3 How do you get to these places? Choose another way to get there.

____

4 Choose one of the places from Activity 1. Calculate the time it takes to get there in two different kinds of transportation.

____

5 Create a map with a new route to the place you chose in Activity 4. Include the places in the neighborhood.
Have your home as the starting point.

6 Compare the kinds of transportation you would recommend to get to those places.

____

7 What action verbs would you use to describe your learning objective today? Explain your choice.

____

____

Video

In My City

Before You Watch

1 What do you remember from the video in the #Discover section? Make notes and share them with a classmate.

Emma	Matt

While You Watch

2 Watch the video and check your notes in Activity 1. ▷ 02

After You Watch

3 Work in groups. You are going to make a video about yourself and your school's neighborhood. Make notes before you begin.

4 In groups, make your video and share it with your classmates. Use the checklist to review your video script. Make sure you:

- ☐ introduce yourself.
- ☐ say how you go to school.
- ☐ say what there is in your school's neighborhood.

5 In groups, provide feedback to your classmates about their video.

Language	
Presentation	
Layout	

Learn to Learn

My Classroom

1 What words can you remember from the past units?

Countries / Nationalities

Numbers

Places in the City

Classroom Objects

Colors

2 Classify the words in Activity 1. Next to each word, write 1 if you always use it and 5 if you never use it. Compare your answers with a classmate and discuss your choices.

3 Plan how you could use the words from Activity 1 in a game to review vocabulary.

4 List the words from the past units that you think are difficult to remember.

5 Explain to your classmates how you think a game could be helpful to review or learn new vocabulary.

6 Design a vocabulary memory game.

7 Which category did you use the most to perform your tasks today? Circle.

Analyze Apply Create
Evaluate Remember Understand

Video

In the Library

Before You Watch

1 What do you remember from the video in the #Discover section? Make notes and share them with a classmate.

Classroom Objects	Questions

While You Watch

2 Watch the video and check your notes in Activity 1. 03

After You Watch

3 Work in groups. You are going to make a video about your classroom. Make notes before you begin.

In my classroom,

there is... ______________________________

____

there are... ______________________________

____

4 In groups, make your video and share it with your classmates.

5 In groups, provide feedback to your classmates about their video.

Language	
Presentation	
Layout	

Learn to Learn

A Story

1 **Name** the people in your family.

2 In pairs, **explain** how these family members are related to you.

Taylor is my sister.

3 What do you know about your parents' story? **Make notes**.

4 **Decide** on the information you want to share about your family with your classmates.

5 **Use** pictures to tell the story of your family.

6 **Revise** your story and make any necessary changes.

7 Can you list the steps needed to create a story?

Video

My Family

Before You Watch

1 What do you remember from the video in the #Discover section? Answer the questions and share the answers with a classmate.

Who is... ?

How old is he / she?

What's his / her job?

Emily	Linda	Tom	Mirian	Claudio

While You Watch

2 Watch the video and check your notes in Activity 1. 04

After You Watch

3 Work in groups. You are going to make a video about your extended family. Make notes before you begin.

____

____

____

____

4 In groups, make your video and share it with your classmates.

5 In groups, provide feedback to your classmates about their video.

Language	
Presentation	
Layout	

Learn to Learn

Study Routine

1. **List** the tasks in your daily routine that are related to studying.

2. **Extend** your list by adding a 30-minute activity that is related to what you learned at school. It can be reading a book, surfing the Internet, etc.

3. **Plan** a new schedule, indicating when you are going to add this new 30-minute activity during your day.

Sunday	Monday	Tuesday	Wednesday	Thursday	Friday	Saturday

4. **Compare** your new schedule with the one from the past week. What is different? Talk to a classmate.

5. **Decide** on the studying-related tasks you are going to include in your daily routine. Write them down.

6. **Develop** a 15-day plan for a study routine.

7. How did you decide to make the changes to your study routine? Make notes. Share your ideas with a classmate.

Video

Daily Routines

Before You Watch

1 Check (✓) the things that Hugo does in the morning.

1. ☐ brush teeth
2. ☐ get dressed
3. ☐ have breakfast
4. ☐ go on social media
5. ☐ go to school
6. ☐ take a shower
7. ☐ watch TV

While You Watch

2 Watch the video and check your answers in Activity 1. ▷ 05

After You Watch

3 In pairs, write a dialogue between two friends. One friend has a healthy daily routine, and the other friend has an unhealthy daily routine.

____

____

____

____

____

____

____

____

____

____

____

____

____

4 Use the checklist to review your dialogue. Make sure you included:

- ☐ the healthy daily routine.
- ☐ the unhealthy daily routine.
- ☐ why it is important to have a healthy daily routine.
- ☐ possible consequences of having an unheathy daily routine.
- ☐ what people can do to change.

5 In groups, make your video and share it with your classmates.

6 In groups, provide feedback to your classmates about their video.

Language	
Presentation	
Layout	

Learn to Learn

Different Homes

1 Look around the classroom. Write down five items you can remember seeing.

2 Classify how the items in the classroom are organized.

3 Experiment with building blocks to show how the classroom could be reorganized.

4 Describe how the changes could benefit students and the teacher. Talk to your classmates.

5 Organize the classroom to make it more comfortable for everyone. Make notes.

6 In groups, evaluate the results of this new classroom organization.

7 Why did you choose this setting for the classroom and not another one?

Video

Where I Live

Before You Watch

1 Complete the chart with information about each person's home.

Hugo	
Katya	
Hugo's grandma	

While You Watch

2 Watch the video and check your answers in Activity 1. ▷ 06

After You Watch

3 In groups, write a description of your ideal house or apartment.

My ideal house is a mansion. There are ten bedrooms and 15 bathrooms. There is a TV and a video game console in all the bedrooms.

____

____

____

4 In groups, make your video and share it with your classmates.

5 In groups, provide feedback to your classmates about their video.

Language	
Presentation	
Layout	

Learn to Learn

Talent Show

1 **Tell** your classmates about a talent you have.

2 **Explain** how you discovered it and why you like it.

3 **Interview** your classmates and find out about their talents.

Name	Talent	How you discovered it

4 **Analyze** how you could categorize your classmates' talents.

____

____

5 **Decide** on the talents that will be presented.

6 **Plan** a talent show with your classmates. Make notes.

____

____

____

____

____

____

____

7 How do you explain what it takes to prepare a show?

Video

What I Can Do

Before You Watch

1 Complete the Venn diagram with information about each person's abilities.

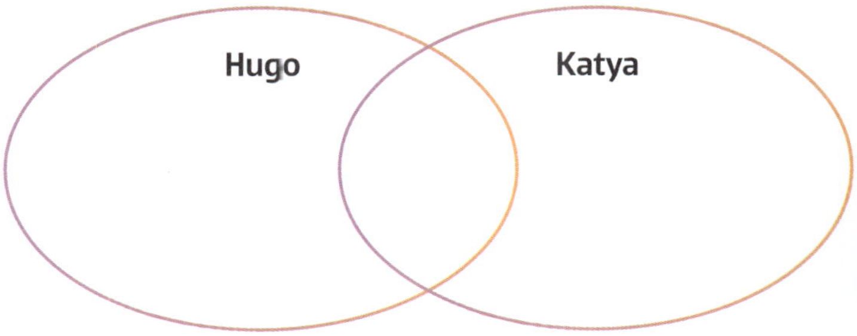

While You Watch

2 Watch the video and check your answers in Activity 1. ▷ 07

After you Watch

3 In groups, write a list of your abilities. Include two abilities for each group member.

____

____

____

4 Work in groups. You are going to make a video about your abilities. Make notes before you begin.

____

____

____

5 In groups, make your video and share it with your classmates. Try to demonstrate the abilities using body language, too.

6 In groups, provide feedback to your classmates about their video.

Language	
Presentation	
Layout	

Learn to Learn

Donation Box

1 **List** some items that can be donated.

2 **Give examples** of places that could receive donations. If there are some in your region, name them. Share them with your classmates.

3 **Identify** some items in your house that can be donated. Write them down and compare them with your classmates.

4 Do some research and **discover** where you could donate these items.

5 **Make up** your donation box. Make notes in your notebook.

6 **Decide** on the place you would like to donate your items.

7 How can you organize information with items for donation in a mind map?

Video

When Is Earth Day Again?

Before You Watch

1 Work in pairs. What information do Hugo and Katya include on their poster about Earth Day?

While You Watch

2 Watch the video and check your answers in Activity 1. ▷ 08

After You Watch

3 Work in groups. Write a dialogue for a video presenting different days during the year that promote climate action and celebrate planet Earth.

4 Use the checklist to review your dialogue. Make sure you included:

- ☐ the name of the special day.
- ☐ the date of the special day.
- ☐ why it is important.
- ☐ what people can do.

5 In groups, make your video and share it with your classmates.

6 In groups, provide feedback to your classmates about their video.

Language	
Presentation	
Layout	

Learn to Learn

Bloom's Taxonomy in Life

1 **Match the verbs to their definitions.**

analyze apply create
evaluate remember understand

1. ______________ – exhibit memory of something learned.
2. ______________ – demonstrate knowledge of facts and ideas.
3. ______________ – use knowledge in a different way.
4. ______________ – look closely at something to understand it.
5. ______________ – present opinions by making judgment about information.
6. ______________ – combine elements in a new pattern.

2 **Choose one topic and summarize how you could use the verbs in Activity 1 when you learn something new.**

____
____
____
____
____
____
____
____

3 **Select another unit other than Unit 8. Can you identify the steps in the unit according to the verbs in Activity 1?**

4 **Get to a conclusion on how the sequence of verbs helped you to reach your learning objectives. You can use the information from Activities 2 or 3.**

____
____

5 **Write about what you learned today. Use the definitions in Activity 1 and see how Bloom's Taxonomy was applied to Unit 8.**

____
____
____
____

6 **Assess what you learned. Reflect on your answer to Activity 4 and see how much you have progressed so far.**

7 **How can the previous activities from today help you understand that you are progressing as a better learner?**

Video

An Adventure Field Trip

Before You Watch

1 **What do you remember from the video in the #Discover section? Answer the questions and share your answers with a classmate.**

1. Where are Hugo and Katya?

____

2. Who is Katya talking to on her cell phone?

____

3. What activities are there?

____

While You Watch

2 **Watch the video and check your answers in Activity 1.** ▷ 09

After You Watch

3 **In groups, talk about what you are doing now. Ask and answer questions about your favorite hobbies, too.**

What are you doing?

I'm exercising with my hula hoop.

4 **In groups, make a video about hobbies and activities going on at the moment and share it with your classmates.**

5 **In groups, provide feedback to your classmates about their video.**

Language	
Presentation	
Layout	

#VIDEO & AUDIO TRACKS

Unit	Track	Page	Activities
Video Tracks			
0	01	10	2 and 3
		137	2
1	02	24	3 and 4
		139	2
2	03	38	2 and 3
		141	2
3	04	52	2 and 3
		143	2
4	05	66	2 and 3
		145	2
5	06	80	2, 3, and 4
		147	2
6	07	94	2, 3, and 4
		149	2
7	08	108	2 and 3
		151	2
8	09	122	2 and 3
		153	2
Audio Tracks			
-	01	Introduction	
0	02	10	1
	03	11	5
	04	13	4
	05	15	8
	06	16	2
	07	16	3
	08	16	4
1	09	25	6
	10	25	8
	11	27	4
	12	30	1
	13	30	3
	14	30	4
	15	30	5
	16	31	8
2	17	39	6
	18	39	9
	19	41	5
	20	43	5

Unit	Track	Page	Activities
Audio Tracks			
2	21	44	4
	22	44	5
	23	44	6
	24	45	9
	25	45	10
3	26	53	6
	27	53	8
	28	55	6
	29	58	1
	30	58	3
	31	58	4
	32	58	5
	33	59	7
4	34	67	7
	35	67	9
	36	69	5
	37	72	3
	38	72	4
	39	72	5
	40	73	9
5	41	81	7
	42	81	9
	43	83	6
	44	84	2
	45	86	3
	46	86	4
	47	89	5
6	48	95	7
	49	95	9
	50	97	6
	51	97	7
	52	99	8
	53	100	2
	54	100	3
	55	100	4
	56	101	8
7	57	108	1
	58	109	6
	59	109	7

Unit	Tracks	Page	Reference
Audio Tracks			
7	60	109	8
	61	109	9
	62	111	5
	63	111	6
	64	114	1
	65	114	3
	66	114	4
	67	115	8
8	68	123	8
	69	125	5
	70	128	1
	71	128	3
	72	128	4
	73	128	5
	74	129	7
	75	129	8

UNIT ZERO

Video Script 01

K: Katya H: Hugo

Part 1

K: Hello!

H: Oh, hi! What's your name?

K: My name's Katya.

H: Nice to meet you, Katya. I'm Hugo.

K: It's nice to meet you, too. How old are you?

H: I'm 13. And you, Katya?

K: I'm 12 years old.

H: Nice. Oh, look! This is Joel. He's my friend from Brazil.

K: Cool.

Part 2

H: Where are you from?

K: I'm from Lima in Peru.

H: Ah, you're Peruvian.

K: Yes, I am. Where are you from, Hugo?

H: I'm from Osny, France. I'm French.

K: A French, a Brazilian, and a Peruvian!

H: Yes, international friends! Cool! Oh, ok, bye, Katya!

K: Goodbye, Hugo.

Audio Scripts

Activity 1 02

Joel:I'm Joel. I'm 13 years old. I'm Brazilian.

Activity 4 04

M: Mike L: Lucy R: Raúl

M: Hi, Lucy.

L: Oh, hi, Mike!

M: This is Raúl.

L: Hello, Raúl. How are you?

R: Great, thanks!

M: Lucy is from China.

L: What about you, Raúl? Where are you from?

R: I'm Brazilian.

L: Wow! Brazil!

R: How old are you? Oh, sorry, my cell phone... Hello, Mom...?

M: Oh, look, there's your brother, Lucy. He looks happy.

L: It's his birthday today. He's 15 years old.

M: Nice! OK, it's time for class. Goodbye, Lucy.

L: Bye, Mike!

Activity 8 05

1. My name's Danny.
2. Her best friend is from Chile.
3. His English teacher is from the United Kingdom.
4. What's your brother's name?
5. What is his nationality?
6. Its name is Sheba.

Activities 2 and 3 06 and 07

I: Interviewer L: Lucas

I: Hello! What's your name?

L: Hey! My name's Lucas.

I: How old are you, Lucas?

L: I'm 12 years old.

I: Where are you from?

L: I'm Brazilian. I'm from Sao Paulo.

I: Do you like Sao Paulo?

L: Yes! It's a big city. I speak Portuguese, and I want to learn English.

I: Thank you, Lucas.

I: Interviewer A: Aby

I: What's your name?

A: Hello! I'm Aby.

I: Hello, Aby. How old are you?

A: I'm 13 years old.

I: And where do you live?

A: I live in Padstow, in the United Kingdom. It's an island, so we live near the sea. I want to learn French.

I: Why do you want to learn French, Aby?

A: France is near my town. There are British and French tourists in my town.

I: That's a good idea. Thanks, Aby.

I: Interviewer A: Alberto

I: Hello! What's your name?

A: Hi! I'm Alberto.

I: How old are you, Alberto?

A: I'm 13 years old.

I: Are you Brazilian?

A: No, I'm Mexican.

I: Where in Mexico do you live?

A: I live in a small town near Guadalajara.

I: So, do you like Brazil?

A: Yes, I do. I want to visit Rio de Janeiro one day!

I: That's great! Thanks, Alberto.

UNIT ONE

Video Script 02

Part 1

K: Katya   H: Hugo   E: Emma

K: Hey, Hugo.

H: Hi, Katya. What's that?

K: It's a video from my new e-pal, Emma. You know, from our school's e-pal scheme.

H: Oh, cool. Let's watch it.

E: Hi, Katya! I'm so excited to be your e-pal. My name's Emma and I'm 14. I'm from Portland, Oregon. There are malls, movie theaters, and restaurants in Portland. The public transportation system in Portland is excellent. There are bike lanes and bridges. There is a good bus service, and there are streetcars.

K: She's really nice!

H: Yeah!

Part 2

H: Hugo   K: Katya   M: Matt

H: Maybe there's a video for me from my e-pal, too.

K: Check your DM!

H: Look, here it is.

M: Hi, I'm Matt. I'm 13, and I'm from Silverton, Colorado, in the United States. There's a bank, and there are two restaurants here, but there aren't any shopping malls. There isn't a hospital. The public transportation system isn't very good. I go everywhere by car, or I walk, or I go by bike. There isn't a sports center, but there are lots of parks. I love nature.

K: He's cool!

Audio Scripts

Activity 6 09

1. restaurant
2. hospital
3. movie theater
4. supermarket
5. shopping mall
6. park
7. bank
8. school

Activity 4 11

1. My name's Brad, and I'm from Staten Island, New York. My school is in Manhattan, so I go to school by ferryboat. It is free, so I pay zero dollars!
2. My name's Gabriela, and I'm from Rio de Janeiro. I go to school by train. The ticket is one dollar.

Activity 3 13

G: Teenage Girl

G: Hello, everyone. It's me, Samira. Welcome back to my radio show. Today's episode is about our towns and cities. My town is Manchester, in England. The streetcar system is very fast, but it is very expensive. Now let's hear from some of you, my listeners!

Activity 4 14

G: Teenage Girl   G1: Teenage Girl 1   G2: Teenage Girl 2

G: Hello, everyone. It's me, Samira. Welcome back to my radio show. Today's episode is about our towns and cities. My town is Manchester, in England. The streetcar system is very fast, but it is very expensive. Now let's hear from some of you, my listeners!
Hello, what's your name, and where are you from?

G1: Hi! I'm Cecilia, and I'm from Juneau, Alaska.

G: Tell me about your town, Cecilia.

G1: Well, there are lots of parks, but the shopping mall isn't very good. It's expensive.

G: Thanks, Cecilia. Now our next caller. What's your name, and where are you from?

G2: Hey, Samira. I'm Angel, I'm a big fan of your show! I'm from Buenos Aires, Argentina. My city is awesome. There are movie theaters, restaurants, supermarkets. There is a subway system, too, but it is very old. Some of the subway cars are old and slow.

G: That's not good, Angel. Thanks for your call. Now, let's listen to some music...

UNIT TWO

Video Script 03

Part 1

K: Katya   H: Hugo

H: Here, let's go in.

K: Look, a poster! Sit down. Put down your backpacks. Take out your books, notebooks, pens, pencils, and erasers.

H: Cool, let's sit down.

Part 2

H: Can you help me?

K: Of course.

H: How do you say this in English?

K: Errr... A desk?

H: Can you repeat that, please?

K: A desk.

H: Thank you! And this?

K: That's a chair.

H: How do you spell it?

K: C-h-a-i-r.

H: Great! Thanks.

Audio Scripts

Activity 5 19

D: Debesh

I'm Debesh, and I'm from Bangladesh. My classroom is very different because it's on a boat! My town is very rural, and the traditional schools are very far away. There are 20 floating classrooms in my district, on eight different rivers. In my classroom, there isn't a desk for the teacher, but there are desks for the students. There is one desk for every two students. There is a whiteboard and a TV. There isn't Internet access in my classroom, but in some boat classrooms there are laptops and Internet. I hope there is Internet in my boat soon! My classes are fun and interesting.

Activities 4 and 5 21 and 22

MM: Mr. More M: Mark

MM: Can you turn your cameras on, please? That's better. Mark, can you turn your microphone on, please?

M: Oh, sorry, Mr. Moore.

MM: That's OK. Can you show us your backpack, please?

M: Yes. Here it is.

MM: What's there in your backpack?

M: A pencil, an eraser, two pens, and three notebooks.

MM: Good! And how do you spell eraser?

M: E – R – A – S – E – R.

MM: Great!

Activities 9 and 10 24 and 25

A: Alejandro

A: All of my classes are online. There is a desk and a chair in my bedroom. Both the desk and chair are blue. On my desk, there is a white tablet and two notebooks. The notebooks are black. Oh, and there are two pens. A green pen and a red pen.

UNIT THREE

Video Script 04

K: Katya H: Hugo

Part 1

K: Thanks! Bye.
Hi, Hugo.

H: Hey, Katya. Who's that?

K: My sister.

H: Your sister? But Emily is six!

K: Yes, my sister Emily is six years old. My sister Miriam is 22. She's a student at college in a different city.

H: Got it. What does she study?

K: She's at medical school. Her dream job is a doctor.

H: That's an important job!

K: Your brother is a student, too, right?

H: Yes. Tom's 24. He's in his final year. His dream job is a teacher.

K: This job is important, too!

H: Yep. Look, here is a picture of him.

K: Cool! And who are those people?

H: Our grandparents. They're in Tanzania now.

K: Wow! On vacation?

H: No, they're volunteers. My grandpa, Claudio, is a construction worker, and my grandma, Linda, is a chef.

K: That's awesome. How old are they?

H: They're 68.

K: Cool!

Audio Scripts

Activity 6 26

H: Hugo

H: This is a picture of my family. Those are my grandparents. My grandpa's name is Claudio, and my grandma's name is Linda. And there's my dad, next to me. His name is Lucas. On the other side of me is my mom, Helen. And look, there's my big brother Raul and my baby sister Sara.

Activity 6 28

1. Miriam is my sister, and she's also my best friend. She isn't at home every day because she is at college far away. But that isn't important; we chat every day on a messaging app on our cell phones.
2. My sister is in the military. I am very happy about this, and I love telling everyone all about my sister. She's only 20, so she's still in her training period. She's away now, but she'll be back soon.
3. My sister is very quiet, but that's just her! I think she prefers reading books to talking to people, but she's so intelligent. And she's still only six years old!
4. My sister is an excellent artist. Her sketches are so beautiful. At the moment, her art is only online, but she has a lot of followers on her Instagram page.

Activity 1 29

I'm Bill, and this is my family tree. My grandparents' names are Jane and Jo. This is my uncle Jack. He's my mother's brother. My aunt's name is Sandy, and this is their son. He's my cousin Adam. That's my father. His name's Mike. My mother's name is Lilian. Oh, and this is me!

Activities 3 and 4 30 and 31

P: Paulo M: Melanie

P: Whose car is that, Melanie?
M: What car?
P: That red sports car on your Instagram post.
M: Oh, that's my cousin Lidia's car.
P: Your cousin Linda? But she's in high school!
M: No, not Linda. Lidia. She's my aunt Genny's daughter.
P: Your aunt Genny?
M: Yes! My dad's sister.
P: Oh, aren't they your family from Guadalajara?
M: Yes, that's right. That's why you don't know them.
P: So, is your cousin really rich?
M: I guess so. She's a businesswoman, and she's very successful. She loves her job and her car!
P: Cool.
M: Look, Paulo. These are my new sunglasses. They're a gift from Lidia. They're my new favorites.
P: Nice! My favorite thing is still my video game console.
M: Of course it is. Let's play after school.
P: Deal!

UNIT FOUR

Video Script 05

K: Katya H: Hugo

K: Oh, I'm tired.
H: You're always tired!
K: It's because I go to bed late. I chat online to my friend Becca every night. We usually watch a movie together, too.
H: Your friend, Becca... Oh!
K: That's right. She goes to school in the morning and in the afternoon, so she does her homework and goes on social media after school. And in the evening, we watch a movie.
H: I see, so you don't sleep much.
K: No, I don't...
H: What do you do in the morning? You get up, and then...?
K: First, I go on social media.
H: Again?! I don't go on social media in the morning.
K: What do you do?
H: Hmm... I take a shower and I brush my teeth. Then I get dressed and I have breakfast.
K: I don't have breakfast.
H: Huh?
K: I don't have breakfast.
H: Seriously? Breakfast is important!
K: I'm not hungry in the morning.
H: All right. Hmm, then what do you do?
K: We go to school together, remember?

Audio Scripts

Activity 9 35

I'm Jon, and I'm Brazilian. I go to school in the afternoon. I get up in the morning and brush my teeth. Then I do my homework and play with my baby brother. I have lunch with my grandma and my brother. I take a shower and get dressed. Then I go to school by bus. I have a snack at school before I go home.

Activity 5 36

M: Man J: Johanna W: Woman G: Gabriel

1.
M: Where are you from, Johanna?
J: I'm from Finland.
M: How old are you?
J: I'm 15.
M: When do you go to school?
J: I go to school in the morning and in the afternoon.
M: Where do you have lunch?
J: I have lunch at school.
M: Do you do homework?
J: No, we don't have homework in Finland.

2.
W: Where are you from, Gabriel?
G: I'm from the Philippines.
W: How old are you?
G: I'm 13.
W: When do you go to school?
G: I go to school in the morning and in the afternoon.
W: Where do you have lunch?
G: I have lunch at home.
W: Do you do homework?
G: Yes, I do homework in the evening.

Activity 3 37

B: Boy W: Woman

Part 1

B: Hi, everyone! I'm Samuel, and welcome to today's podcast. Today, Dr. Hilaria Lopes is here. Hello, Dr. Lopes.
W: Hello, Samuel.
B: Let's talk about being healthy. Our routine is important for this. I have a few messages here from some of our listeners. Gabriela says, "I am always tired. In the evening, I do my homework, and then I watch my favorite series."

W: My question to Gabriela is: Do you watch series for many hours? It's not a problem to watch series every day, but sleeping is very important for everyone.

B: That's true. I sometimes watch series, but I go to bed early. I usually sleep nine hours every night, so I have energy for school.

Activity 4 38

B: Boy W: Woman

Part 2

B: OK, next message. It's from Daniel. "I go to school in the morning and in the afternoon. I always go on social media and chat with my friends in the evening, but I am sometimes sad. I don't know why."

W: It's important to have balance in our lives. My question to Daniel is: Do you exercise? Exercise is good for us. We feel good when we exercise. The Internet is great, but it's good to have a break, too.

B: Good idea! I never exercise. But when I have dinner, I always chat with my family. I never go on social media at dinnertime. I like this little time in the real world! All right, let's see another message...

Activity 5 39

/iz/	/s/	/z/
brushes	gets	goes
watches	sleeps	does
		has

Activity 9 40

1.

A: I don't go on social media in the morning.

B: Me neither.

2.

A: I have lunch at school.

B: Me too.

UNIT FIVE

Video Script 06

K: Katya H: Hugo

K: Hello?

H: Hi, Katya. It's me.

K: Oh, hey, Hugo. What's up?

H: I'm OK, but I need some help with my homework.

K: Sure. What's wrong?

H: Well... argh, hang on. That's better!

K: Are you in your apartment?

H: No, I'm at my grandma's.

K: Does you grandma live in an apartment?

H: Yes, she does. She lives in a small apartment downtown. It's a nice apartment, but it's near the main street, so it's noisy sometimes! I'm on the rooftop now.

K: On the rooftop?!

H: Yeah... but don't worry, it's not dangerous! Look! There's a rooftop garden here.

K: Cool!

H: It's a community garden so all the residents help. There's a vegetable garden and some chairs, too.

K: Haha.

H: What's funny?

K: Well, I'm in my vegetable garden now!

H: Do you have a vegetable garden, too?

K: Yes, I do. I live in a house, so my vegetable garden isn't on the roof. It's in our yard. Let me show you. It's small, but we grow a few vegetables. I love it! So do you live with your grandma now?

H: No, I don't. I visit her sometimes. Who do you live with?

K: I live with my mom, dad, sister, aunt, and cousins.

H: That's a lot of people!

K: I know! But we have a big house. Now, about that homework.

H: Oh, no!

K: What?

H: My homework is downstairs, in my grandma's bedroom!

Audio Scripts

Activity 6 43

I'm Lauren, and I live on a narrowboat in London, England with my aunt, Julie. We aren't always in the same place on the river because we move the boat every two weeks. Narrowboats are small. Usually, there is a couch and a table – they transform into two beds. There is a small kitchen with a sink, a stove, and a mini refrigerator. There is also a very small bathroom with a toilet and a shower. My aunt and I have a small vegetable garden on the roof of our narrowboat. Sometimes life is difficult on the boat because there isn't a lot of space, but I prefer a narrowboat to an apartment. Life is an adventure!

Activity 2 44

K: Kate O: Oli

K: Does Miguel live on a narrowboat?

O: No, he doesn't. Do you live in an apartment?

K: No, I don't.

S: Sally T: Ted

S: Do you live with your grandparents?

T: Yes, I do.

S: Do you live in a house?
T: No, we don't. We live in an apartment.

Activities 3 and 4 45 and 46

W: Woman G: Girl
W: Where do you live, Ana?
G: I live in North Carolina, in the United States.
W: Do you live in a house or an apartment?
G: I live in a house. Actually, it's a tiny house!
W: What is a tiny house?
G: A tiny house is just like a normal house, but a lot smaller!
W: Who do you live with?
G: I live with my mom and dad, and my brother.
W: What rooms are there in your tiny house?
G: Well, there are only three rooms in the house. There is one big room, which is the kitchen and the living room all in one. There is a very small bathroom, but it only has a toilet and a shower. We use the sink in the kitchen to brush our teeth and wash our faces.
W: What about bedrooms?
G: Above the kitchen there is a second floor – that's where my brother and I sleep.
W: Do you share a bedroom with your brother?
G: Yes, I do. Our beds are under a window, so I look at the stars at night.
W: Do you like your tiny house?
G: Yes, I do! I think my house is cool because the furniture transforms into other things. For example, the table and couch transform into my parents' bed. There aren't any kitchen cabinets – we use boxes. In the evening, I move the boxes and I climb up to my bed. Also, tiny houses are very good for the environment – they don't use a lot of energy or space, and they're cheap.
W: Is there anything you don't like about your tiny house?
G: Uh, well, we don't have a washing machine, so we go to town to wash our clothes. That is not so nice!

UNIT SIX

Video Script 07

K: Katya H: Hugo
K: Wow, that picture is incredible. You can draw really well.
H: Thanks.
K: Look, there's the art teacher. Show Mrs. Ramirez your drawing.
H: No, please...
K: Why not? I'll show it to her.
H: Don't touch my book!
K: OK, sorry!
H: No, *I'm* sorry. I'm not very confident about my drawing.
K: Well, I think they are amazing. I can't draw! I can't do anything, really. My big sister is the talented one in my family. She can speak three languages, she's good at sports, she can dance tango very well...
H: But you can swim! You're on the school team, and you can play the violin, too.
K: Yeah, I guess.
H: Can you sing well?
K: Yes, I can. Why?
H: Me too! It's my brother's birthday on Saturday. Come to his karaoke party with me?
K: Karaoke? Count me in! I can dance, too.
H: Oh no, no dancing...

Audio Scripts

Activity 7 48

1. speak a foreign language
2. use sign language
3. cook
4. play sports
5. dance
6. code

Activity 9 49

W: Woman M: Man
1.
W: No, like this... up, down, left, right.
M: Jessica, what's that smell?
W: Oh... eh... it's dinner, sorry!

W: Woman B: Boy
2.
W: Amazing! Thanks, Riley. OK, next audition for the talent show...
B: Hello, I'm Eric.
W: All right, Eric. Show us your talent.
B: "Near, far, wherever you are..."
W: I don't *think* so...

G: Girl B: Boy
3.
G: Eh... um... I'd like... two... eh... deux... coffee... café... eh... milk.
B: Deux cafés au lait, s'il vous plait.
G: Thanks! My French is terrible.

SC: Sports Commentator

4.

SC: And it's Mendez with the ball... she gets past Cruz... oh, there's Rodrigues... but she's past Rodrigues... can she do it... yes, I think she can... Gooooaaaaaal!
An incredible performance by Mendez... oh, and what's she doing now? A victory dance! Well, it's a good thing she's an excellent soccer player, because she's not a great dancer!

G: Girl B: Boy

5.

B: Can you do it?

G: Ssh! I need to concentrate.

B: Sorry... sorry. I'm just nervous.

G: I'm almost...

B: Oh, no...

G: Calm down, I just need to... There... no more video!

B: You're amazing with computer codes! Thank you. It is such an embarrassing video.

G: It's pretty funny... but your singing is really bad...

Activities 6 and 7 50 and 51

Millicent Simmonds is an 18-year-old actress from the United States. She is deaf, so she can't hear. She is famous because she is a good actress. She doesn't speak in the movies; she uses sign language!
Aaron Fotheringham is from the United States. He's 30 years old. Aaron can't walk; he uses a wheelchair, but he can do some incredible things with his wheelchair! He does wheelchair tricks like BMX bike tricks and skateboard tricks, too.

Activity 8 52

G: Girl B: Boy W: Woman M: Man

1.

G: Mom, don't sing. It's awful!

2.

B: Hey! Don't sleep now. This is my favorite part of the movie!

3.

W: Brush your teeth, Alex. It's time for bed.

4.

M: Open your books, please.

5.

W: Don't go on social media now. It's dinnertime!

Activities 2 and 3 53 and 54

FR: Female Reporter MR: Male Reporter

FR: And now for our news report on some talented teens. Our county is home to several teenagers with amazing talents. Pedro Queiroz is going to tell us more.

MR: La Cruz High School has some very talented teenagers. For example, Angela Garcia. She can run 100 meters in 12 seconds! That's fast! She wants to go to the Olympics.
In the school, all students study foreign languages. Some students can speak two or three languages because their parents are from different countries. But Henrique Lopes can speak ten different languages! He uses apps on his cell phone and watches movies without subtitles.
Now let's talk about Patty Morales. She is the school's Spelling Bee champion. She has a very good memory – she reads long and difficult words in a dictionary once or twice, and then spells them with no problem. Amazing!

UNIT SEVEN

Video Script 08

K: Katya H: Hugo

K: All right, let's get started...

H: Cool. When is Earth Day, again?

K: It's next week, on April 22. Every year, people all over the world celebrate Earth Day. We need to make a poster with some ideas to protect our planet. What do you think?

H: Well, a big problem today is trash. There's so much trash everywhere!
People buy too many unnecessary things and companies still use a lot of pollutant materials, like plastic.

H: That's a good point! There's also a lot of plastic in the ocean, and that's bad for marine life.

K: Let's talk about that on our poster!

H: OK... Let's write something about plastic bags.

K: Yeah! You don't need a new bag every time you buy something! The same for plastic straws. What else?

H: Plastic bottles...

K: Take a reusable water bottle to school.

H: Yes! What time is it?

K: It's ten to five. Why?

H: Because I have soccer practice on Mondays and Wednesdays at 5:30. My mom is going to drive me there.

K: I think that's all the information we need, right?

Audio Scripts

Activity 5 62

L: Liz H: Hugo

L: Hurry up, Hugo! We're late!

H: What do you mean? It's only 7 o'clock. It takes ten minutes to get to school.

L: Ten minutes by car, but today we're walking.

H: What?!

L: We can't go to school by car. Today is all about air pollution. Cars pollute the air. You can only go by bike, subway, or on foot.

Activity 6 63

M: Man **W:** Woman

1.

M: Every February, this celebration commemorates the struggles and victories of millions of Americans over the most awful obstacles – slavery, bigotry, and poverty – as well as their contributions to the cultural and political life of the country.

2.

W: Many schools commemorate the life of Martin Luther King in January by bringing his words and dream to life. Martin Luther King wanted a more accepting society than the one he knew.

3.

M: On this special day, established in 1950, the United States and the world community recognize people who work to promote and protect the fundamental freedoms set forth in the Declaration.

UNIT EIGHT

Video Script 09

K: Katya **H:** Hugo

K: Hi, Hugo!

H: Hello, Katya. How's your group in the field trip? Are you having a good time?

K: Yes, it's great! I enjoy being outdoors with fresh air. Everyone is very nice, too.

H: That´s great! I can see you are eating now.

K: Yes, it´s lunch time now. The food here is delicious.

H: What are you eating?

K: I am eating a vegetable quiche and chips – the vegetables in the quiche are leftovers from dinner last night. And the chips are also leftovers from last night – they were deep-fried to make chips.

H: That's a great way to avoid waste.

K: I know!

H: I like your T-shirt, too.

K: Thank you! We are all wearing them. These are the official field trip T-shirts, and they are made of 100 % recycled cotton.

H: That's interesting. And where are you guys now?

K: We are hanging out in the lounge right now because we have lunch break at 1 p.m. There are four groups and each group has break at different times. We take turns doing each activity, so group 1 is kayaking right now and group 2 is rock climbing. I am in group 3, and it's our turn for a break. What about group 4? What is group 4 doing? Oh, of course! So, group 4 is horseback riding, which will be our next activity. I can't wait for it!

H: So, do you have your boots on?

K: Yes, I do. And I have thick socks and my coat on. It's cold here!

H: Wow, that's awesome! Enjoy it!

Audio Scripts

Activity 8 68

1. I like taking pictures.
2. I love reading books.
3. I don't like playing video games.
4. I like shopping.

Activities 3 and 4 71 and 72

G1: Girl 1 **G2:** Girl 2

G1: Look at my new bag, Elena.

G2: I love it! Is that from the new store at the shopping mall?

G1: No, it's from the thrift store.

G2: From the thrift store?!

G1: Yes! I love that store. They have great stuff there.

G2: But those are other people's clothes!

G1: They are second hand, yes, but so what? They're clean and in good condition. It's good for the environment to shop at a thrift store.

G2: Hmm.

G1: Come on. The store is just across the street. Let's go inside.

G2: Oh, look at these dresses. Wow, only ten dollars? They are so cheap!

G1: You love shopping. I can't believe you never come here.

G2: Hmm, this... And this...

G1: Elena! Are you buying all these clothes?

G2: I think so. These skirts are only five dollars each.

G1: But you have so many skirts! Don't buy things just because they're cheap.

G2: Hmm, you're right. But look at this beautiful dress! I want it so badly!

G1: But do you need it? I mean, where are you going to wear it? It's so fancy!

G2: You are right. The only thing I need is socks for basketball practice.

G1: Here are some, look.

G2: They are new!

G1: Yeah! Thrift stores sometimes have new clothes, like socks and underwear.

G2: Only 50 cents! I'll definitely buy those. They are cheap, and I need them!

NOTES

NOTES

PICTURE CREDITS

Front cover (A) Krakenimages.com/Shutterstock/Shutterstock / (B) Artistdesign29 /Shutterstock/Shutterstock / (C) Studio Harmony/Shutterstock/Shutterstock / (D) S_L/Shutterstock/Shutterstock / (E) Maslakhatul Khasanah/ Shutterstock/Shutterstock / (F) Spasiblo/ Shutterstock/Shutterstock / (G) Macrovector/Shutterstock/Shutterstock / (H) Net Vector/ Shutterstock/Shutterstock; Page 9 LightField Studios/Shutterstock; Page 10 (A) HBRH. Shutterstock/Asset Library / (B) Atores/Olive Tree Filmes / (C) Olive Tree Filmes / (D) Apirakthanakorn/ Shutterstock; Page 11 (A) charnsitr. Shutterstock/Asset Library / (B) Peter Etchells. 123rf.com/Asset Library / (C) Fotogroove. Shutterstock/Asset Library / (D) T. Lesia. Shutterstock/Asset Library / (E) Anatoly Tiplyashin. Shutterstock/Asset Library / (F) Magi Bagi. Shutterstock/Asset Library; Page 12 (A) AnnaStills/Shutterstock / (B) Irina Bobreshova/Shutterstock; Page 13 dolgachov/123RF; Page 15 (A) Jon Barlow. Pearson Education Ltd/Asset Library / (B) Gareth Boden. Pearson Education Ltd/Asset Library / (C) Panat_b. Shutterstock/Asset Library / (D) wizdata. Shutterstock/Asset Library / (E) DFree/Shutterstock / (F) CarlaVanWagoner/Shutterstock / (G) DFree/Shutterstock; Page 16 (A) zstockphotos/123RF / (B) CYSUN. Shutterstock/Asset Library / (C) Debbie Rowe. Pearson Education Ltd/Asset Library; Page 17 wavebreakmedia. Shutterstock/Asset Library; Page 18 manuta/123RF; Page 20 (A) Алексей Бутенков. 123rf.com/Asset Library / (B) shin sang eun/Shutterstock; Page 23 Ryan Deberardinis/Alamy Stock Photo/Alamy; Page 24 (A) Jules Selmes. Pearson Education Ltd/Asset Library / (B) Nick Starichenko. Shutterstock/Asset Library / (C) Anna Khomulo. 123rf.com/Asset Library / (D) Stephen Coburn/123RF / (E) John_T/Shutterstock/Asset Library / (F) melissamn/shutterstock/Shutterstock / (G) Rigucci/Shutterstock/Asset Library; Page 25 (A) Beresnev/Shutterstock/Asset Library / (B) Mix3r/Shutterstock/Asset Library / (C) artinspiring/123rf/123RF / (D) Pixel Embargo/Shutterstock/Asset Library / (E) neyro2008/123rf/Asset Library / (F) elenabsl/123rf/123RF / (G) avian/Shutterstock/Asset Library / (H) abscent/123rf/123RF / (I) Kryvenok Anastasiia/Shutterstock/Asset Library / (J) Coleman Yuen/ Pearson Education Asia Ltd/Asset Library / (K) MindStudio/Pearson Education Ltd/Asset Library / (L) Coleman Yuen/ Pearson Education Asia Ltd/Asset Library / (M) Radu Bercan/shutterstock/Shutterstock / (N) Darren Hedges/Shutterstock/Asset Library / (O) Mikhail Gnatkovskiy/Shutterstock/Asset Library / (P) MSSA/Shutterstock/Asset Library / (Q) Ekaterina Pereverzeva/123rf; Page 26 (A) Debbie Rowe/ Pearson Education Ltd/Asset Library / (B) Diego Vito Cervo/123rf.com/Asset \Library / (C) Jarretera/shutterstock/Shutterstock / (D) EGT-1/shutterstock/Asset Library / (E) Brainsil/Shutterstock/Asset Library / (F) morrowlight/Shutterstock/Asset Library / (G) Daniel Ernst/123rf/123RF; Page 27 (A) Markus Gann/123rf/123RF / (B) Cathy Yeulet/ 123rf/Asset Library; Page 28 elenabsl/123rf/123RF; Page 29 Minerva Studio/Shutterstock/Asset Library; Page 30 (A) Coleman Yuen/ Pearson Education Asia Ltd/Asset Library / (B) Alexander Smirnov/123rf.com/Asset Library / (C) rawpixel/123rf/Asset Library / (D) Chevanon Wonganuchitmetha/123rf/Asset Library / (E) kathleenru/123rf/123RF / (F) Marco Rubino/123rf/123RF; Page 32 david tiberio/123rf/123RF; Page 34 (A) Tiwat K/shutterstock/Shutterstock / (B) pisaphotography/Shutterstock/Asset Library; Page 37 stockfour/Shutterstock; Page 38 (A) maroke/shutterstock/Shutterstock / (B) valzan/Shutterstock/Asset Library / (C) sum43/123rf/123RF / (D) Cheuk-king Lo/Pearson Education Asia Ltd/Asset Library / (E) MOSO IMAGE/Shutterstock/Asset Library / (F) spaxia/123rf/123RF / (G) Syda Productions/Shutterstock/Asset Library; Page 39 (A) Artisticco LLC/123rf/Asset Library / (B) Oxy_gen/Shutterstock/Asset Library / (C) MSSA/Shutterstock/Asset Library / (D) Billion Photos/Shutterstock/Asset Library / (E) Martin Kemp/Shutterstock/Asset Library / (F) RTimages/Shutterstock/Asset Library / (G) jessmine/123rf/Asset Library / (H) Dimedrol68/Shutterstock/Asset Library / (I) Oleg suhenco/Shutterstock/Asset Library / (J) cloki/Shutterstock/Asset Library / (K) Alexander Kharchenko/123rf/Asset Library / (L) Shutter_M/Shutterstock/Asset Library / (M) bryljaev/123rf/Asset Library; Page 40 (A) Gorodenkoff/shutterstock/Shutterstock / (B) SaMBa/shutterstock/Shutterstock / (C) Mark Bowden/123rf/123RF / (D) AVAVA/Shutterstock/Asset Library; Page 41 Pack-Shot/shutterstock/Shutterstock; Page 42 Oleksii Rashevskyi/123RF/123RF; Page 43 (A) Muhammad Mostafigur Rahman / Alamy Stock Photo/Alamy / (B) NADIIA POLIASHENKO/123rf/123RF / (C) Paul Beebee, C/O Beehive Illustrations/ Pearson Education Ltd/Asset Library; Page 44 (A) Wafiq Sharif Mohammed/123RF / (B) rana raheel abbas/123rf/123RF; Page 45 (A) MarcoVector/shutterstock/Shutterstock / (B) VH-studio/Shutterstock/Asset Library; Page 46 (A) iimages/123rf/Asset Library / (B) notkoo/shutterstock/Shutterstock / (C) franzidraws/123rf/Asset Library / (D) Artisticco LLC/123rf/123RF / (E) robuart/123rf/Asset Library / (F) Incomible/Shutterstock/Asset Library; Page 48 (A) filmfoto/123rf/Asset Library / (B) ILUSTRA CARTOON/ Pearson Brasil/Asset Library; Page 51 ephotocorp / Alamy Stock Photo/Alamy; Page 52 michaeljung/Shutterstock/Asset Library / (B) Dmitry Kalinovsky/Shutterstock/Asset Library / (C) Blend Images/Shutterstock/Asset Library / (D) mangostock/Shutterstock/Asset Library / (E) Lisa F. Young/ Shutterstock/Asset Library / (F) Wavebreak Media Ltd./ 123rf/Asset Library; Page 53 (A) ahasoft2000/123rf/Asset Library / (B) Kostyantine Pankin/123rf/Asset Library / (C) tulpahn/Shutterstock/Asset Library / (D) i3alda/Shutterstock/Asset Library / (E) SimpleEPS/Shutterstock/Asset Library / (F) Malinovskaya Yulia/Shutterstock/Asset Library / (G) Carla Viana/ Pearson Brasil/Asset Library; Page 54 (A) Shutterstock/Asset Library / (B) michaeljung/Shutterstock/Asset Library / (C) Gorodenkoff/Shutterstock/Asset Library / (D) Marmolejos/Shutterstock/Asset Library / (E) cheapbooks/Shutterstock/Asset Library; Page 55 Tudor Photography/ Pearson Education Ltd/Asset Library; Page 56 (A) Pack-Shot/shutterstock/Shutterstock / (B) Tono Balaguer/Shutterstock/Asset Library; Page 57 (A) Matteo Santos/ Pearson Brasil/Asset Library / (B) Shutterstock/Asset Library / (C) Jon Barlow/ Pearson Education Ltd/Asset Library / (D) Shutterstock/Asset Library; Page 58 akiradesigns/Shutterstock/Asset Library; Page 59 Igor Zakharevich/123rf/Asset Library; Page 60 Shutterstock/Asset Library; Page 62 Tetiana Kozachok/123rf/123RF; Page 65 lightfieldstudios/123rf/123RF; Page 66 (A) Andrey tiyk/ Shutterstock/Asset Library / (B) Africa Studio/Shutterstock/Asset Library / (C) miya227/Shutterstock/Asset Library / (D) vadymvdrobot/123rf/123RF / (E) Stuart Monk/Shutterstock/Asset Library / (F) LightField Studios/Shutterstock/Asset Library; Page 67 (A) stockbroker/123rf/Asset Library / (B) eakasarn/Shutterstock/Asset Library / (C) Stock Rocket/Shutterstock/Asset Library / (D) Renata0s/Shutterstock/Asset Library; Page 68 (A) Graphic design/Shutterstock/Asset Library / (B) stillfx/123rf/123RF / (C) Svetlana Larina/ Shutterstock/Asset Library / (D) Studio 8. Pearson Education Ltd/Asset Library / (E) wittkephotos/123rf/123RF; Page 69 (A) somartin/123rf/123RF / (B) eugenekh/123rf/123RF; Page 70 (A) Shutterstock/Asset Library / (B) AJR_photo/Shutterstock/Asset Library; Page 71 (A) imtmphoto/Shutterstock/Asset Library / (B) Maya Kruchankova/Shutterstock/Asset Library; Page 72 (A) Svitlana Bezuhlova/Shutterstock/Asset Library / (B) sasha2109/Shutterstock/Asset Library / (C) Iakov Filimonov/Shutterstock/Asset Library / (D) Andriy Popov/123rf/Asset Library / (E) Cathy Yeulet/123rf/Asset Library; Page 74 kakigori/123rf/123RF; Page 76 Roshini Pochont/ Pearson India Education Services Pvt. Ltd/Asset Library; Page 79 Roberto Lo Savio/shutterstock/Shutterstock; Page 80 (A) Andrew Lam/Shutterstock/Asset Library / (B) Katarzyna Białasiewicz/123rf/Asset Library / (C) YuRi Photolife/Shutterstock/Asset Library; Page 81 (A) Artazum/Shutterstock/Asset Library / (B) Mostphotos/Shutterstock/Asset Library / (C) Artazum/Shutterstock/Asset Library / (D) iriana88w/123rf/Asset Library / (E) Jules Selmes/ Pearson Education Ltd/Asset Library / (F) Anna Andersson Fotografi/Shutterstock/Asset Library / (G) hkeita/123rf/Asset Library / (H) Suti Stock Photo/Shutterstock/Asset Library / (I) Africa Studio/Shutterstock/Asset Library / (J) New Africa/Shutterstock/Asset Library / (K) Andrey_Popov/shutterstock/Shutterstock / (L) 565474/Shutterstock/Asset Library; Page 82 (A) Geoff Wols/shutterstock/Shutterstock / (B) Martin Silva Cosentino/shutterstock/Shutterstock / (C) valerybocman/123rf/123RF / (D) dikobrazik/123rf/Asset Library; Page 83 Alicia G. Monedero/Shutterstock/Asset Library; Page 84 (A) Sophie Bluy/ Pearson Education Ltd/Asset Library / (B) Gelpi JM/Shutterstock/Asset Library; Page 85 (A) 332206/Shutterstock/Asset Library / (B) Photographee.eu/Shutterstock/Asset Library / (C) VikiVector/

Shutterstock/Asset Library; Page 86 (A) V. J. Matthew/Shutterstock/Asset Library / (B) Elnur/Shutterstock/Asset Library / (C) Pixel-Shot/Shutterstock/Asset Library / (D) bilanol/123rf/Asset Library / (E) Lowphoto/Shutterstock/Asset Library; Page 88 fizkes/Shutterstock/Asset Library; Page 89 Baksiabat/Shutterstock/Asset Library; Page 90 (A) ppa/Shutterstock/Asset Library / (B) Aeesha Norm/shutterstock/Shutterstock; Page 93 Cristina Conti/Shutterstock/Asset Library; Page 94 (A) Rey Borlaza/Shutterstock/Asset Library / (B) olegdudko/123rf/Asset Library / (C) Microgen/Shutterstock/Asset Library / (D) serezniy/123rf/Asset Library; Page 95 (A) stunningart/123rf/123RF / (B) Daisy Daisy/Shutterstock/Asset Library / (C) Jan H Andersen/Shutterstock/Asset Library / (D) MaszaS/Shutterstock/Asset Library / (E) dolgachov/123rf/Asset Library / (E) Dinis Tolipov/123rf/123RF / (F) mrwebhoney/Shutterstock/Asset Library; Page 96 (A) struna/Shutterstock/Asset Library / (B) Pixel-Shot/shutterstock/Shutterstock / (C) Hafiz Johari/shutterstock/Shutterstock / (D) Piti Tan/Shutterstock/Asset Library; Page 97 (A) Kathy Hutchins/shutterstock/Shutterstock / (B) WENN Rights Ltd / Alamy Stock Photo/Alamy; Page 99 (A) milkos/123rf/123RF / (B) Shutterstock/Asset Library / (C) Casezy idea/Shutterstock/Asset Library / (D) panitanphoto/Shutterstock/Asset Library / (E) Dejan Dundjerski/Shutterstock/Asset Library; Page 100 (A) PhotoByToR/Shutterstock/Asset Library / (B) LightField Studios/Shutterstock/Asset Library / (C) Paulus Rusyanto/123rf/123RF / (D) Aaron Amat/Shutterstock/Asset Library; Page 101 Dragon Images/Shutterstock/Asset Library; Page 102 Milica Nistoran/Shutterstock/Asset Library; Page 103 Daisy Daisy/Shutterstock/Asset Library; Page 104 (A) Syda Productions/Shutterstock/Asset Library / (B) RioPatuca/Shutterstock/Asset Library / (C) AnnGaysorn/shutterstock/Shutterstock / (D) Juan Ci/Shutterstock/Asset Library; Page 107 Halfpoint/shutterstock/Shutterstock; Page 108 (A) Daisy Daisy/Shutterstock/Asset Library / (B) New Africa/shutterstock/Shutterstock / (C) nito500/123rf/Asset Library / (D) Coleman Yuen/ Pearson Education Asia Ltd/Asset Library / (E) Andriy Popov/123rf/123RF / (F) Orgus88/ Shutterstock/Asset Library / (G) AVS-Images/Shutterstock/Asset Library; Page 109 Lana Nikova/Shutterstock/Asset Library; Page 110 (A) Iakov Kalinin/Shutterstock/Asset Library / (B) Chatcharin Sombutpinyo/Shutterstock/Asset Library / (C) Chinnapong/Shutterstock/Asset Library; Page 111 (A) tharun15/123rf/Asset Library / (B) Basheera Designs/Shutterstock/Asset Library / (C) Orakunya/Shutterstock/Asset Library; Page 112 Jörg Carstensen/ Pearson Education Ltd/Asset Library; Page 113 (A) VikOl/Shutterstock/Asset Library / (B) A. Singkham/123rf/Asset Library; Page 114 (A) Renan Teuman/Shutterstock/Asset Library / (B) Pand P Studio/Shutterstock/Asset Library; Page 115 (A) olivier/Shutterstock/Asset Library / (B) Pressmaster/Shutterstock/Asset Library / (C) stewie/Shutterstock/Asset Library / (D) Roman Samborskyi/Shutterstock/Asset Library / (E) KarepaStock/Shutterstock/Asset Library; Page 116 (A) Alexander Raths/Shutterstock/Asset Library / (B) Pressmaster/Shutterstock/Asset Library; Page 118 Sanjay Charadva/ Pearson India Education Services Pvt. Ltd/Asset Library; Page 121 Friends Stock. Shutterstock/Asset Library; Page 122 (A) Skumer. Shutterstock/Asset Library / (B) tcsaba. Shutterstock/Asset Library / (C) Artur Didyk. Shutterstock/Asset Library / (D) apolinarias/123rf/123RF; Page 123 (A) dzein. 123rf.com/Asset Library / (B) Rvector. Shutterstock/Asset Library / (C) robuart. 123rf.com/Asset Library / (D) Creative Stall. Shutterstock/Asset Library / (E) Lorelyn Medina. Shutterstock/Asset Library/ (F) Paul Beebee, C/O Beehive Illustrations. Pearson Education Ltd/Asset Library / (G) Incomible. Shutterstock/Asset Library / (H) Amplion. Shutterstock/Asset Library / (I) Paul Beebee, C/O Beehive Illustrations. Pearson Education Ltd/Asset Library; Page 124 Elena Kozlova/123rf/123RF / (B) Gareth Boden. Pearson Education Ltd/Asset Library / (C) Maria Dryfhout. Shutterstock/Asset Library / (D) Vanessa Van Rensburg. 123rf.com/Asset Library; Page 125 (A) mangostock. Shutterstock/Asset Library / (B) nullplus. Shutterstock/Asset Library / (C) trattieritratti. Shutterstock/Asset Library / (D) serezniy. 123rf.com/Asset Library / (E) Leyla Ismet. Shutterstock/Asset Library; Page 126 (A) Jacek Chabraszewski. Shutterstock/Asset Library / (B) Daniel Zuckerkande/ Shutterstock/Asset Library / (C) Stokkete. Shutterstock/Asset Library / (D) Patricia_studioX. Shutterstock/Asset Library / (E) Riznychenko Oksana. Shutterstock/Asset Library; Page 128 (A) Ludmila Baryshnikova. 123rf.com/Asset Library / (B) tarzhanova. 123rf.com/Asset Library / (C) gogoiso. Shutterstock/Asset Library / (D) eightstock. Shutterstock/Asset Library / (E) gogoiso. Shutterstock/Asset Library / (F) Voronina Svetlana. Shutterstock/Asset Library / (G) Pakhnyushcha. Shutterstock/Asset Library / (H) Stocksnapper. Shutterstock/Asset Library / (I) Alexlukin. Shutterstock/Asset Library / (J) Karkas. Shutterstock/Asset Library / (K) laur7411. 123rf.com/Asset Library / (L) Kanstantsin Prymachuk. 123rf.com/Asset Library / (M) Danilo. Red Dragon. Pearson Brasil/Asset Library / (N) Andrienko Anastasiya/ Shutterstock/Asset Library; Page 129 Chaim Devine/Shutterstock/Asset Library; Page 130 (A) Africa Studio. Shutterstock/Asset Library / (B) Kheng Guan Toh. Shutterstock/Asset Library / (C) Studio 8. Pearson Education Ltd/Asset Library / (D) Julinzy. Shutterstock/Asset Library / (E) SpeedKingz. Shutterstock/Asset Library / (F) Anatoly Tiplyashin. Shutterstock/Asset Library; Page 132 (A) Pictures_for_You. Shutterstock/Asset Library / (B) Ian Allenden. 123rf.com/Asset Library / (C) Yuliia Blazhuk. 123rf.com/Asset Library; Page 136 smuay/Shutterstock/Asset Library; Page 138 (A) foamfoto/Shutterstock/Asset Library / (B) Pete Spiro/Shutterstock/Asset Library / (C) Werayuth Tes/Shutterstock/Asset Library / (D) Sylvie Bouchard/Shutterstock/Asset Library / (E) Ferenc Szelepcsenyi/ Shutterstock/Asset Library; Page 139 Wasim Muklashy/shutterstock/Shutterstock; Page 141 wavebreakmedia/shutterstock/Shutterstock; Page 142 incomible/123rf/123RF; Page 143 Monkey Business Images/shutterstock/Shutterstock; Page 145 Bearnika/shutterstock/Shutterstock; Page 147 Kent Weakley/Shutterstock/Asset Library; Page 148 Anek Suwannaphoom/123rf.com/Asset Library; Page 150 White bear studio/Shutterstock/Asset Library; Page 153 wavebreakmedia/Shutterstock/Asset Library